# Irish Fiction

**Also available in this series:**

*Native American Literatures: An Introduction,* by Suzanne Lundquist
*American Gothic Fiction: An Introduction,* by Allan Lloyd-Smith

**Forthcoming in this series:**
*Fantasy Fiction: An Introduction,* by Lucie Armitt
*Horror Fiction: An Introduction,* by Gina Wisker
*Crime Fiction: An Introduction,* by Alistair Wisker
*Science Fiction: An Introduction,* by Pat Wheeler

CONTINUUM STUDIES IN LITERARY GENRE

# Irish Fiction: An Introduction

KERSTI TARIEN POWELL

continuum
NEW YORK • LONDON

2004

The Continuum International Publishing Group Inc
15 East 26 Street, New York, NY 10010

The Continuum International Publishing Group Ltd
The Tower Building, 11 York Road, London SE1 7NX

www.continuumbooks.com

Printed in the United States of America

Library of Congress Cataloging-in-Publication Data

Powell, Kersti Tarien.
    Irish fiction : an introduction / Kersti Tarien Powell.
        p. cm. — (Continuum studies in literary genre)
    Includes bibliographical references and index.
    ISBN 0-8264-1596-2 (alk. paper) — ISBN 0-8264-1597-0
(pbk. : alk. paper)
        1. English fiction—Irish authors—History and criticism.
2. Northern Ireland—Intellectual life.   3. Northern Ireland—In literature.
4. Ireland—Intellectual life.   5. Ireland—In literature.
I. Title.  II. Series.
    PR8797.P69 2004
    823.009'9417—dc22

                                                    2004013386

# Contents

# Chapter One

# What Is Irish Fiction?

"What ish my Nation? Who talks of my Nation?": The Irish Captain MacMorris challenges the Welsh Captain Fluellen in Shakespeare's *Henry V* (1600). Both serve in the same English army. Both fight a common French enemy. And yet Shakespeare, an English author, takes pains to show their differences, both from each other, and from the English characters of the play. Shakespeare intends for MacMorris's question, "what ish my nation" to reflect back upon England, which claims to include both Ireland and Wales, but it also turns back to Ireland. The question "what ish my nation" expresses a critical difficulty for students of Irish literature, culture, and history. MacMorris rightly implies that the answer partly depends upon "who talks of my nation." How do we understand "Irishness" when it has so often been written by others, including the English (such as Shakespeare) who ruled parts of the Irish island for centuries, and by visitors "touring" the country? For us, MacMorris's questions cascade into a series of further questions. What does it mean to be Irish? What makes a writer an Irish writer? What is Irish fiction?

This book will not offer concrete answers to these questions. Rather, bearing in mind the difficulties involved, it will attempt to negotiate its course not past but through the problems of language, national identity, and representation. These problems become more urgent when dealing with a small nation that has suffered under foreign rule, as a consequence of which it has had to define and re-define its cultural and national identity.

In other words, on which side of the Irish Sea do we locate the point of departure for our quest for definition? And will this definition be determined by linguistic markers? Separated from

England by the sea, the two islands are connected by a linguistic umbilical cord—the English language. And yet, as Shakespeare's MacMorris implies (through the unusual spelling of *is* as *ish*), the same language does not imply the same usage, in accent or even in meaning.

## Language

The linguistic dilemma faced by every Irish writer is most famously expressed by Stephen Dedalus, the protagonist of James Joyce's *A Portrait of the Artist as a Young Man* (1916). Talking with the Dean of Studies, or, as Dedalus refers to him, a "countryman of [the English poet and playwright] Ben Jonson," Joyce's aspiring artist thinks to himself:

> "The language in which we are speaking is his before it is mine. How different are the words *home*, *Christ*, *ale*, *master*, on his lips and on mine! I cannot speak or write these words without unrest of spirit. His language, so familiar and so foreign, will always be for me an acquired speech. I have not made or accepted its words. My voice holds them at bay. My soul frets in the shadow of his language" (Joyce, *A Portrait* 159).

Dedalus's statement reflects the dual nature of the language question; an Irish author writing in English is always uncomfortably aware of composing in the shadow of another tradition.

This shadow is evident already at the level of the name Ireland. Ireland was first mentioned by the Alexandrian Greek geographer Ptolemy who, writing in around A.D. 100, called the island *Ierne*, a version of the Irish word for the island, *Ériu*, which later became *Éire*. The Irish are often referred to as Celts who, commonly seen as the "original" inhabitants of Ireland, were in fact preceded by other tribes. The Anglo-Norman invasion was the first serious challenge faced by the Gaelic-speakers. To simplify matters, we could say that English-speaking settlers arrived in Ireland in two waves: first the so-called Old English or Anglo-Norman invaders, and then the New English who appeared during the Tudor reconquest (sixteenth century). Although the Old English did not manage to conquer Ireland linguistically, the Irish-speaking population was aware of the threat that the newcomers represented for their cultural identity. This is evident from the lament of one of the finest thirteenth-century Irish poets, Gíolla Bríghde Mac Con Mighde:

> If poetry were to be extinguished, my people,
> If we were without history and ancient lays
> Forever . . .
> Everyone will pass unheralded.[1]

The poet identifies his responsibility for recording historical facts as well as celebrating his people. Depicting the fate of Irish poetry as inextricably bound up with the fate of his people, Mac Con Mighde implies that a nation can be conceived through literary means. Belonging to the oral tradition, the poet sees individual memory—or a story—as a link in the great communal story. However, this communal story can take two possible paths: an idealized version of the (lost) Irish past or a turn to the new language. In the latter case it is important to note that Irish English (or Hiberno-English as it is commonly referred to) is an inherently problematic mode. As the Irish critic Seamus Deane has said, it was "not only a dialect or patois; it was one that was consistently characterized as suffering from deformity—excess, illogic, mispronunciation. . . . Verbose, inaccurate, melodramatic, unreliable, in sad need of some form of sobriety, Irish speech and the Irish political condition required a rational articulation that was beyond the capacity of the national character to produce" (Deane, *Strange Country* 55). In short, the dilemma that faced nineteenth-century Irish authors was that their claim to authenticity and accurate representation of (Irish) reality depended upon an extensive use of Irish speech. At the same time, for Irish problems to gain credence and relevance in England, an (Irish) story had to be contained within a framework of (English) logic and accuracy, without taking refuge in justifications such as "it's an Irish story, and may therefore be gently irregular."

According to Joyce's Stephen Dedalus, the fate of every English-speaking Irish soul is to fret in the shadow of another language. Yet any language is an "acquired speech" for a writer. To recall the words of John Banville, a writer is like an infant, having to learn in order to assimilate the world around him. However, Banville continues,

the artist must learn and unlearn, for he must "leap, executing grace-
ful somersaults as he goes, but look down, always, no matter how
vertiginous the view" (Banville, "A Talk" 13). Looking "down" at the
history of Irish literature, one can picture it as a story of a loss but
also as a tale of a successful survival. Having lost some of the Gaelic
world, the Irish created a new mold for their linguistic and cultural
identity within the English-speaking tradition.

## National Identity

Bearing the words of Shakespeare's MacMorris in mind, when
speaking of "my nation" we speak of a nation that contains varieties
of Irishness. The English-speaking settlers, having provided and
forced upon the natives a new linguistic scheme, simultaneously
attempted to claim their own Irishness—the right to belong to this
island. Edward Said claimed that nationalism is "an assertion of
belonging to a place, a people, a heritage. It affirms the home created by a community of language, culture, and customs" (Said,
*Reflections* 177). In the case of Ireland it is difficult to find a community united by language, culture, and customs. Instead, this unity
is a locus of desire for a number of different communities, making
it more of an imagined state than actual reality. In order to give it
cultural and ideological currency, Irish nationalist thought has traditionally anchored the idea of cultural unity not in historical fact
but in the material of legends. This is evident, for instance, during
the Irish cultural revival in the late nineteenth and early twentieth
centuries, and was most famously exemplified by W. B. Yeats's ide-
alization of the Irish peasantry. During the revival, the West of
Ireland came to represent a geographical and cultural location from
which political and cultural unity was seen as originating, for the
national character of Ireland was believed to have been preserved in
the still largely Irish-speaking West. The following chapters will
show that at different times such a repository of (historical or leg-
endary) unity was seen as consisting of Roman Catholicism, the
Irish language movement, the Irish revival, or even the protectionist trade policy. A strong claim for national authenticity is characteristic of colonized countries. Yet, in the case of Ireland, the lines
of division are less clear-cut, as the multilayered colonization

process has left the Irish grappling with a fractured presence within which several communities compete for authenticity. Perhaps the most obvious example is that of Northern Ireland, where the disastrous results of a violent clash between republican and loyalist, Protestant and Catholic allegiances can easily be seen. Another example is the problematic relationship between the Anglo-Irish—the English-speaking settlers who arrived during the Tudor reconquest—and the Irish.[2] The dilemma facing the Anglo-Irish population is most poignantly exemplified in a scene from John Banim's novel *The Anglo-Irish of the Nineteenth Century*:

> "After more than seven hundred years of identity with this country—"
> "Not identity, Grady; that almost makes you speak a paradox," said the Secretary.
> "Connexion, Sir?"
> "No."
> "Then, Sir, conjunction?"
> "Not even that, unless you mean our grammatical anomaly, a disjunctive conjunction . . ."[3]

Attempting to locate a grammar for Anglo-Irish relations, Terry Eagleton described the text of this relationship as indecipherable, since "there is a fundamental opacity or equivocation built into it, a subtle mismatching of perceptions by which it refuses to add up to some luminously intelligible whole" (Eagleton, *Heathcliff* 126). Eagleton's outlook is bleak, denying us the hope of ever reaching this sense of luminous wholeness. However, it could be argued that rather than attempting to locate an unequivocal definition, it would be more fruitful to attempt to discern different perceptions of Irishness. To quote an Irish writer, poet, and translator from Gaelic, Thomas Kinsella: "It is not as though literature, or national life, were a corporate, national investigation of a corporate, national experience—as though a nation were a single animal, with one complex artistic feeler. . . . especially in this present . . . it seems that every writer has to make the imaginative grasp at identity for himself; and if he can find no means in his inheritance to suit him; he will have to start from scratch" (Kinsella 66). Irish (literary) heritage can emerge in a number of different forms—including that mentioned by Kinsella, in other words, starting from scratch. In this case, the "luminous intelligible whole" becomes a possible, if kaleidoscopic, image. Here we must refer to MacMorris once more, for if the final picture is kaleidoscopic, it is imperative to consider the question "who speaks of my nation," and how the intended audience determines and influences national self-image.

## Representation

The British colonization of Ireland became a political reality in 1800 with the Act of Union between Great Britain and Ireland. The piece of land that until then had been an overseas colony now became part of the kingdom. Already at the level of its definition, the Union gave rise to a series of problems. As Ina Ferris astutely remarked, the name itself—the United Kingdom of Great Britain and Ireland—contained a dilemma, as Ireland is "at once a part of the kingdom (a political subject) but not a part of Great Britain (not a national subject)" (Ferris 1). Interestingly, the same year, 1800, also saw the publication of Maria Edgeworth's celebrated debut, *Castle Rackrent*, which marks the birth of the regional novel in English. Thady Quirk, the idiosyncratic narrator of *Castle Rackrent*, presents the story of the decline of his landlords so vividly that even king George III is said to have rubbed his hands and noted with pleasure: "What what, I know something now of my Irish subjects." One can choose whether to interpret this incident as fact or fiction, but it is worth noting that not only the king, but the English audience in general needed an introduction to this new part of the kingdom. So far Irish subjects had occupied the English theaters as "stage Irishmen," presenting the Irish as a conglomeration of loquacious drunkards who kept the rest of the cast and the audience entertained. They were believed to be "wild"; a nation of great storytellers and drinkers, unpredictable, effeminate, and childlike in their passionate nature. Thus it became necessary for the Irish to claim not only political independence but also national subjecthood, so as to exert control over their national self-image in artistic representations. In short, instead of a caricature, an accurate representation was needed. However, the physical distance of Ireland from Britain never quite made the Irish presence an everyday reality for the English, and throughout the nineteenth century we see Irish writers struggling to "explain" the Irish people to an English audience. In other words, Irish writers felt a need to move away from the portrayal of an encounter, which too often remained on an anecdotal or introductory level, to an inside view of the Irish experience. That this "anxiety of accuracy" was occasionally overwhelming is evident in the plethora of footnotes with which Maria Edgeworth furnished her Irish novels. Extensive explanations and footnotes are characteristic traits of these attempts to introduce regional heroes to the (inter)national stage, and offer a point of contact with readers from outside Irish geographical and cultural borders. However wild and wondrous the Irish tales and tours were, realism became a fashionable literary article, a tendency evidenced by another nineteenth-century Irish author, Gerald Griffin. Writing from London, Griffin informed his brother: "Reality you know is all the rage now" (Cronin 114). In order to satisfy this demand for reality, Griffin asked his brother to furnish him with materials for a few short stories which later became the *Tales of the Munster Festivals* (1827). His attempts to provide material to satisfy the "rage" were counterbalanced by his endeavors to educate the English audience. Thus he asked rhetorically in the concluding note to the *Tales*: "Will England, then, remain insensible to the personal afflictions, to the continued agonies of this long-suffering and long-neglected class of men?" (Cronin 114). This concern with the intended audience and its feelings, however, had adverse effects, as most of the Irish fiction composed in Ireland was directed toward an audience outside Ireland. That writing about Ireland to an Irish audience was far from an easy task is attested by statements such as Maria Edgeworth's famous complaint: "It is impossible to draw Ireland as she now is in a book of fiction—realities are too strong, party-passions too violent to bear to see, or care to look at their faces in the looking-glass. The people would only break the glass, and curse the fool who held the mirror up to nature —distorted nature, in a fever" (Zimmern 185). The need to "draw Ireland" or make the Irish themselves look into the looking-glass grew and deepened, so that a hundred years later another author wrote to his wavering publisher, begging him not to back out of publishing his book and saying: "I seriously believe that you will retard the course of civilization in Ireland by preventing the Irish

people from having one good look at themselves in my nicely polished looking-glass" (Joyce, *Letters* 63–4). The young James Joyce
was uncompromising in advocating and executing his style of
"scrupulous meanness," regarding *Dubliners* as a representative work
that reflected the Irish experience with almost clinical accuracy.
That this inward glance reflected a deep-seated need for the Irish
nation is attested by W.B. Yeats, who wrote at the time of a national
and cultural renaissance, arguing for the self-sufficiency of the Irish
self-image: "If you would know Ireland—body and soul—you must
read its poems and stories. They came into existence to please
nobody but the people of Ireland. . . . They are Ireland talking to
herself" (Yeats, *Tales* 25).

To summarize, one could say that instead of a looking-glass the
Irish writer needed a convex mirror in which both the outsider and
the insider would be supplied with a reflection of an accurate (Irish)
reality. However, representation is also a question of focus and perspective. In other words, when reading Irish fiction one has to be
aware of who is holding the mirror, where one is being made to look,
and who is the intended audience. Maria Edgeworth found Irish
realities too strong for the neutrality of a looking-glass. A mirror,
however, is never neutral, for it offers an artificial means to contain
and frame the subject matter—"Irish fiction."

## Irish Fiction

Even a cursory glance at the dates chosen by literary historians as a
point of departure indicates the difficulties involved in providing a
temporal framework for Irish literature. To give a few examples,
Norman Vance's *Irish Literature: A Social History* (1999) starts with
the seventeenth century; Seamus Deane's *A Short History of Irish
Literature* (1986) begins in 1690; Norman Jeffares's *Anglo-Irish
Literature* (1982) in the early eighteenth century; David Cairns and
Shaun Richards use Spenser and Shakespeare as their starting point
in *Writing Ireland: Colonialism, Nationalism and Culture* (1988);
James M. Cahalan's *The Irish Novel: A Critical History* (1988) effec-
tively begins with Maria Edgeworth; Declan Kiberd in *Inventing
Ireland: The Literature of the Modern Nation* (1995) chooses Oscar
Wilde as his starting point; and Terry Eagleton in *Heathcliff and the*

*Great Hunger: Studies in Irish Culture* (1995) begins the chapter on the Anglo-Irish novel with Jonathan Swift.

In his "Introduction" to the *Penguin Book of Irish Short Stories*, Benedict Kiely claims that "Irish prose fiction, properly so called and written in English . . . , begins with the start of the nineteenth century, with, to be exact, Maria Edgeworth's *Castle Rackrent*" (Kiely 8–9). In this statement Kiely simplifies the matters greatly; as this introduction has already shown, nothing is that clear-cut in Irish studies. However, *Castle Rackrent* can indeed be seen as one of the first truly important landmarks in the field of Irish fiction. Not only did the publication of Edgeworth's novel coincide with momentous events in Irish history—the year of the Union—but it also introduced a number of features that later became characteristic of many Irish novels. For instance the Hiberno-English dialect that Edgeworth for the first time put to such an extensive use in a novel functions on two levels; first, Edgeworth's tale acquired its realist air through Old Thady's colloquial speech and, second, it introduced the deceiving voice of a servant and an unreliable Irish storyteller. In the thematic and structural center of Edgeworth's novel stands the Rackrent estate, the dilapidated Big House par excellence which later becomes a symbol of the decline of the Protestant Ascendancy and reappears in the Gothic novels of Sheridan Le Fanu, but also in Somerville and Ross, only to make its fictional comeback in contemporary Irish novels by authors like Jennifer Johnston, Aidan Higgins, and John Banville. Edgeworth's "rotting house" becomes particularly fertile ground for a point of departure in a quest for things Irish as it stands in the middle of a fictional and historical road, affording us not only an opportunity to gaze forward, into the future, but also backward at things past. As Edgeworth herself said in the "Preface" to *Castle Rackrent*, these were "tales of other times." As the following chapters will demonstrate, the extinction of the race of Rackrents was hardly the case, but in order to avoid the too strong realities of the present, a backward look into the past became a staple excuse to claim, as Joyce put it so aptly in *Ulysses* (1922), "it seems history is to blame."

The objective of this book is not to provide a comprehensive account of literary history in Ireland. Instead, it offers beginning students an overview of the central themes and key questions that continue to enchant and enchain fiction writers in Ireland. However, to measure the exact amount to which history is to be "blamed," the following chapters give a brief explanation of relevant historical events, and outline the course of Irish history.

This book does not examine fiction written in Irish. On this subject students might wish to consider such valuable studies as James M. Cahalan's *The Irish Novel*, Declan Kiberd's *The Irish Classics* (2000), and Joep Leerssen's *Mere Irish and Fior-Ghael* (1997)—to name but a few.

The "Preface" to *Castle Rackrent* "warned" its readers, "totally unacquainted with Ireland," that these memoirs "will perhaps be scarcely intelligible" or "appear perfectly incredible." Like the incredible reality of Rackrents, almost every Irish story seems to require the suspension of disbelief. And not because of an overabundance of leprechauns or shamrocks, but rather because of the incredible story of survival and success that they contain.

---

## Notes

1. Deane, Seamus, *A Short History of Irish Literature* (London: Hutchinson, 1986) p. 16.

2. While in social and political terms, the term "Anglo-Irish" is mainly used for the Protestant English settlers, under whose control Ireland was from 1690s till mid-nineteenth century, in literary terms "Anglo-Irish" usually denotes the literature produced by that class but also the literature composed by other non-Anglican and non-English-settler classes.

3. Eagleton, Terry, "Changing the Question," in *Heathcliff and the Great Hunger: Studies in Irish Culture* (London: Verso, 1995) pp. 125–126.

# Chapter Two

# Timeline

| | |
|---|---|
| 8000 B.C. | First tribes arrive to Ireland |
| c. 200 B.C. | Arrival of the first Gaelic-speakers |
| c.130–80 B.C. | Ptolemy's account of Ireland |
| 432 | St. Patrick arrives in Ireland |
| 795 | First Viking raid on Iona, Rathlin, Inishmurray, and Inishbofin |
| 975–1014 | Brian Boru King of Munster's reign |
| 1002–1014 | Brian Boru King of Ireland, until his death at the Battle of Clontarf |
| 1170 | "Strongbow" arrives in Ireland |
| 1175 | Treaty of Windsor between Henry II and Rory O'Connor, High King of Ireland, who submits to rule as a vassal |
| 1366 | Statues of Kilkenny, which sought to prevent English settlers from adopting the Irish language |
| 1541 | A Parliamentary meeting declares Henry VIII the King of Ireland |
| 1591 | The founding of University of Dublin (Trinity College) |
| 1595 | Hugh O'Neill, earl of Tyrone, proclaimed traitor, at war with English forces under Mountjoy, defeated at the Battle of Kinsale in 1601, submits in 1603 |
| 1597 | Edmund Spenser's *A View of the Present State of Ireland* |
| 1603 | New Testament translated into Irish |

| | |
|---|---|
| 1607 | The Flight of the Earls to Spain |
| 1641 | Catholic rebellion in Ulster |
| 1649–1651 | Cromwellian conquest, massacres, and implementation of plantations |
| 1690 | William of Orange wins the Battle of the Boyne |
| 1691 | Treaty of Limerick |
| 1695–1725 | Penal laws against Catholics |
| 1726 | Jonathan Swift's *Gulliver's Travels* |
| 1729 | Jonathan Swift's *A Modest Proposal* |
| 1768 | Maria Edgeworth born |
| 1771 | Abolition of penal laws begins |
| 1775 | Henry Grattan becomes the leader of Patriot Party |
| 1782 | Irish Parliamentary Independence ("Grattan's Parliament") |
| 1785 | The founding of Royal Irish Academy |
| 1791 | Wolfe Tone's *Argument on Behalf of the Catholics of Ireland*; The foundation of the Society of United Irishmen |
| 1792 | Relief Act allows Catholics to practice law; Edmund Burke's *Reflections on the French Revolution* |
| 1794 | William Carleton born |
| 1796 | Michael Banim born |
| 1798 | The rebellion of the United Irishmen; John Banim born |
| 1800 | Act of Union; Maria Edgeworth's *Castle Rackrent* |
| 1803 | Robert Emmet's rising, trial, and execution; Lady Morgan's *St. Clair, or the Heiress of Desmond*; Gerald Griffin born |
| 1805 | Lady Morgan's *The Novice of Dominick* |
| 1806 | Lady Morgan's *The Wild Irish Girl*; Charles Lever born |
| 1812 | Maria Edgeworth's *The Absentee* |

| | |
|---|---|
| 1814 | Lady Morgan's *O'Donnel, a National Tale*; Sheridan Le Fanu born |
| 1817 | Maria Edgeworth's *Ormond* |
| 1818 | Lady Morgan's *Florence Macarthy* |
| 1820 | Charles Robert Maturin's *Melmoth the Wanderer* |
| 1823 | Catholic Association founded under the leadership of Daniel O'Connell |
| 1825 | Michael Banim's *Crohoore of the Bill-Hook* |
| 1826 | John Banim's *The Nowlans*; John and Michael Banim's *The Boyne Water* |
| 1827 | Lady Morgan's *The O'Briens and the O'Flaherties*; Gerald Griffin's *Tales of the Munster Festivals* |
| 1828 | O'Connell elected as an MP for County Clare |
| 1829 | Catholic Emancipation; Gerald Griffin's *The Collegians* |
| 1830–1833 | Tithe War; William Carleton's *Traits and Stories of the Irish Peasantry* |
| 1832 | Reform Bill |
| 1839 | Charles Lever's *Confessions of Harry Lorrequer* |
| 1840 | Gerald Griffin dies |
| 1840–1842 | Daniel O'Connell's Repeal Campaign |
| 1842 | John Banim dies |
| 1845–1849 | The Great Famine |
| 1847 | William Carleton's *The Black Prophet: A Tale of Irish Famine* |
| 1848–1849 | Rebellion by Young Ireland movement |
| 1849 | Maria Edgeworth dies |
| 1858 | James Stephens establishes the Irish Republican Brotherhood; The Fenian Brotherhood formed in the USA; Edith Somerville born |
| 1859 | Lady Morgan dies |
| 1861–1863 | Sheridan Le Fanu's *The House by the Churchyard* |

| | |
|---|---|
| 1862 | Violet Martin (Ross) born |
| 1864 | Sheridan Le Fanu's *Uncle Silas* |
| 1867 | Attempted Fenian rising; Matthew Arnold's *On the Study of Celtic Literature* |
| 1869 | Disestablishment of the Church of Ireland; William Carleton dies |
| 1872 | Charles Lever's *Lord Kilgobbin*; Charles Lever dies |
| 1873 | Sheridan Le Fanu dies |
| 1874 | Michael Banim dies |
| 1875 | Charles Stewart Parnell elected to the Parliament |
| 1878–1880 | Standish James O'Grady's *History of Ireland: Heroic Period* |
| 1879 | Irish National Land League formed |
| 1882 | Phoenix Park murders, the Chief Secretary and Under-Secretary murdered in Dublin; James Joyce born |
| 1886 | Home Rule Bill; George Moore's *A Drama in Muslin* |
| 1889 | Somerville and Ross's *An Irish Cousin* |
| 1891 | Oscar Wilde's *The Picture of Dorian Gray* |
| 1893 | The foundation of Gaelic League; Second Home Rule Bill |
| 1894 | George Moore's *Esther Waters*; Somerville and Ross's *The Real Charlotte* |
| 1896 | Liam O'Flaherty born |
| 1897 | Bram Stoker's *Dracula*; Kate O'Brien born |
| 1898 | United Irish League founded |
| 1899 | Elizabeth Bowen born |
| 1900 | John Redmond elected chairman of Irish Parliamentary Party and United Irish League; Sean O'Faolain born |
| 1902 | Francis Stuart born |
| 1903 | George Moore's *The Untilled Field*; Frank O'Connor born |

| | |
|---|---|
| 1905 | The foundation of Sinn Féin; George Moore's *The Lake*; James Joyce sends the first five stories of *Dubliners* to Grant Richards |
| 1906 | Samuel Beckett born |
| 1911 | Flann O'Brien born |
| 1912 | Home Rule Bill; Ulster Rebellion; James Stephens's *The Charwoman's Daughter* and *The Crock of Gold* |
| 1914 | James Joyce's *Dubliners* |
| 1915 | Violet Martin (Ross) dies |
| 1916 | The Easter Rebellion; James Joyce's *A Portrait of the Artist as a Young Man* |
| 1918 | Sinn Féin's electoral triumph |
| 1919–1921 | Anglo-Irish War |
| 1920 | The Government of Ireland Act introduces partition between two Home Rule states; Dublin's "Bloody Sunday" |
| 1921 | December, Anglo-Irish Treaty; Brian Moore born |
| 1922 | Irish Free State established, Northern Ireland excluded; James Joyce's *Ulysses* published in Paris |
| 1922–1923 | Civil War |
| 1923 | Irish Free State admitted to the League of Nations |
| 1924 | Daniel Corkery's *The Hidden Ireland* |
| 1925 | Partition of Ireland confirmed by tripartite agreement; Liam O'Flaherty's *The Informer*; Somerville's *The Big House of Inver* |
| 1926 | Eamon de Valera founds Fianna Fáil |
| 1928 | William Trevor born |
| 1929 | Proportional representation abolished in Northern Ireland; Elizabeth Bowen's *The Last September* |
| 1930 | Edna O'Brien born; Jennifer Johnston born |
| 1931 | Banning of the IRA in Free State; Frank O'Connor's *Guests of the Nation*; Kate O'Brien's *Without My Cloak* |

| | |
|---|---|
| 1932 | de Valera forms government; Sean O'Faolain's *Midsummer Night Madness and Other Stories* |
| 1933 | Kate O'Brien's *The Ante-Room* |
| 1934 | Samuel Beckett's *More Pricks than Kicks*; Sean O'Faolain's *A Nest of Simple Folk*; John McGahern born |
| 1935 | Importation and sale of contraceptives banned in the Free State |
| 1936 | Sean O'Faolain's *Bird Alone*; Kate O'Brien's *Mary Lavelle* |
| 1937 | Constitution of Éire replaces Free State; Liam O'Flaherty's *Famine* |
| 1938 | Samuel Beckett's *Murphy* |
| 1939–1945 | Irish neutrality in the Second World War |
| 1939 | James Joyce's *Finnegans Wake*; Flann O'Brien's *At-Swim-Two-Birds* |
| 1940 | Frank O'Connor's *Dutch Interior*; Sean O'Faolain's *Come Back to Erin* |
| 1941 | James Joyce dies; Flann O'Brien's *An Béal Bocht* (*The Poor Mouth*); Kate O'Brien's *The Land of Spices* |
| 1945 | John Banville born |
| 1946 | Liam O'Flaherty's *Land* |
| 1948 | Republic of Ireland declared; Francis Stuart's *The Pillar of Cloud* |
| 1949 | Edith Somerville dies; Elizabeth Bowen's *The Heat of the Day*; Francis Stuart's *Redemption* |
| 1950 | James Stephens dies; Liam O'Flaherty's *Insurrection*; Francis Stuart's *The Flowering Cross* |
| 1951 | Samuel Beckett's *Molloy* and *Malone Meurt* (*Malone Dies*) published in Paris |
| 1953 | Samuel Beckett's *Watt* appears in English and *The Unnamable* in French |
| 1954 | IRA attacks in Armagh |
| 1955 | Brian Moore's *Judith Hearne*; Colm Tóibín born |

| | |
|---|---|
| 1956–1962 | IRA campaign in North |
| 1958 | William Trevor's *A Standard of Behaviour*; Roddy Doyle born |
| 1960 | Edna O'Brien's *The Country Girls* |
| 1961 | Eoin McNamee born |
| 1962 | Edna O'Brien's *The Lonely Girl*; Anne Enright born |
| 1963 | John McGahern's *The Barracks*; Flann O'Brien's *The Dalkey Archive* |
| 1964 | Sean Francis Lemass and Terence O'Neill, prime ministers of North and South, meet; Edna O'Brien's *Girls in Their Married Bliss* |
| 1965 | John McGahern's *The Dark* published and banned under the Censorship Act |
| 1966 | Aidan Higgins's *Langrishe, Go Down*; Flann O'Brien dies; Frank O'Connor dies; William Trevor's *The Day We Got Drunk on Cake* |
| 1967 | Flann O'Brien's *The Third Policeman*; Samuel Beckett's *Stories and Texts for Nothing* |
| 1968 | First Civil Rights march; Clash in Derry between IRA and police; Northern Ireland breaks down in violence |
| 1969 | People's Democracy march from Belfast to Derry in January, a series of explosions follows the march, British troops sent in; James Plunkett's *Strumpet City*; Samuel Beckett awarded the Nobel Prize for Literature; Emma Donoghue born |
| 1970 | Splits in Sinn Féin and IRA lead to the forming of provisional fractions; John Banville's *Long Lankin* |
| 1971 | Ian Paisley's Democratic Unionist party founded; First British soldier killed by IRA in Belfast; Francis Stuart's *Black List, Section H*; John Banville's *Nightspawn* |
| 1972 | "Bloody Sunday" in Derry; Direct Rule from Westminster imposed; Jennifer Johnston's *The Captains and the Kings*; Brian Moore's *Catholics*; William Trevor's *The Ballroom of Romance* |

| | |
|---|---|
| 1973 | Ireland enters EEC; Sunningdale Agreement; Economic recession in North and South; John Banville's *Birchwood*; John McGahern's *Nightlines*; Elizabeth Bowen dies |
| 1974 | Guildford and Birmingham pub bombings; Jennifer Johnston's *How Many Miles to Babylon*; Kate O'Brien dies |
| 1975 | Brian Moore's *The Great Victorian Collection* |
| 1976 | British ambassador in Dublin killed; John Banville's *Doctor Copernicus* |
| 1979 | Earl Mountbatten and relations killed in County Sligo; 18 soldiers killed in County Down; John McGahern's *The Pornographer*; Brian Moore's *The Mangan Inheritance*; Jennifer Johnston's *The Old Jest* |
| 1981 | John Banville's *Kepler* |
| 1982 | Soldiers killed at Knightsbridge and Ballykelly |
| 1983 | Referendum bans abortion in Republic; William Trevor's *Fools of Fortune* |
| 1984 | Liam O'Flaherty dies; John Banville's *The Newton Letter* |
| 1985 | Brian Moore's *Black Robe* |
| 1986 | Confirmation of Republic's ban on divorce; John Banville's *Mefisto* |
| 1987 | Eleven people killed before Remembrance Service in Enniskillen; Brian Moore's *The Colour of Blood*; Roddy Doyle's *The Commitments* |
| 1988 | Samuel Beckett's *Stirrings Still* |
| 1989 | Fianna Fáil forms coalition cabinet with Progressive Democrats, with Charles Haughey remaining Taoiseach; Samuel Beckett dies in Paris; John Banville's *The Book of Evidence*; Robert McLiam Wilson's *Ripley Bogle* |

| | |
|---|---|
| 1990 | Mary Robinson elected the seventh President of Ireland; Roddy Doyle's *The Snapper*; John McGahern's *Amongst Women*; Colm Tóibín's *The South* |
| 1991 | Sean O'Faolain dies; Roddy Doyle's *The Van*; Anne Enright's *The Portable Virgin*; Joseph O'Connor's *Cowboys and Indians* |
| 1993 | Roddy Doyle's *Paddy Clarke Ha Ha Ha* published and wins the Booker Prize; John Banville's *Ghosts*; Colm Tóibín's *The Heather Blazing* |
| 1994 | IRA and Loyalist paramilitary groups announce ceasefire; Eoin McNamee's *Resurrection Man*; Emma Donoghue's *Stir-fry* |
| 1995 | Seamus Heaney awarded Nobel Prize for Literature; Jennifer Johnston's *The Illusionist*; John Banville's *Athena*; Anne Enright's *The Wig My Father Wore*; Emma Donoghue's *Hood* |
| 1996 | The IRA bomb attack on Canary Wharf in London and the end of ceasefire; A constitutional referendum to permit civil divorce and remarriage passes; Roddy Doyle's *The Woman Who Walked Into Doors*; Robert McLiam Wilson's *Eureka Street* |
| 1997 | Mo Mowland appointed first woman Secretary of State for Northern Ireland; Bertie Ahern's Fianna Fáil-PD coalition comes to power; IRA declares the resumption of the 1994 ceasefire; John Banville's *The Untouchable*; Emma Donoghue's *Kissing the Witch* |
| 1998 | Omagh bombing |
| 1999 | Roddy Doyle's *A Star Called Henry*; Colm Tóibín's *The Blackwater Lightship* |
| 2000 | Francis Stuart dies; John Banville's *Eclipse*; Anne Enright's *What Are You Like?* |
| 2001 | Eoin McNamee's *The Blue Tango* |

2002    The referendum conducted in the Republic votes
        for the undoing of the laws regarding abortion; John
        McGahern's *That They May Face the Rising Sun*
        (published in the United States under the title *By
        the Lake*); John Banville's *Shroud*

# Chapter Three

# Getting Started with Irish Fiction

It is difficult to give a tried and tested recipe of how to read an Irish novel or a short story. There are innumerable ways of approaching an Irish text (as the chapter on Irish criticism will show). Central to all of these are the skills of close reading and literary analysis. But Irish fiction can present unusual problems for readers. Opening an Irish novel, you may feel as if you are eavesdropping a conversation that has been going on for centuries. James Joyce's *Finnegans Wake* is an extreme example of the difficulties one may encounter. Consider for instance its opening sentence: "riverrun, past Eve and Adam's, from swerve of shore to bend of bay, brings us by a commodius vicus of recirculation back to Howth Castle and Environs." The only thing that seems certain when reading this sentence is the need for different reading strategies than, let's say, a novel by John Grisham or Danielle Steele (and by this I do not mean to diminish the achievement of these two authors). The "riverrun" sentence raises a plethora of pressing questions: Why does the novel begin in medias res, or in the middle of a sentence? What does Joyce mean by "riverrun"? Why is the standard expression "Adam and Eve" reversed? Why are the punctuation and sentence structure so strange? What is commodius vicus? And where is Howth Castle, and which river are we talking about?

*Finnegans Wake* is a notoriously difficult text, and the task of unraveling its intricacies has kept scholars busy for decades. However, if read carefully, every Irish text is capable of raising just as many questions (although perhaps not quite so complex). This book is designed to help you approach Irish texts, and, if done with an open and curious mind, also to enjoy the process.

## Some Suggestions for Getting Started

First, place the text within its particular political, cultural, and social framework. Try to determine the perspective(s) of the story: urban or rural, Protestant or Catholic, female or male, Protestant Anglo-Irish nationalist or Catholic Irish nationalist. Start by considering the author's background. You will find Chapter Four especially helpful in this respect, as it introduces you to the best and the best-known authors and texts from 1800 to 2002.

Then explore the central themes of the book. Is the text concerned with family relations? Is the text trying to analyze a specific segment or event from Irish history? Is the book centered around a discussion of a contentious historical or political issue, such as the Northern crisis? These and many other thematic, social, and cultural preoccupations are immensely important factors in an Irish text.

In other words, another story lies beneath the one you read—the story of a small nation struggling to define itself. It is a story of divided loyalties, frictions that have influenced religious, familial, political, cultural, and personal commitments. The religious divide between Protestants and Catholics has characterized the everyday reality of Ireland for centuries. But influence does not always lie with loyalty. For instance, while James Joyce was outspokenly anti-Catholic, images and references to Catholic tradition permeate his works. More often we see only part of the story. Authors such as Sheridan Le Fanu were writing about the problems that accompanied the life of Protestant Ascendancy, a minority in Ireland that for centuries was more powerful than the majority of inhabitants. And despite some prominent exceptions, women were often underrepresented in the Irish literary tradition.

As each faction endeavors to construct a personal identity of Ireland (often portraying as the definitive depiction), even place becomes politically freighted. The countryside, especially the West of Ireland, has traditionally been seen as the site of "true Irishness." The urban environment, by contrast, is frequently deployed to criticize the loss of an authentic living experience. The city becomes the site of crime and violence. Chapter Five gives an overview of these and similar themes, pointing toward further discussion.

Insofar as possible, consider the texts to which the author refers. Irish fiction turns outward as well as in. We may very productively analyze Irish fiction in the context of international influence. There are good editions of many nineteenth-century authors (such as the Pickering editions of Maria Edgeworth's works and Lady Morgan's *The Wild Irish Girl*) and most of Joyce's prose texts, which identify the more important references. Make sure to read these textual notes closely. English, French, Russian, and German writers (to name but a few traditions) have left indelible marks on the literature of Ireland. Certainly, British literary traditions remain a first point of contact, not only because of language, but also because of Ireland's long history under Britain. In studying Maria Edgeworth, one might compare her to her Irish contemporary, Lady Morgan, but also to the English (women) writers—not to mention the Scottish Sir Walter Scott, who openly acknowledged Edgeworth's influence upon him. Lady Morgan, in turn, compares well with a French writer, Madame de Staël (in fact, Lady Morgan was hailed as "the Irish de Staël"), an early promoter of women's rights and an outspoken opponent of Napoleon. Furthermore, in addition to contemporary references and historical, social, and political allusions, Irish writers are—as are all writers—prone to weave references to other authors' works into the texture of their fiction. James Joyce was famous for adding such references to the draft versions of his texts. Contemporary Irish authors frequently employ references to his work, as well as to those of European authors. An awareness of this is important while reading authors like John Banville, John McGahern, Edna O'Brien, and Anne Enright. At first, tracing these references may seem daunting. Consider them as possible avenues to a better understanding of Irish fiction.

Some knowledge of historical background is essential for every student of Irish literature, so that the stories told by the Irish prose writers would not appear "perfectly incredible" or "scarcely intelligible." Ireland's history is long and complex, and, similarly to its literature, has frequently been the site of contesting interpretations. This book examines Irish fiction from the publication of Maria Edgeworth's *Castle Rackrent* (1800) onward. By no means do I wish to suggest that Irish history began in 1800. While *Castle Rackrent* marks a suitable starting point for an overview of Irish fiction, Ireland and its history prior to the publication of Edgeworth's masterpiece offer an intriguing picture of the struggle for self-identity.

## An Outline of Irish History

### Celts to Romans

As we know, the first Celtic people appeared in Ireland during the Iron Age, but there is no evidence of a large-scale invasion.[1] The signs of the earliest inhabitants, who might have migrated from Britain, date to 8,000 B.C. These people lived in small huts in hunting camps and might have been migrating seasonally. There is no evidence of agricultural activity or artistic production of any sort, both of which seem to have arrived with the appearance of Neolithic peoples who came from Britain or Europe about 6,000 years ago. They built dolmens, passage-tombs and court-cairns, developed pottery, and manufactured axes. The first metal-workers appeared during the Bronze Age (2,500–600 B.C.). From this period survive beautifully ornamented objects such as earrings, fibulae (dress fasteners), and other types of jewelry. Approximately 200 B.C., around the time when iron came to replace bronze as the main material for tools and weapons, the first Celtic peoples arrived in Ireland and with them came the Irish language and La Tène style artwork. Although the Celtic peoples had developed means of written communication of sorts, such as Ogham (an alphabetic script), the art of writing arrived in Ireland with Christianity in the fifth century. The monastic settlements brought Latin (written) culture into contact with Gaelic (oral) civilization. From this period survives a substantial corpus of literature both in Latin and Irish. The learned Irish men were at first uneasy in developing a relationship with the Christian clergy, but the encounter was remarkably smooth. The sixth and seventh centuries saw the flowering of a friendly cohabitation of Christian and Irish culture. The preservation of folk traditions, which so far had been the poets' function, became the concern of the monastic scribes who were eager to make the local lore part of Christian belief. They recorded the stories of the "origins" of Irish history but also the great sagas such as the Ulster cycle, the Fenian cycle, the Cycle of the Kings, and the Mythological cycle, as well as the group of Voyages. All these sagas were recorded in original Irish, as a consequence of which Irish became one of the oldest vernacular literatures in Europe. On the social ladder, the highest position was occupied by the kings (kings of petty local kingdoms, over-kings ruling several kingdoms, and the kings of over-kings who ruled a whole province). It seems that during the early historic period the leading dynasty was the Uí Néill, whose primacy was shattered around the eleventh century. Starting from the ninth century, Ireland's kingdoms began to suffer from Viking invasions, which were partially responsible for the fall of the Uí Néill and the rise of Brian Boru, who famously beat the Vikings at the battle of Clontarf in 1014, where he lost his own life. The Battle of Clontarf was in later "historical accounts" construed as a victory by the High King of Ireland over foreign invaders, but the Vikings were by this time already playing a minor role in Ireland's war-torn domestic policy. Subsequent antiquarian movements have attempted to portray early Ireland as an independent country with a centralized culture, but the political centralization was brought to Ireland by the Norman invaders in the twelfth century.

### Norman Invasion to 1640

The Normans came at the instigation of Diarmait MacMurchada (Dermot MacMurrough), the king of Leinster (a region in Ireland) who had been expelled by the reigning high king Ruaidrí Ua Conchobair (Rory O'Connor). The expelled MacMurchada sought help from south of Wales, and found his ally in Richard de Clare, also known as Strongbow, under whose leadership the French-speaking Norman invaders arrived in Ireland. Strongbow brought a professional army of 1,000 men and captured Wateford and Dublin. Henry II, having become uneasy seeing the success of Strongbow's conquest, arrived near Waterford with his fleet, and granted Leinster to Strongbow to thank him for his service—and also to make sure that he stayed faithful to the Crown. Before leaving Ireland, Henry gave a substantial piece of land from Shannon to the Boyne to Hugh de Lacy and his family. Although the country had not yet been systematically colonized, the English established their presence and now ruled the area around Dublin, mostly known as the Pale (the expression "beyond the pale" is believed to derive from that time). The majority of the population still lived according to the old Irish customs and laws, but the country was politically and culturally divided into English (the Pale around Dublin and south) and Gaelic (west and north) parts. During the same period, missionaries from the continental religious orders such as Cistercians and Franciscans started to arrive in Ireland. These orders became absorbed in Irish culture and they recruited their members from the dominant literary families. The great influence that Irish culture and society had on the colonists is evident from the colonists' attempts to defend themselves against that influence; for instance, the Statues of Kilkenny (1366) prohibited the English from speaking Irish, marrying Irish, or fostering children with Irish families. A full-scale conquest of Ireland was unfeasible because of the great cost it would involve; at the same time the English were also reluctant to leave this half-conquered "wild" bogland, as the French or Spanish could take it over and turn it into their military stronghold. Henry VIII tried to come up with a middle way to resolve the "Irish problem"; having declared himself the king of Ireland in 1541, Henry tried to persuade the Gaelic chieftains to accept the English rule, offering them titles and governmental positions in return. Progress was slow during the Henriqean era and also under Edward VI and Mary, so Elizabeth I inherited a situation that did not satisfy any parties. The army installed in Ireland was a growing financial burden for the Old English, the Irish chieftains were getting more concerned about the conduct of the army and feared the full-scale takeover, the army captains were annoyed with Elizabeth's reluctance to deal with the situation decisively and eagerly awaited the opportunity to establish themselves as local gentry.

The first plantations began in east Ulster (1572–1573) and Munster (1584), and the result was escalating violence: the latter was the cause of the Desmond rebellion (1579–1583) and the former led to the Nine Years War (1594–1603). The Ulster colony was reestablished when, on Christmas Day 1601, at the Battle of Kinsale, Lord Mountjoy's English army defeated the Irish force under Hugh O'Neill. By 1607 there were no leaders of Gaelic Ireland left on the island; in the famous Flight of the Earls they all had fled to continental Europe. Many scholars also emigrated and joined the continental seminaries. The central institutions of England became effective throughout Ireland. The New English Protestant community, predominantly Anglican, found itself partly supported and partly opposed by other non-Catholic groupings such as the Presbyterian Scots who had settled mainly in the North of Ireland.

### Cromwell to Eighteenth Century

Old English families grew restless seeing the anti-Catholic measures being taken, and a rebellion broke out in Ulster in 1641. The rising served for Protestants as a justification for the confiscation of land from the Catholics. Charles I's alleged support to the rebels gave another reason for Oliver Cromwell's army to land in Ireland in 1649. The Cromwellian massacres that followed prepared the ground for the next step in Ireland's colonization, as more than 150,000 English Protestant emigrants arrived in Ireland during the next 20 years.

The Cromwellian regime of the 1650s effected substantial changes in landholding and political rights. The penal legislation was instituted, as a consequence of which most of the Irish land was owned by the new Protestant élite. The 1650s saw important changes in parliamentary politics; the Irish parliament was abolished and replaced by an inadequate Irish representation at Westminster. After the collapse of the Cromwellian regime in 1659, Charles II was proclaimed king in Dublin in May 1660. In 1685, the Catholic James II succeeded to the English throne, a development that made Irish Protestants nervous about their privileged status and property. James appointed a Protestant Lord Deputy, Lord Clarendon, who was recalled after two years and replaced by the earl of Tyrconnell, a maneuver which signaled James's pro-Catholic sympathies. The English political élite, growing more and more worried about his leniency toward Catholics, invited James's son-in-law, William of Orange, to take the English throne, thus instigating another war centered upon Ireland. James landed in Ireland in March 1689. Four months later William's forces arrived in Ulster, and the two armies met at the Battle of the Boyne on July 1, 1690. William won the battle and the defeated James fled to France. The war was ended by the Treaty of Limerick, after the siege of that city, in October 1691. The military triumph of the Williamites meant that political authority was restored to the Protestants.

During the eighteenth century, Ireland became subordinate to England. The head of the Irish administration (the Lord Lieutenant) was appointed by the Crown on the recommendation of the English government, and most of the important offices were filled by

Englishmen. The Crown could avail of Poynings' Law (1494), which gave the English (from 1707, the British, after Scotland became part of the kingdom) Privy Council the power to respite and to amend all legislation that came from the Irish parliament, as well as the Declaratory Act (1719), which made the House of Lords at Westminster the final court of legal appeal in Irish law cases and gave the British parliament the power to make laws for Ireland.

Protestant settlers had come to regard Ireland not only as their new home but also as their country, and this encouraged them to regard themselves as the rightful and historic inhabitants of Ireland. The best example of the national feelings of the New English Protestant landholders can be found in William Molyneux's tract *The Case of Ireland's Being Bound by Acts of Parliament in England Stated* (1698). Molyneux, born and educated in Dublin, was the first Secretary of the Dublin Philosophical Society and sat as an MP for Dublin University, and, most importantly, during the time the Lord Justices were absent, 1697–1698, shared responsibility for the Irish government. Molyneux's tract exemplifies the ideas prevalent among Irish Protestant Patriots and their desire to be equal with Britain. The Protestant élite did not want separation from Britain, just the power to govern. In his tract Molyneux claimed: "The great Body of the present People of *Ireland* are the Progeny of the *English* and *Britains* [Britons], that from time to time have come over into this kingdom; and there remains but a mere handful of the Ancient *Irish* at this day, I may say, not one in a thousand" (Foster 161). Although historically and sociologically questionable, the tract indicated the depth of the nationalist feelings among the settlers.

The Irish situation was complicated because the religion of the landowning élite—the Protestant Church of Ireland—differed from the majority of the population. The minority élite secured its economic, social, and political position by implementing discriminatory legislation (Penal Laws). Penal Laws were not devised systematically, yet step by step they achieved the exclusion of Catholics from the political life and constituted a serious hindrance to their economic advancement. For instance, the adoption of an English oath (in 1692) precluded Catholics from sitting in Parliament. The 1703 act for registering clergy deprived Catholics of religious leadership and limited the number of Catholic clergy in Ireland. Restrictions also applied to the freedom of Catholics to educate their children; to carry arms; to inherit, own, lease, and work land; to trade and employ; to enter the major professions; and, as of 1728, to vote.

### Grattan's Parliament to the Famine

In May 1782, Irish parliamentary independence was recognized (it was ratified by the British parliament on January 22, 1783). As Henry Grattan famously said, Ireland was now a nation. However, given the deprivation of the Catholic civic rights, this was essentially a "Protestant Nation" and the parliament became known as "Grattan's parliament." Under the rule of the Protestant élite, the country's economy advanced significantly. One of the best networks of roads in Europe was created: cities like Dublin, Cork, Limerick, and Wateford gained new public buildings and streets. However, the sectarian loyalties remained strong; for example, a grouping called the Catholic Defenders was formed in County Armagh in the 1780s as a response to the Protestant Peep O'Day Boys and their disarmament raids. In 1791, an organization called the United Irishmen was created, the members of which mainly came from the Protestant and Presbyterian middle classes who wanted to reform the representative system. Their name was inspired by Wolfe Tone, a Republican and revolutionary who believed that Ireland's problems could only be overcome if Catholic, Protestant, and Dissenter joined their forces and Ireland broke the connection with England. The United Irishmen formed an alliance with the Catholic Defenders, and their revolutionary hopes were running high, especially since they were extremely successful in recruiting new members and were even able to enlist the French among their supporters. It seemed likely that a successful rebellion could be organized. However, when a large-scale invasion tried to land near Bantry Bay in 1796, the rebels were detained due to bad weather, and the authorities gained sufficient time to gather forces for a ruthless counterattack. When the rebellion broke out in May 1798, it was fragmented and localized, and the French help came too late. After the defeat of 1798, political power remained strongly in the hands of the ruling Protestant class, and instead of independence the new century began with a legislative union with Britain.

Between the years 1778 and 1792, most of the laws restricting the liberty of Catholics were abolished, and the major obstacle to granting full civil rights for Catholics remained the prohibition of their becoming members of the Parliament. Protestant conservatives both in England and Ireland were firmly opposed to granting full Catholic emancipation; however, eager to be part of the kingdom, the Protestants tried to "calm" the Catholic nationalists by promising them a full emancipation. In 1800, the Irish Parliament passed the Act of Union, thus voting itself out of existence and giving birth to the United Kingdom of Great Britain and Ireland. Ireland was from now on to be represented by about 100 MPs in Westminster Palace in London. Part of the trade-off was full Catholic emancipation, but the Prime Minister William Pitt failed to overcome King George III's opposition.

That the Union and the accompanying promises did not satisfy everyone in Ireland is evident from another attempt at rebellion in 1803, this time instigated by young Robert Emmet, who was sentenced to be hanged, drawn, and quartered. His last words are believed to have been: "Let no man write my epitaph. . . . When my country takes her place among the nations of the earth, then, and not till then, let my epitaph be written. I have done." The country Emmet dreamt of was slow to materialize, and even slower was the arrival of the eagerly awaited Catholic emancipation. After a long campaign and pressure, Daniel O'Connell finally won the emancipation in 1829. O'Connell was the leading figure in the Catholic Association, founded in 1823. After the success of 1829, he launched a campaign to repeal the Act of Union, but this new campaign failed to produce the desired outcome. However, O'Connell's organization gave birth to a new movement—first led by Thomas Davis and, after his death, by an Ulster Presbyterian John Mitchel—the United Irishmen movement agitated for an independent Irish republic and was responsible for a rebellion in 1848.

The failure of the United Irishmen rebellion was due to the fact that at the time the population was undergoing one of the most tragic events in nineteenth century: the Great Famine. Between 1800 and 1845, there had been 16 food crises because of bad weather. Despite the fact that emigration was growing more popular, the poorest classes were still susceptible to a natural disaster. In

1845, an incurable fungal disease arrived in Ireland from Europe, affecting most the staple of the poorest people's diet: the potato crop. In three of the following four years this "potato blight" hit again, as a consequence of which tens of thousands died of malnutrition and epidemic diseases. The total number of Famine victims was, according to recent calculations, close to one million. The Famine and mass emigration affected the poorest classes, which were also predominantly Irish speaking. Due to malnutrition and unemployment, emigration during the time of Famine became massive; it has been estimated that annual emigration to North America exceeded 65,000. The reasons why the Famine had such a disastrous effect and why it was not prevented are still a contentious topic. In popular opinion, the Famine was perpetuated by the British, who failed to help this not-so-remote part of their kingdom.

### The Aftermath of Famine and Home Rule

The aftermath of Famine saw the rise of political and cultural nationalism. The revolutionary wing of the nationalist movement formed its own organization, the Irish Republican Brotherhood (Fenians), in 1858. The British government responded to the developing Irish nationalism by implementing wide-ranging social reforms, including Land Acts, which transferred the ownership from landlord to tenant. The government's policy was commonly described as "killing Home Rule by kindness." The campaigns for Land League (a mass movement aimed at tenant defense and at making the peasants proprietors of their land) caused large-scale unrest in rural Ireland, which climaxed with British Prime Minister William Gladstone's introduction of land law reform in 1881. The League was declared unlawful in 1881, and Charles Stewart Parnell (a Protestant and an active supporter of Home Rule) was subsequently imprisoned. This indicated that the government was prone to use violence whenever the political situation in Ireland showed signs of tenseness, a tendency particularly evident during the so-called Land War of 1879–1882, when the members and the leaders of the Land League were subjected to harassment and threats.

From the political perspective, the Irish Parliamentary Party at Westminster under Isaac Butt and Charles Stewart Parnell (both

Protestants) was the sole political organization working for independence through parliamentary means after the failed rebellions in 1848 and 1867.

The rise of nationalist feelings culminated in 1893, when the Gaelic League (*Conradh na Gaeilge*) was founded. The revival of the Irish language was accompanied by renewed demands for political independence. In 1884, the Gaelic Athletic Association was founded, an organization dedicated to promoting traditional Irish sports. Lady Gregory, W. B. Yeats, and others founded the Irish Literary Theatre in 1898, which later became known as the Abbey Theatre. The following year Arthur Griffith began the newspaper *United Irishmen*. All these developments were directed toward the goal of achieving cultural (and political) independence.

In 1885 Gladstone introduced a "Home Rule" Bill, which would have granted power, albeit very limited, to an all-Ireland Parliament. This, however, turned out to be too much for the Unionists and the Conservatives, who launched a campaign to oppose the bill. In 1893, Gladstone's second attempt to pass the bill failed, as the conservative House of Lords voted against it. However, at that time the Home Rule question became less important on the political agenda, and the attention was focused more on economic and social problems, mainly due to the Liberal Party having lost the majority to the Conservatives.

In 1905, Sinn Féin ("Ourselves") was founded, an organization with a broadly based nationalist membership and with its own economic agenda. It became more and more evident that the idea of Home Rule was insufficient and complete independence was on the agenda.

### World War I and Independence

The terms introduced by yet another Home Rule Bill of 1912 were similar to those expressed in earlier proposals. However, this bill was received with even more aggressive opposition. This was especially evident in Ulster, where the concentration of Protestants was the highest, and the Unionist support the strongest in Ireland. The tactics deployed by the opposition were such that a civil war was thought to be on the verge of breaking out. The crisis was temporarily "forgotten" with the outbreak of the First World War in 1914, as the bill was passed in the Parliament but suspended thereafter. Among the terms were the special conditions for some or all of the nine Ulster counties, which were to be excluded from the bill. This development was met with a strong opposition from the nationalists whose leader, John Redmond, had allowed temporary exclusion in order to pass the bill. The Ulster unionists and their problems remained an unresolved question, hanging threateningly over Ireland during the First World War.

Over 270,000 Irishmen (40% of the adult population) served in the British army during the war, and thousands contributed to the war effort by working in munitions factories. Many nationalists participated, hoping that their contribution would help Ireland to get Home Rule. At the same time, unionists volunteered to join the Ulster Volunteer Forces, believing that by sacrificing for Britain, they might help to prevent Home Rule. Dissatisfaction among the nationalists escalated into the Easter Rising of April 1916. The rebellion was doomed to failure as it lacked organization and tactical planning. It was to be facilitated by an arms shipment from Germany, but the interception of the German ship caused chaos among the insurgents. Only about a thousand people came out on Easter Monday to take over some government buildings in central Dublin. Although an Irish Republic was declared outside the occupied General Post Office, the rising was over in less than a week. The insurgents signed an unconditional surrender, and their leaders were executed. The Easter Rising revealed the organizational failures of the nationalist insurgency, but it also showed the insufficiency of Home Rule as a response to Irish problems. Despite the lack of public support during the insurrection, the executions galvanized public sympathy for the rebels. The radical nationalist wing reorganized their forces, the volunteer movement changed their name to Irish Republican Army (IRA), and Sinn Féin became the main outlet for radical nationalist ideas. They won the 1918 general elections, and in January 1919, Dáil Éireann, a Republican assembly, was founded. At the same time, the IRA began a guerrilla war against the British forces, also known as the "Troubles." Having declared English military occupation illegal, the IRA attacked the symbolic representations of British control, such as the Big Houses belonging to the

Protestant Ascendancy. The government retaliated by sending in special units, the most infamous of which were known as the "Black and Tans." A truce was finally introduced in July 1921, after which the country was formally partitioned and the Government of Ireland Act established the statelet of Northern Ireland. Arthur Griffiths and Michael Collins led the republican negotiating team that signed the treaty with the British government in December 1921. The treaty turned out to be unacceptable for many staunch Republicans, among whom the most prominent was Eamon de Valera, the leader of underground republican government during the War of Independence.

The disagreements proved strong enough to cause the outbreak of the Civil War in June 1922, when the provisional government forces attacked the republican-held Four Courts in Dublin. The war lasted little over a year, with casualties on both sides, but the government's victory was quite evident. Despite its relatively short duration, historians have seen the Civil War as more traumatic and influential than the Independence War (also referred to as the "Anglo-Irish War") of 1919–1921. For the outcome of the Civil War—the separation of the six Northern counties from the Free State—constituted a permanent fracture in Irish politics, history, and families.

### The Free State

Under these circumstances it is understandable why the policy of new Cumann na nGaedheal government, consisting of the treaty supporters under the leadership of William Thomas Cosgrave, was characterized by caution, continuity, and tradition. The civil service, legal system, army, and education system of the Free Irish State (later the Republic of Ireland) were modeled after the British example. The Free State remained a predominantly agricultural country, exporting mainly to Britain and importing most manufactured goods from its old colonizers. In 1930, the government established the five-person Censorship Board, which banned thousands of books by Irish and international authors. Northern Ireland remained an issue until the border between the north and south of Ireland was finally ratified in 1925. The Free State had to deal with a fragile internal stability, as an army mutiny was narrowly averted in 1924, and the IRA was still not ready to accept the partitioning of Ireland that resulted from the Civil War.

De Valera founded his own party, Fianna Fáil ("Soldiers of Destiny") in 1926, and after the 1932 general election became the Taoiseach (Prime Minister). De Valera saw this as an opportunity to implement his rather radical views on politics and economics. For instance, he decided to give priority to developing small industries and to enforce severe protectionist measures with regard to import and export issues with Britain. In 1937, he successfully introduced a new constitution. During the Second World War (or "Emergency" as it was called in Ireland), de Valera adopted a policy of military neutrality. After the war, the government's unpopularity rose, as the country was suffering from economic hardship and de Valera's party's name was tarnished by numerous scandals. He lost the 1948 elections, after which a period of political instability followed with a succession of three short-lived governments. The immigration rate started to rise, reaching the level of the Famine years.

Finally, under the leadership of Seán Lemass, elected in 1959 as Taoiseach and the leader of Fianna Fáil, Ireland became less reluctant to let in foreign influences and more prone to open up the country to an influx of new ideas in economics and politics. In this respect, the major step was the publication of T. K. Whitaker's white paper, *Economic Development* (1958), followed by the First Programme for Economic Expansion in 1958 (followed by the Second in 1963), which heralded the abandonment of self-sufficiency in favor of free trade policy, and the encouragement of foreign investment and increase in export. The Broadcasting Authority Act of 1960 was followed by the opening of a national television service in 1962. That same year saw Ireland's initial application for European Economic Community (EEC) membership. The Second Vatican Council (1962–1965) decreed radical renewals in Catholic worship, which in Ireland meant worshipping both in Gaelic and English, and involved lay participation in Church affairs. These developments were followed by the relaxation of censorship in 1967, the installation of free second-level education in

1967–1968, and tax breaks for artists in 1969. In short, the 1960s were a dynamic period that culminated in 1973 with the government's decision to enter the EEC. However, due to the oil price rise on the world market, the same year also saw a new set of severe financial difficulties that continued to affect the country over the next 15 years. The economic instability was accompanied by political insecurity; between 1973 and 1989 Ireland again had a series of short-term governments and saw seven general elections.

### Northern Irish Conflict and the Republic in the EU

The presence of substantial Catholic communities, especially in the border areas, had been causing difficulties in Northern Ireland from its foundation in 1920. Over the years, the North experienced a particularly tense atmosphere due to recurrent confrontations between Catholic Civil Rights demonstrators and their Protestant opponents. In 1969, the events escalated into open communal violence, and the British army intervened in an effort to restore peace. Implementing the Falls Road curfew and internment without trial caused an eruption of violence that was beyond containment, and culminated in 1972 with bombings and shootings. Paramilitary groupings, most notably the Provisional IRA (an extreme republican organization) and the Ulster Defence Association (an extreme loyalist organization), were particularly active in the rapidly deteriorating situation. The British government commenced "direct rule" from Westminster, and a series of initiatives to restore peace followed, most notably the Sunningdale Agreement in 1973, the Power Sharing Executive in 1974, and the "Rolling Devolution" plan in the early 1980s. In 1994, a major breakthrough seemed to have occurred with the calling of a ceasefire, but hopes for peace were dashed by the IRA bomb attack on Canary Wharf (London) in February 1996. On August 15, 1998, a bomb was detonated in the center of Omagh city; 28 people were killed, 200 were injured. The Omagh bombing was the most disastrous evidence of the ongoing nature of the problems in the North. Following many attempts to resume peace talks, the Northern Ireland Executive was finally formed with considerable help from former U.S. Senator George Mitchell. The power was passed from Westminster to Belfast at midnight on December 1, 1999, and the government of the Irish Republic removed its territorial claim to Northern Ireland from its constitution. Unfortunately, tension started to grow over arms decommissioning, and in February 2000, the Secretary of State for Northern Ireland, Peter Mandelson, suspended the Assembly. The international efforts to implement the Good Friday Agreement and to achieve the decommissioning of weapons continue today.

While peace in the North still seems somewhat precarious, the South has demonstrated that its economic success and prosperity are stronger than ever. Change has come quickly, as evidenced by the election of Mary Robinson, the first female president of the Republic of Ireland, in 1990. Liberal and youthful, she signaled a new beginning and a new challenge to the South. The Ireland of the 1990s is mostly characterized by the "Celtic Tiger" phenomenon. The prosperity of the Republic is based on such industries as electronics and computer components, but the Celtic Tiger, as the country's sudden economic growth within the EU framework has been called, is also apparent in the literary, theatrical, and musical spheres. The "liberalization" of Irish society is becoming more evident; for instance, the laws regarding abortion were undone in 2002 (after the legalization of divorce in 1995), and the influence of the Catholic Church has grown less pronounced. The Republic's Law Reform Act of 1993 established equal age of consent for homosexuals and heterosexuals. The inclusion of sexual orientation in the Unfair Dismissals Act guaranteed rights for lesbian and gay workers.

One could end this brief overview of Ireland's history by mentioning that the Irish Prime Minister Bertie Ahern and the Fianna Fáil party scored a sweeping victory in the latest general elections in May 2002. The Republic's growing success in the EU also seems like a suitably upbeat note on which to end. However, in order to bring us back to the intricacies of the story of Ireland and its literature, I would like to consider the final passage from Joyce's *Finnegans Wake*: "End here. Us then. Finn, again! Take. Bussofthlee, mememormee! Till thousendsthee. Lps. The keys to. Given! A way a lone a last a loved a long the"

Scholars have noted how the ending here seems to complete the beginning of the book: "riverrun, past Eve and Adam's, from swerve of shore to bend of bay, brings us by a commodius vicus of recirculation back to Howth Castle and Environs." *Finnegans Wake* seems to bring us back where we started—"back to Howth Castle and Environs"—trying to "end here," the text finds itself continuing along the riverrun path of past towards the future (the keys to which we have been given).

---

## Notes

1. This overview of Irish history is indebted to the following books: R. F. Foster, *Modern Ireland, 1600–1972,* (New York: Penguin, 1989); Séan Dutty et al., *Atlas of Irish History* (Dublin: Gill & Macmillian, 1997); Seamus Deane, *A Short History of Irish Literature* (London: Hutchinson, 1986).

# Chapter Four

# The Best and the Best Known

## Maria Edgeworth (1768–1849)

Already a celebrated author, Maria Edgeworth was asked to compose a biographical sketch to be included as a preface to her novels. She refused, saying that "as a woman, my life, wholly domestic, cannot afford anything interesting to the public . . . I have no story to tell" (Zimmern 218). This refusal can be attributed to the shyness of one of the greatest nineteenth-century storytellers in Ireland, but it also indicates what was considered to be a "woman's place" in society at that time.

Maria Edgeworth was born in England where her father, Richard Lovell, was living at the time.[1] She participated in English Enlightenment culture and her first publications were, rather fittingly, didactic tales for children and stories of fashionable English society. Her first novel is often referred to by its short title, *Castle Rackrent*.

## *Castle Rackrent* (1800)

The full title—*Castle Rackrent: an Hibernian Tale: Taken from Facts, and from the Manners of the Irish Squires; before the Year 1782*— emphasizes the period in which the novel is set, that is "before the year 1782." This statement, however, cannot be taken at face value; as critics have noted, *Castle Rackrent* contains numerous references to the political situation around the time of the novel's publication. So this claimed "historicity" should be read as an excuse rather than fact. Furthermore, as critics have noted, the juxtaposition of "Hibernian" and "Irish" in the title indicates the author's intention to relate a tale of Irish social life ("Irish facts") in a Hibernian manner ("vernacular idiom").

In the "Editor's Preface," Edgeworth declares her preference for the "worthless and insignificant" over the great and famous, and criticizes conventional histories for their stylistic pomposity and unreliability. She claims that these "memoirs"—as *Castle Rackrent* is presented to its readers—are more authentic and genuine, constituting a "plain unvarnished tale." The narrator, an old "faithful" servant of the Rackrent family, Thady M'Quirk, represents the quintessential unreliable narrator in the history of Irish literature, and is modeled on the Edgeworths' steward John Langan. The fluctuating nature of Thady's self-image is evident already on the level of his name, which evolves during the tale from "honest Thady," to "old Thady" and finally to "poor Thady." Not only is the narrator's name in flux, but he also appears to be "disguised," for Thady begins his tale by describing the long greatcoat that he wears "winter and summer." Thus the reader is never given a full description of him, as he remains hidden behind his cloak. Edgeworth inserts a footnote concerning Thady's cloak, which can be traced back to the traditional old Irish cloak or *brat*, and includes a quotation from Edmund Spenser stating that this historic garment can be a "fit house for an outlaw, a meet bed for a rebel, and an apt cloak for a thief." The coat thus implicates Thady from the beginning of his story as a potentially subversive character.

Thady relates the tale of the rise and fall of the Rackrent family, formerly known as the O'Shaughlins. By saying that the O'Shaughlins were "related to the kings of Ireland," Edgeworth suggests that her fictional landholders were originally native Irish who were forced to change their Irish (Catholic)-sounding name in order to become proprietors of their estate. The "Editor's Preface," "Glossary," "Footnotes," and "Afterword" frame Thady's story but also constitute a story in their own right—the "editor" comments on Thady's tale and introduces the authoritative voice of the landholding class, which, despite being absent from the main narrative, still exerts control over the tale of the Rackrents.

Thady's narrative gives an overview of three generations of Rackrents: Sir Patrick, a convivial host, drinks himself to death; the skinflint Sir Murtagh bursts a blood vessel and dies in a fit of rage after a dispute over a lawsuit; Sir Kit marries a Jewish heiress, locks her up because she refuses to hand over her diamonds to him, and dies after a duel. Finally Sir Condy, a kindhearted would-be politician loses his land and the Rackrent estate to Old Thady's son Jason. A minor character until the very end of the novel, Jason lurks on the outskirts of Thady's narrative, and although Thady emphatically proclaims the cold nature of their relations, critics have seen the two as conspiring together to get the better of the Rackrents. Having spread false rumors about his death in order to observe his own wake, Sir Condy finally dies penniless. Although the fate of the Rackrent estate remains uncertain, as Lady Rackrent is still alive and disputing Jason's claims for the estate, the end of the novel is generally seen as the fulfillment of the ultimate peasant dream—a M'Quirk taking over the castle and the land.

*Castle Rackrent* initially met with a mixed response, for Thady's vernacular idiom was something that reviewers had not previously encountered, but critics admired the humor and the spirit of the story. The second edition was welcomed in England as a successful representation of "our Irish neighbors," but the response in Ireland veered more and more toward the negative. Edgeworth family reports show that some readers had taken the novel as satire, others as an "authentic" account of the absurdities of life in Ireland, and many Irish squires were furious about the irreverent portrayal of their class.

Edgeworth wrote several other novels, most of which were not set in Ireland. Of her other "Irish tales," the most notable are *Ennui* (1809), *Belinda* (1810), *The Absentee* (1812), and *Ormond* (1817). The *Essay on Irish Bulls* (1802, written in collaboration with her father) is a collection of jokes, anecdotes, puns, epigrams, allegories, personal memoirs, conversations, and dialogues. After Richard Lovell's death in 1817, Maria edited and completed his *Memoirs* (1820), but her literary production declined significantly in the later years of her life as she missed her father greatly and was also occupied by running the Edgeworthstown estate until her death in 1849.

## Lady Morgan (Sydney Owenson) (1776?–1859)

I accuse Miss Owenson of having written bad novels, and worse poetry—volumes without number, and verses with-

out end—nor does my accusation rest upon her want of
literary excellence—I accuse her of attempting to vitiate
mankind—of attempting to undermine morality by
sophistry—and that under the insidious mask of virtue, sensibility and truth (Connolly, "I Accuse Miss Owenson" 98).

As exemplified by this quotation from a contemporary review
attacking both the author and her literary production, Sydney
Owenson was a controversial figure in Irish literature. Born into the
family of actor-manager Robert Owenson, Sydney accompanied her
father on his theatrical tours around Ireland. As for Maria
Edgeworth (to whom Sydney Owenson has often been compared
to and contrasted with), her father played a pivotal role in
Owenson's life. She often claimed that she was born while her
English mother was crossing the Irish Sea; the in-between-ness and
indeterminacy implied in this description make it an apt image for
her largely self-manufactured identity. She came to fame first by
singing, dancing, and harp playing, and in 1805 published a collection entitled *Twelve Original Hibernian Melodies*. Her first two novels, *St Clair, or the Heiress of Desmond* (1803) and *The Novice of
Dominick* (1805) achieved no great success, which only arrived with
the publication of her third novel, *The Wild Irish Girl*.

### The Wild Irish Girl (1806)

Set in Connacht, the novel tells the story of Glorvina (the name
derives from the Irish *glór-bhinn*, "sweet voice"), an Irish princess,
and a somewhat mysterious hero referred to as M— (or Mortimer).
Mortimer is a nobleman, the younger son of an absentee Anglo-Irish
landlord and his letters to a friend, referred to as J. D., tell the story
of his "tour" in Ireland. Mortimer "discovers" Ireland very much like
Columbus discovers America. Owenson strives to present a country untouched by foreign glances, and to show Ireland "as it really
is." For Owenson, this means an exotic Celtic past with wild and
romantic natural scenery as a backdrop. Her novel presents Ireland
through a double lens, one belonging to Mortimer, and the other
emerging through the extensive footnotes, quotes, mottos, and comments. Thus the novel is left wavering between the authenticity of
the lush romantic plot and the accuracy aspired to in the footnotes.

Having arrived at his father's estate, Mortimer discovers an old Gaelic Prince and his daughter, Glorvina, living on the remote island of Inismore. Learning that during the Cromwellian plantation of new settlers his own family had taken over what used to be the Prince's lands and estate, Mortimer seeks access to his secluded family pretending to be a traveling painter and is eventually hired as Glorvina's teacher. Mortimer finds Glorvina accomplished not only in harp playing but also conversant in a number of foreign languages and well informed despite her secluded existence (she reads English newspapers). However, Mortimer persuades Glorvina to read Rousseau, Goethe, and Chateaubriand in order to "know herself and the latent sensibility of her heart." Glorvina, for her part, takes it upon herself to instruct Mortimer in the Irish language and introduces him to the magical world of Irish history and literature. A shadow is cast on their blissful existence when Mortimer learns that the family has a mysterious benefactor, and suspects that the latter's true interest is Glorvina. The benefactor turns out to be Mortimer's father, who, having come to regret the injustices done to the Prince and his family, has contrived to educate Glorvina and by marrying her, to secure her future and give her back her rightful inheritance. The "true" lovers are united in the end, and Mortimer's marriage to Glorvina is rendered as an allegory of the Act of Union of Britain and Ireland. Sanctioning their love, Mortimer's father wishes the names of Inismore and M— to be "inseparably blended, and the distinctions of English and Irish, of protestant and catholic, for ever buried."

The Gaelic culture into which Glorvina initiates Mortimer is mainly mediated through footnotes and Glorvina's epistles. This is a portrayal of past greatness, contemporaneously rendered as exotic and authentic. Interestingly, it is not Mortimer who instructs Glorvina but vice versa, the visitor "touring" Ireland is made aware of his lack of knowledge, and directed toward a better understanding of Irish culture and of his own identity. On numerous occasions Mortimer is portrayed as an outsider; for instance, whenever the conversation turns into Irish, he is unable to follow it. Even if the Irish speak English, the language sounds different to Mortimer; we are told that the Prince of Inismore is not so much speaking English as translating from Irish. Thus, what at first seems a position of power—a better-educated and more worldly visitor, culturally superior to the other characters—turns out to be a limited and potentially vulnerable viewpoint.

The publication of *The Wild Irish Girl* made Sydney Owenson a social celebrity. She frequently appeared in society dressed as Glorvina, even carrying a harp with her. Such attempts at self-fashioning had both nationalistic and commercial interests at heart. Owenson was a passionate and romantic nationalist, but she had to work (and write) for her living. She was employed as a governess at the Marquis of Abercorn's house where she met her future husband, Sir Charles Morgan, the family surgeon whom she married in 1812. Lady Morgan, as she was from then onward known, published a few more Irish novels, which all enjoyed great commercial success —*O'Donnel, a National Tale* (1814), *Florence Macarthy* (1818), and *The O'Briens and the O'Flaherties* (1827).

## John (1798–1842) and Michael (1796–1874) Banim

John and Michael Banim are often referred to as Ireland's first Catholic novelists. They were born into the family of a Kilkenny tenant farmer. Michael remained in Kilkenny all his life. He became a shopkeeper first and then a postmaster. John had a more romantic life; he fell in love with a Protestant girl who died of tuberculosis, after which he went to live in London only to return to Kilkenny a few years later to meet with his own premature death from a spinal disease.

The Banim brothers emerged on the literary scene in the early 1820s under the pseudonym "the O'Hara brothers." Their major subject was peasant life in their native Kilkenny (Michael provided John with all the local detail and lore, similarly to Stanislaus Joyce who supplied his brother James with detailed information on Dublin) but they were equally interested in Irish history and the historical causes of Protestant-Catholic strife. It has often been said that the Banim brothers represent a link between Maria Edgeworth, the Ascendancy lady, and William Carleton (who was of peasant birth). Indeed, the brothers shared similar concerns with numerous other nineteenth-century Irish novelists, as they were trying to write both for their Irish audience and to satisfy the demands of their English publishers. The Banims' novels occasionally suffer from an overly didactic mode, and their stories tend to succumb to sentimentality. However, they managed to paint a convincing picture of life in nineteenth-century Ireland, an achievement for which they are occasionally referred to as the first national authors.

Michael and John collaborated on most of the O'Hara brothers' tales, but critics have determined that we can assign *Crohoore of the Bill-Hook* (1825) to Michael alone. The less talented of the two, Michael wrote *Crohoore* while John was trying to make his fortune in London. The novel depicts rural violence in nineteenth-century Ireland, centering around the story of the peasant Crohoore who, adopted by a farming family, is later accused of having murdered his adoptive parents. He is found innocent and turns out to have been the farmers' true son. Although less sophisticated literarily, Michael Banim makes up for his shortcomings by his keen observation of social detail, customs, and habits of Irish peasantry, and with his psychological insight. Michael's description of an ex-priest or a "spoiled priest" in one of his letters inspired John to write a novel that eventually became one of his best works, *The Nowlans* (1826).

*The Nowlans* depicts a farming family that at first sight seems quite prosperous. As a "Black Protestant" married to a Catholic, Mrs. Nowlan thinks of herself as "more of an aristocrat than her husband or even than her children." John, their son, feels the tension at home and buries himself in his studies. His scholarly pursuits are interrupted when his wealthy uncle takes him under his somewhat dubious patronage. In his ramshackle household John meets his cousin Maggie who confuses his priestly conscience. She does not rob him of his virginity but his purity of mind is irrevocably lost. Trying to bury his awakening sexuality beneath the scrupulous observance of his religious duties, John resumes his studies to become a priest. All goes well until he accidentally meets a cultured Protestant girl, Letty Adams. His attraction to Letty springs not only from her polished manners or her higher social status; Banim makes it clear that John is also taken by her physical beauty. The psychological depth and detailed descriptions make this portrait of a young priest's emotional struggles a much more believable picture than, for instance, Gerald Griffin later achieves in *The Collegians*. John and Letty run away and try to make a living in Dublin, but their marriage is doomed and their financial situation becomes desperate as word gets out that John is a "spoiled priest." Letty dies in childbirth and the heartbroken John returns home. As a convincing in-depth depiction of the inner struggles—and the eventual damnation—of a Catholic priest, with *The Nowlans* Banim enters new fictional terrain, later to be explored by such famous Irish writers as James Joyce and George Moore.

John Banim's second best known novel is considered one of the finest historical novels to have emerged from nineteenth-century Ireland, *The Boyne Water* (1826). The novel is heavily influenced by Walter Scott, whom John greatly admired and whom he considered an ideal national novelist. *The Boyne Water* centers around a pivotal event in Irish history, the Battle of the Boyne, which took place during the Jacobite-Williamite War of 1689–1691. Banim deploys a familiar device; his narrator is a visitor to Ireland through whose eyes events are described. His Protestant protagonist, Robert Evelyn, is an exemplar of religious and political tolerance. The author's didactic aim of educating his English readers is evident throughout the novel. However, by choosing one of the most contentious moments in Ireland's tempestuous history, Banim also attempts to disentangle the causes of violence and strife among his fellow countrymen. His Protestant heroes, Robert Evelyn and his sister Esther, while traveling in the north of Ireland, meet and fall in love with the Catholics Eva and Edmund O'Donnell. The ensuing war separates the lovers, whose tolerance is put to a difficult test. The novel tries to show how sectarian violence ruins the country, as it destroys the lives of the young lovers; Esther does not survive the siege of Derry, and Robert and Eva have to flee to the continent. The didactic aims of *The Boyne Water* were not directed solely toward an English audience but encompassed the Irish as well. This is evident from the final passage of the novel where Robert writes to Edmund from exile:

> From the present hour, Ireland must become a united country, fairly and nobly rivalling England in all that makes England truly great, or remain, for ages, a province of England, poor, shattered, narrow-minded, contemptible, and, party with party as she stands, contemned by the world,

and by England, too. A little time will teach this lesson. When it is taught, the union indispensable to avoid the evil will be endeavoured by a recantation of old slanders, and a concession of old rights. Man cannot always be unjust to man (Banim 563–564).

Modern critics have found the Banim brothers' descriptions of landowning classes lacking in authenticity; their upper-class characters tend to remain "cardboard" figures and are less believable than the lower class (or Irish) characters. The successful portrayal of the new, post-Emancipation Catholic upper-middle-class was left to the Banims' colleague, Gerald Griffin.

## Gerald Griffin (1803–1840)

Gerald Griffin was born and educated in Limerick. In 1820, when he was seventeen, his parents had to emigrate to Pennsylvania, while Gerald remained behind under the care of his elder brother, Dr. William Griffin. He remained a devoted son to his parents, presenting his father with the 800 pounds he earned from his novel *The Collegians*.

In 1823, Gerald left Ireland to seek fame and fortune in London, where he hoped to become a playwright. During his years in London, Griffin earned his living as a journalist and songwriter. Reading the Banim brothers' *Tales by the O'Hara Family* inspired him to abandon his theatrical ambitions and start writing regional stories—as he wrote to his brother, reality was all the rage in London. A few years later he returned to Ireland and went to live with his brother in Dublin. His most successful novel was *The Collegians*.

### *The Collegians* (1829)

The novel is based on a real-life murder case that took place in County Limerick in 1819, when a young girl's body was washed ashore. The son of one of the leading county families and his boatman were arrested and brought to trial for the murder. Daniel O'Connell himself acted as defense attorney for the accused nobleman, and came close to influencing the jury's verdict by claiming that the boatman was to be blamed for the murder. The trial attracted enormous public interest around the time when Griffin was sixteen years old.

*The Collegians* is the story of a beautiful country girl, Eily O'Connor, who runs away to secretly marry the upper-middle-class Hardress Cregan. Hardress and his college friend, Kyrle Daly (the two "collegians"), have both been rejected by heiress Anne Chute. The proud and passionate Hardress marries Eily instead, thinking that he prefers her "natural" looks and character to Anne's cold and polished manners. However, he soon discovers that he is revolted by the "bashfulness, the awkwardness and the homeliness" of Eily's speech and accent. He is particularly perturbed by a nightmare in which she peels a potato with her fingers during a fashionable dinner party. Hardress's passionate and melodramatic character is set off against Kyrle Daly's rationality and good common sense. In fact, Griffin was concerned about this polarization of characters, worrying that his readers were bound to prefer Hardress "just because he is a fellow of high mettle, with a dash of talent about him." It is true that Hardress the villain is the more complex character of the two. Having married Eily, he keeps her hidden in a cottage under the pretext that he needs to introduce this news slowly to his parents. In the meanwhile, he realizes that winning Anne Chute's love is not an impossible goal. Encouraged by his socially ambitious mother, Hardress proposes to Anne, who accepts his proposal, thus cementing his predicament. When his faithful boatman Danny Mann suggests that by removing Eily, Hardress's problems would be over, the latter does not have the moral courage to stop him. Soon after Danny Mann drowns Eily, both Hardress and Mann are brought to justice, and the deserving Kyrle Daly marries Anne Chute.

One of the important features of this novel is the wide range of characters it introduces, as critics have aptly said, Griffin had not written a novel *about* Ireland but "an Irish novel." *The Collegians* was later used by Dion Boucicault for his stage play *The Colleen Bawn* (1860). Having published three other novels and collections of stories—the most famous of which was the *Tales of the Munster Festivals* (1827)—Griffin came under the influence of one Mrs. Lydia Fisher, a confirmed Quaker. Convinced of the futility of writing, he burned his manuscripts and joined the Christian Brothers.

He was transferred to Cork and soon afterward died of typhus. Griffin's novels depict the time when the penal codes had just been lifted and the Catholic middle class had started to make full use of their newly won political and economic rights. Griffin's Ireland remains heavily affected by rural instability, but with the marriage of Kyrle Daly and Anne Chute a happier prospect is introduced in *The Collegians*. This possibility of a "happy ending" for Ireland was unfortunately to be removed by the catastrophic effect of the Great Famine, most famously and poignantly depicted by William Carleton.

## William Carleton (1794–1869)

Born into a family of Irish-speaking farmers in County Tyrone, William Carleton was the youngest of four children. He was an ambitious boy with scholastic promise. He studied at various hedge schools (before Catholic Emancipation, these were run by Catholic schoolmasters for a small fee, as according to the penal laws Catholics were not permitted to run or teach in state schools). His family was evicted and Carleton spent a couple of years on the road, teaching in various parts of Ireland. He arrived in Dublin, where he met the Reverend Caesar Otway in 1828, under whose influence he converted to Protestantism and became a contributor to an anti-Catholic periodical run by Otway, the *Christian Examiner*. Here Carleton published his first tales and novellas, mainly consisting of a bitter attack on Catholicism. These sketches formed the basis for his *Traits and Stories of the Irish Peasantry*, published in Dublin in five volumes (1830–1833). The sympathy and power with which he evokes Irish peasant life are often marred by his desire to impress readers with his learned style and the wide range of his English vocabulary. A native Irish-speaker, he also studied Latin and, as critics have noted, the three languages combine in his fiction, often producing a rather incongruous effect. He excelled in short forms, sketches, and short stories, but had difficulties sustaining a longer narrative, as a result of which his novels appear either melodramatic or dry. Of his short fiction, one of the best examples (and one of the best in Irish literature) is the short story "Wildgoose Lodge," first published under the title "Confessions of a Reformed Ribbonman" in the *Dublin Literary Gazette* and later revised for *Traits and Stories of the Irish Peasantry*. "Wildgoose Lodge" portrays a harrowing scene of revenge of Catholic Ribbonmen (a secret Catholic society) on a Protestant farmer who had informed the authorities about a theft of arms from his house. "Captain" Patrick Devann, a schoolteacher and parish clerk, makes the men gathered for a secret meeting swear an oath on the Bible to wreak revenge on the offender. The nameless narrator depicts his disgust and horror at the lengths to which these men are prepared to go, and the near bestiality of the actions of the Captain and his gang. The farmer's house is set on fire and he is made to watch how his wife, half burnt, throws their baby out of the window in an attempt to rescue it, only for the Captain to thrust his bayonet into the child and throw it back into the flames. The narrator finishes the tale by reporting that he later witnessed the Captain and his gang gibbeted near the scene of their horrible crime; he himself has but narrowly escaped. With such a detailed exposition of this horrifying material, no wonder the English audience found many of Carleton's stories unpalatable to their taste.

"Wildgoose Lodge" is not directly autobiographical, although it is based on a real-life event that took place in County Louth in 1816; similarly, Carleton's most famous novel, *The Black Prophet: A Tale of Irish Famine* (1847) is inspired by real-life tragedy, the Great Famine that plagued Ireland in the 1840s. The novel is often praised for its rendering of peasant dialogue, unfortunately marred by the awkwardness of the main narrative in standard English. *The Black Prophet* is a story of the "prophecy man," Donnel Dhu, who commits the murder of which the peasant family Dalton is suspected. The murder becomes eventually less significant than bringing together a young couple, happy and deserving of their happiness, which even the dark villain, Donnel the black prophet, cannot prevent. The novel is mainly praised for the depictions of Famine-stricken Ireland and the terrible conditions in which peasants lived, based on Carleton's own experience. His other novels inspired by his Famine experience are *The Emigrants of Ahadarra* (1848) and *The Tithe Proctor* (1849). Carleton was a prolific author who continued to write throughout his life but his later fiction suffers from overly long and melodramatic plots.

It is difficult to pinpoint Carleton's place in the Irish literary tradition; a Catholic, Irish-speaking and rural, he is seen as occupying a pivotal role. Yet, his conversion to Protestantism and his criticism of both religions make him a difficult case. He does not lend himself easily to the nationalist cause, as in 1852 he famously proclaimed that a "greater curse could not be inflicted on the country than to give it a Parliament of its own making." His bilingualism and his intimate knowledge of the country and its people nevertheless make him one of the most interesting writers to have emerged from nineteenth-century Ireland.

## Charles Lever (1806–1872)

. . . is by far the greatest of that group of writers who, by education and sympathies, are identified with the English element in Ireland. He was untouched by the Gaelic spirit, was a Tory in politics, and a Protestant. He had no sympathy with the religious aspirations of Catholics, and his pictures of their religious life are sometimes offensive. These are his limitations. On the other hand, his books are invariably clean and fresh, free from vulgarity, morbidness, and mere sensationalism. His first four books overflow with animal spirits, reckless gaiety, and fun (Brown 197).

Harsh criticism accompanied Charles Lever from the outset of his literary career. Labeled as "the English element in Ireland," a Protestant, anti-nationalist, Tory, and painter of pictures of reckless gaiety and fun, Lever was castigated as a non-Irish Irish writer, most famously by W. B. Yeats. Recent criticism has seen an upsurge of interest in one of the most prolific authors of the nineteenth century, who, like so many others, sought to make his fortune with his pen, and, as only a few could claim, succeeded in the attempt.

Lever was born in Dublin and educated at Trinity College; he traveled widely in Europe and Canada before returning to Ireland to resume his studies at the Royal College of Surgeons. In 1832, he worked in County Clare, trying to relieve the sufferings of the victims of a cholera epidemic. He was then appointed as doctor at a spa in County Derry, where he met and befriended William Maxwell, whose *Wild Sports of the West* (1832) inspired Lever's own early literary efforts. His first novel, *The Confessions of Harry Lorrequer* (1839) became his most well-known work, and, unfortunately, was also believed to be representative of the style of his entire *oeuvre*. This novel is a portrayal of the comic adventures of a young subaltern in Ireland and Europe during the Napoleonic wars. It is a good example of an "overflow with animal spirits, reckless gaiety, and fun." Lever was entirely unpretentious about his work, writing to Maria Edgeworth: "I have no constructiveness in my head; the most I am capable of is the portraiture of certain characters with more or less of contrast of 'relief' between them. These once formed, I put them *en scène*, to die out in an early chapter when their vitality is weak— if stronger, to survive to the end of the volume" (Cahalan 64). The plots of his early novels rely more on character and anecdotes than on a consistent storyline. His rollicking novels were extremely popular in England, but the Irish could not forgive him for making them the target of his ridicule.[2] William Carleton, for example, was relentless in his attacks; in 1843 he wrote about Lever's "disgusting and debasing caricatures of Irish life." It was not the critical response to his novels, but his own restless character and dissatisfaction with the small, close-knit society in Portstewart that prompted Lever to leave Ireland for Brussels in 1839. He returned in 1842 to edit the *Dublin University Magazine* for the next 3 years, but left again in 1854, settling this time in Italy. The year of the Famine, 1845, marks the emergence of a new Lever; the novels that appeared in this period, *The O'Donoghue* and *St. Patrick's Eve*, show a more serious side of "Dr. Quicksilver," as Lever was also known in England. In these novels he presents a darker picture of Ireland, especially in *St. Patrick's Eve*, which was inspired by his own experiences as a doctor during the cholera epidemic in County Clare. His later novels, especially *The Martins of Cro Martin* (1856) and *Lord Kilgobbin* (1872) are, as critics have now started to note, as nationalistic as anything that Carleton produced.

*Lord Kilgobbin* differs from the novels discussed so far, as it emphatically draws attention to its contemporary nature with the subtitle "Tale of Ireland in Our Time." Kilgobbin Castle is the site of ancient feuds; it was originally inhabited by the O'Caharneys family, but was then taken over by Hugh de Lacy (de Lacy is the name of one of the first Anglo-Norman families to settle in Ireland after the twelfth-century conquest) and subsequently won back by the O'Caharneys. Having dropped their Irish allegiances, the

O'Caharneys anglicized their name to Kearney, and later reappropriated their "ancient" (Catholic) faith. The present occupants of the castle can boast of a noble title thanks to a descendant of the family, Michael, who had acted as an aide-de-camp at the Battle of the Boyne and, according to the family annals, conducted the defeated King James to Kilgobbin Castle where the grateful king created him a viscount with the title of Lord Kilgobbin. The title is questionable, as it was bestowed by a king who was no longer a king.

Indeterminacy is characteristic of the castle and the status of its inhabitants. In fact, as critics have often noted, the castle, occupying a "borderland between fertility and destitution," is located in a transitional zone between the terra firma and the Bog of Allen. Mathew Kearney, the current Lord of Kilgobbin, inhabits the castle with his daughter Kate, who is a model daughter and the most down-to-earth of characters, and his son Dick, an ambitious and arrogant youth. Their quiet existence is thrown into turmoil with the arrival of Nina Kostalergi, Mathew's exotic niece. Nina is the child born from Mathew's sister's marriage to Count Kostalergi. Half-Greek, half-Irish, brought up in Italy, Nina personifies a state of transition and in-betweenness. She attracts a number of suitors, among them a young secretary to the Lord Lieutenant in Ireland, Walpole; Dick's college friend Joe Atlee, a self-made journalist and diplomat; and the Fenian leader Daniel Donogan. Having agreed to marry Walpole, Nina eventually runs away with Donogan, leaving the rest of the characters wondering about the mess they find themselves in. When Atlee asks Walpole whether the whole story wasn't very Irish, the latter replies: "So they say down there, and, stranger than all, they seemed rather proud of it."

Aside from its humor and wonderful characterization, Lord Kilgobbin is most notable for the juxtaposition of "old Ireland" and "modernized Ireland." The peasants are not deferential to their landlords and they read newspapers like the rest of the characters (newspapers play a pivotal role in the novel and are used in order to further the action on several occasions). The Bog of Allen represents a transitional territory between the static Kilgobbin Castle and the international world of politics and diplomacy. Irish politics is not swamped by the Bog but taken onto an international stage and discussed and influenced by periodicals published in Turkey, Vienna, and London.

Lever does not offer any solutions to the "Irish problem," but instead of offering a portrayal of the static "old Ireland," he gives a vibrant and convincing picture of Ireland at the threshold of modernity.

## Sheridan Le Fanu (1814–1873)

Although writers like Griffin, Banim, or Lady Morgan were sympathetic to the Catholic cause, they were far from endorsing the Emancipation or, to be more accurate, all the means used for achieving it. Joseph Sheridan Le Fanu is a good example of the isolation that ensued in Protestant circles after the Emancipation, the rise of O'Connell and Fenianism, and the Great Famine.

Le Fanu is best known as a representative of Protestant Gothic writing. His short stories and novels document the growing state of anxiety in the fictional world where the otherworldly atmosphere heightens the almost clinical sensibility of his characters that are frequently oppressed and tortured by their own senses. Hallucinatory, haunting scenes are Le Fanu's trademark, along with vivid and memorable characters. This is best exemplified by his most famous novel, *Uncle Silas: A Tale of Bartram-Haugh* (1864). Although set in England (Le Fanu's publisher was more keen on him depicting an English subject in modern times), *Uncle Silas* exemplifies the anxieties that governed many lives in nineteenth-century Ireland. As Elizabeth Bowen said in her "Introduction" to the reprint of *Uncle Silas*, the novel is "an Irish story transposed to an English setting." The novel is narrated by Maud Ruthyn, who is placed under the guardianship of her uncle after her father's death. Silas is her father's estranged brother, ostracized by society on the account of the somewhat mysterious deaths of his wife and one of his gambling friends. In order to demonstrate his support for Silas, Austin's will requires Maud to be sent to live in his household under his care. If Maud did not live to 21, Silas would inherit her considerable fortune. Silas concocts a plan to marry Maud to his son Dudley, without knowing that Dudley is already married. Discovering this fatal flaw in his plan, Silas conspires to bring about Maud's death, which she narrowly escapes.

Critics have noted that Maud is put through different types of terror—sexual, physical, and psychological. Her isolation at

Bartram-Haugh is a staple feature of Le Fanu's gothic novels. This is evident in his *The House by the Churchyard* (serialized in 1861–1863, published as a book in 1863) where the village of Chapelizod is removed from the rest of the world, and its hermetic existence is pierced only by the mysterious occurrences that disrupt otherwise idyllic village life. The central incident in the novel is a mysterious attack on the life of Dr. Sturk, which leaves him in a coma. Suspicion falls on the newcomer to the village, the Englishman Paul Dangerfield alias Charles Archer, who, as it eventually turns out, is responsible for the murder of which Lord Dunoran's father was accused. There are multiple subplots that help to create a picture of a village seething with life, gossip, and everyday scandals. *The House by the Churchyard* has been criticized for its overly loose plot (the question of the identity of the mysterious attacker on Dr. Sturk's life is almost forgotten by the end of the novel), but paradoxically its main attraction lies in the very diffuseness of its plot(s), and the gentle humor with which this fusion of supernatural and inexplicable events is portrayed. One of Le Fanu's central motifs, guilt, is also the central theme of James Joyce's works, most notably *Ulysses* (1922) and *Finnegans Wake* (1939). The latter is also set in Chapelizod, and the river Liffey is its central thematic concern, as well as its most commented upon and celebrated feadure. The following passage from *The House by the Churchyard* has been seen as a major influence on *Finnegans Wake*:

> "I like the river," says he; "it has a soul, Miss Lily, and a character. There are no river *gods*, but nymphs. Look at that river, Miss Lilias; what a girlish spirit. I wish she would reveal herself, I could lose my heart to her, I believe—if, indeed, I could be in love with anything you know. Look at the river—is not it feminine? it's sad and it's merry, musical and sparkling—and oh, so deep! Always changing, yet still the same. 'Twill show you the trees, or the clouds, or yourself, or the stars; and it's so clear and so dark, and so sunny, and—so cold. It tells everything, and yet nothing. It's so pure, and so playful, and so tuneful, and so coy, yet so mysterious and *fatal*. I sometimes think, Miss Lilias, I've seen this river spirit; and she's like—very like you!" (Le Fanu 126).

The river is here associated with femininity, becoming an example of mutability and change, childish and playful but at the same time also lethal. Le Fanu articulates here the duality that characterizes the daily existence of his protagonists. Duality was also a governing feature of the lives of Anglo-Irish landlords. While Catholics felt liberated and hopeful, Protestants were worried about the end of their domination in Ireland. Estrangement from the present, concern about an uncertain future—these are the fears that fed the sensationalism and heightened sensibility of Le Fanu's fiction. The unnamed narrator of *The House by the Churchyard* is a good example of this sense of inevitability; while "justifying" the death of one of his characters, Lilias Walsingham, the narrator says that his original plan was to "let" Lilias marry her handsome suitor, but, as he claims, "all about her was so linked in my mind with truth, and melancholy, and altogether so sacred, that I could not trifle with the story. . . ." The tragedy of death is in Le Fanu's fictional universe seen as ever-present in life. This passage can be interpreted as a resigned reading of the British situation in Ireland where the rise of the Catholic middle-class threatened the secure-looking position of the Anglo-Irish landholders. The era of Big Houses was to continue to flourish on the pages of novels, which tried to offer a testimony of the glorious past and record the hermetic and lonesome present of the Anglo-Irish Ascendancy.

## Somerville and Ross (Edith Somerville [1858–1949] and Violet Martin [1862–1915])

Edith Somerville and Violet Martin, both descendants of old Anglo-Irish families, met for the first time in 1886. The meeting of these two cousins was a momentous event (Edith was later quoted as saying that it was "the hinge of my life") in Irish literary history. Somerville and Ross, their pen name, was to become immensely popular after the publication of their five collaborative novels, and their literary "blockbuster," the "Irish R. M." stories.

Somerville and Ross were two independent-minded ladies who were avid advocates of women's suffrage. Considering their rather conservative and traditional family background, they fashioned their double self-image with a remarkable courage and defiance of convention. For instance, Violet Martin adopted a man's name for her pen name and Edith sported items of gentlemen's clothing such as ties and collars.

Their first joint venture into the literary marketplace was entitled *An Irish Cousin* (1889). The novel was originally conceived as a sensational Gothic novel or a "shilling shocker" as the two authors referred to it, but it gradually developed into a more realistic picture of Big House life. This became the staple theme of Somerville-Ross fiction. That their aim was realistic representation rather than fanciful entertainment is evident from a letter in which Edith complained about the expectations that their respective families had about literature. She said: "My feeling is that any character is interesting if treated realistically. They care for nothing but belted earls or romantic peasants" (Robinson 88). Belted earls and romantic peasants were not to be found in the literary production of the Somerville-Ross enterprise. On the contrary, their most celebrated novel, *The Real Charlotte* (1894), painted a realistic picture of life at a Big House, and offered character portraits with a psychological depth hitherto lacking in nineteenth-century Irish fiction. The novel tells the story of two women, the plain, common-looking but determined Charlotte Mullen and a feather-headed beauty Francie Fitzgerald. Charlotte is an especially fascinating portrait of a middle-aged Protestant spinster, trying to climb the social ladder of the West Cork village society. As one of Esther's brothers said: "Such a combination of bodily and mental hideosity as Charlotte could never have existed outside of your and Martin's diseased imaginations." The spectacularly hideous Charlotte manages to procure access to the heart and, more importantly, the will of a dying relative, and consequently inherits the fortune meant for Francie. She then tries to marry Francie off to Christopher Dysart, the son of the local Anglo-Irish Ascendancy family, while she herself pursues the land agent Roddy Lambert. She finds her options blocked when Francie falls for the roguish Captain Hawkins who leaves her, after which the heartbroken Francie marries Lambert, who had all along been her admirer. Charlotte tries to blackmail Lambert, who owes her money, but abandons her revenge when Francie dies in a riding accident.

Somerville and Ross obtained somewhat mixed reviews; typically for the Irish writers of their generation, they were loved in

England and condemned in Ireland, or vice versa. Thus, for instance, their somber, realistic novels were not to the taste of the general reading public in England where their humorous stories of *Irish R. M.* were loved and cherished; on the other hand, their comic tales did not earn them praise from Irish nationalist critics who condemned them together with Charles Lever. That Somerville and Ross continued to see (like Edgeworth and Lady Morgan earlier) the accurate portrayal of Irish reality as a complicated task is evident in Edith Somerville's remark in one of her letters: "It gets sadder every day! I can't help it . . . I'm afraid the people who talk so much of our rollickingness will be rather sick. But *how* could a book about Ireland in 1920 rollick?" (Robinson 176).

The riding accident that proved fatal to the fictional Francie turned out to have been a strangely prophetic event, as five years after the publication of the novel, Violet Martin had a similar accident, which left her ailing until her death in 1915. Although they continued to produce stories, their collaboration never produced more sustained forms of fiction again. After Martin's death, Somerville published five more novels. She still used both of their names, as she believed that even after her friend's death they were able to communicate beyond the grave. Out of these five novels one stands out: *The Big House of Inver*, published in 1925.

Similarly to *The Real Charlotte*, at the center of *The Big House of Inver* is a determined and strong-minded middle-aged female character, this time Shibby Pindy (Isabella Prendeville). Shibby is a dispossessed descendant of the once wealthy and famous Prendeville family, trying to restore herself and her family to its former glory (even if this means obtaining the remnants of former glory by purchasing them from village auctions). Shibby conspires to marry her half-brother Kit to a rich heiress, Peggy Weldon. Instead of cooperating with Shibby and her machinations, Kit gets a peasant girl, Maggie Connors, pregnant, and although Shibby murders the girl, Peggy has already found out about Kit's affair and refuses to marry him. The novel ends with the burning down of the Big House, which turns out to have been insured, so that instead of the Weldon family it is Shibby who is ruined. The burning of the Big House is a powerful symbol of the decline of the Protestant Ascendancy, and the death of Big House culture. However, the fiction inspired by

Ascendancy culture shows resistance and longevity, and has now been revived by such contemporary writers as Jennifer Johnson and John Banville.

## George Moore (1852–1933)

As George Moore declared in the *Confessions of a Young Man*: "I came into the world apparently with a nature like a smooth sheet of wax, bearing no impress, but capable of receiving any. Nor am I exaggerating when I say I think I might equally have been a Pharaoh, an ostler, a pimp, an archbishop; and that in the fulfillment of the duties of each a certain measure of success would have been mine" (Hough 167). Indeed, his life before the start of his literary career shows evidence of amazing versatility; the son of a Catholic landowner, young George Moore aspired to such careers as jockey, painter, and (under family pressure) also contemplated joining the army. His father's death left him free to make his own choices and in 1873, Moore arrived in Paris to study art, first at the École des Beaux Arts and then the Académie Julian. He frequented the circles of famous Impressionist artists such as Manet, Degas, Pissarro, and Renoir. Having realized that he possessed little talent for painting, Moore immersed himself in nineteenth-century French literature. He went to the meetings of Symbolist poets; he read, admired, and met Émile Zola. As his family land failed to produce sufficient income to support his life in Paris, Moore returned to England. He first tried making money from poetry; having failed, he tried his hand at prose. Among his literary influences were such authors as Ivan Turgenev, Zola, Honoré de Balzac, Walter Pater, Édouard Dujardin, Charles Dickens, and W. B. Yeats. This cosmopolitanism and evident influence of continental writers were unprecedented in Irish literature. Like one of his own characters (from the novel *The Lake*), Moore's life and his fiction can be seen as a relentless, multi-faceted pursuit of the most elusive of goals—life as such:

> He was not following her, but an idea, an abstraction, an opinion; he was separating himself, and for ever, from his native land and his past life, and his quest was, alas! not her, but—He was following what? Life? Yes; but what is life? (Moore 264–5).

Influenced by Zola's naturalistic portrayals of everyday reality, Moore's first novels tapped into the same, scrupulously realistic vein. *A Modern Lover* (1883), *A Mummer's Wife* (1885), and *A Drama in Muslin* (1886) all concentrate on the depiction of social injustice. While *A Modern Lover* was banned by Mudie's commercial library (one of the most popular circulating libraries at the time), *A Drama in Muslin* managed to irritate a number of representatives of the landholding class in Dublin. Moore courted controversy throughout his career; during the different stages of his life he managed to offend not only the landholders and the Irish nationalists but also his own family and friends (the frank portrayals of his childhood caused an irreparable breach with his brother Maurice).

Somewhat paradoxically, despite an evident French influence, his first books were regarded as "the most English of all novels." His reputation was established by *Esther Waters* (1894), an unflinching portrayal of the hardships of a single working-class mother in late nineteenth-century England. However, both Moore's (French) aestheticism and his "English" novels should be seen as attempts to fashion a certain (literary) persona, rather than ways to classify him as an artist. He was clearly interested in the Irish literary scene, for instance he made a significant contribution to the development of Irish theater, collaborating with W. B. Yeats on *Diarmuid and Grania* in 1901. His interest in the type of theater that Yeats was pursuing at the time, however, was short lived, and, having quarreled with Yeats, Moore immersed himself in the Irish language movement. As there was a real shortage of good modern literature in Irish, Moore saw his opportunity to fill the gap. He composed a collection of short stories, entitled *The Untilled Field* (1903), for translation by Tadhg Ó Donnchadha. He and James Joyce did not become friends at any point during Moore's lifetime (he was even quoted as saying that *Ulysses* is "not art, it's like trying to copy the London Directory," claiming that he never finished the book). However, the influence of both *The Untilled Field* and Moore's later novel, his masterpiece *The Lake*, is clearly detectable in Joyce's fiction.

*The Untilled Field* comprises 13 short stories, all set in Ireland or dealing with Irish subject matter. For Moore, this entailed religion and, specifically, the stultifying effect of Roman Catholicism on the

Irish. The picture Moore paints of Ireland is rather bleak: as a result of unemployment and poverty the country is suffering from mass emigration but also from the lack of vigor and joy. The author's anti-clericalism is especially evident in stories like "In the Clay," "Some Parishioners," and "The Wild Goose." The Catholic clergy seems to have taken over Ireland and squeezed out every life-giving vein from its inhabitants' mental and physical world. In fact, as exemplified by one of the stories, "A Letter to Rome," the Catholic clergy itself realizes the severity of the situation, that the birthrate is declining and the number of exiles growing. In Moore's story, Father MacTurnan writes a letter to the Pope suggesting the revocation of the decree of celibacy. The "overproduction" of nuns and monks and the emigration of Catholics have made the situation such that, as Father MacTurnan reflects, "every Catholic who leaves Ireland helps to bring about the very thing that Ireland has been struggling against for centuries—Protestantism." Although the bishop manages to ease Father MacTurnan's mind with good humor, the overall impression given in the collection is not so compassionate or benign. The first story, "In the Clay," tells the tale of a sculptor whose works are destroyed by a couple of boys who believe that their priest might object to them. This act of vandalism impels the artist to leave Ireland. In "The Wild Goose," an Irish-American, Ned Carmady, tries to settle down in Ireland; but his wife's growing piety and the overall stupor and unquestioning submission to the priests' wishes wreck his marriage and he returns to America. Paralysis is the thematic center of Joyce's *Dubliners*, and Moore's Irish characters can also be seen as paralytic, they hardly seem to move or travel; if they are able to find any mental agility, they use it to leave the country. The homesick Irish-Americans are unable to settle down; they come to Ireland believing that they can stay forever, but are glad to escape soon afterwards. Tradition is in these stories a backward force; it is not the ancient Irish tradition depicted by Lady Morgan but the Catholic one which has overshadowed the earlier historical layer and now dominates everyday reality in Ireland. Comparing *Dubliners* and *The Untilled Field*, one could say that while Moore is realistic in his vision and precise in execution, he is still a step away from Joyce's clinical accuracy. Parallels between the two authors do not end here: *Ulysses* developed from a short story intended for

*Dubliners*; Moore's most famous novel, *The Lake*, was first conceived as a short story in *The Untilled Field*.

*The Lake* is dedicated to Édouard Dujardin and includes a letter (in French) by Moore to Dujardin, the French novelist traditionally credited as the formative influence on Joyce's innovative use of interior monologue. Moore was a good friend of Dujardin, and this dedication acknowledges both their friendship and Moore's artistic debt. In the Preface, Moore explains the problems that the novel's intended style caused for him. His artistic difficulties were due to the fact that

> . . . the one vital event in the priest's life befell him before the story opens, and to keep the story in the key in which it was conceived, it was necessary to recount the priest's life during the course of his walk by the shores of a lake, weaving his memories continually, without losing sight, however, of the long, winding, mere-like lake, wooded to its shores, with hills appearing and disappearing into mist and distance (Moore viii).

First published in 1905, *The Lake* recounts the story of a young priest, Father Oliver Gogarty, and his spiritual and mental awakening leading to the awareness that his true calling is the world rather than the church. Having denounced a young schoolteacher, Nora Glynn, from the pulpit, thus causing her to emigrate to England, Father Gogarty slowly begins to realize that his outburst was caused by his own jealousy; he had been in love with the girl without knowing it, and was outraged not because of her overstepping the boundaries set by the church but because she was carrying another man's child. He sees his only escape as being to stage his own accidental drowning in the lake; the novel ends with him swimming across the lake to seek his fortune in the wide world.

*The Lake* is a fascinating book both because of its stylistic innovations (most of the action takes place in Father Gogarty's mind, a technique that gives a naturalistic accuracy to the protagonist's mental wavering while retaining the symbolist nature of the novel's beautiful descriptive passages) and its daringly chosen subject matter; a "spoiled priest" had appeared in Irish fiction before Moore, but Moore gave his "errors" a lyrical and philosophical depth which had not been previously achieved.

## James Stephens (1880?–1950)

For James Stephens, 1912 was an "annus mirabilis"—a truly remarkable year. He published his second volume of poems, *The Hill of Vision*, and two of his best-known novels, *The Charwoman's Daughter* and *The Crock of Gold*. Both novels present a fascinating fusion of realism and fantasy, exploring the gap between the dream world of desire and actual reality. In this, Stephens was greatly interested in and influenced by William Blake and the ideas of theosophy.

*The Charwoman's Daughter* seems at first glance to be a realistic depiction of life in Dublin slums, however, by calling his protagonist Mary Makebelieve, Stephens signals the fantastic vein of his novel. Mary's story develops on the scale instantly recognizable from fairy tales—it is a Cinderella story about overcoming poverty and squalor, where dreams and dreaming are encouraged, and a gratifying end result is a certainty. Mary becomes infatuated with a policeman whose "affections" undergo a change once he discovers her low parentage. A suitable young prince saves Mary and her rich American Uncle Patrick bequeaths his money to the Makebelieves. The novel is a generic fusion of fairy tale, bildungsroman, and the "coming of age" story. Mary has to come to terms with the everyday reality of social and financial inequalities and the complexities of human relationships in the Dublin of the early twentieth century. Moving away from her mother's dream world of a better life, Mary learns about the secrets of womanhood, and class tensions, but her future will be entwined with another strand of fantasy as she finds her Prince Charming, a young clerk who in his turn nurtures utopian dreams about a socialist future and a free Ireland.

The sexual awakening of a woman is also the central theme of *The Crock of Gold*. The novel has been labeled as "prose fantasy," however, its fictional roots lie in W. B. Yeats's apocalyptic stories from *The Secret Rose*, William Blake's visionary poems, and Nietzsche's philosophy. *The Crock of Gold* has been read as a pastoral idyll, an allegory, a burlesque, a satire about the Puritan Irish, and a comic novel. Indeed, all these genres lend some of their features to Stephens's novel, which tells the tale of the peasant girl Caitilin Ní Murrachu, who oversteps parental constraints in order to marry a god called Angus Og, and the story of the Philosopher, married to the Thin Woman of Inis Magrath, and his quest for "gaiety and music and a dance of joy." The Philosopher and Caitilin transcend the bounds of dry and lifeless morality in order to embrace a joyous and fertile new existence. The cast of characters in this novel is remarkably wide, including talking animals, leprechauns, and their crocks of gold.

In one of his letters, Stephens encapsulates his artistic credo by saying that "I look on certain abstract words such as 'love', 'honour', 'spirit' as prophetic words, having no concrete existence now, but to be forged in the future by the desire which has sounded them" (Martin xii). This constructive desire, based on fantasy and make-believe, is in Stephens's world the force that helps his characters face their present predicaments, but also signals his hopes for a different Ireland of song, dance, and fairy tale. W. B. Yeats admired Stephens greatly, as he felt that Stephens was the author who could "take care of Irish literature." Furthermore, one of the most eminent of Irish writers, James Joyce, also harbored a great respect for him. Joyce saw Stephens as the author to carry on his own fictional enterprise, assigning him the task of completing his most complex masterpiece, *Finnegans Wake*, should anything prevent him from doing so.

Stephens's world of leprechauns and crocks of gold is not only a fantasy or a fairy-tale world of dreams of better life. His Celtic fantasies attempt to forge a philosophy of life in a new world order where justice and stability reign supreme.

## James Joyce (1882–1941)

Ireland's most famous author was born in Dublin into the family of May and John Stanislaus Joyce. The future writer's middle-class father was a great lover of drink, music, and conversation, and was absolutely incapable of holding down a job or providing his family with a stable income. May Joyce was a pious Catholic, who endured 15 pregnancies and died of cancer in 1903. James Joyce was educated by the Jesuits and graduated from the Royal University of Ireland. While at university he spent more time pursuing his arcane literary interests than the subjects on the official curriculum. By the time he graduated from university he was well-read not only in European literature (he gave a paper at the Literary and Historical Society entitled "Drama and Life" and published an article on a Norwegian dramatist Henrik Ibsen (1828–1906) in the *Fortnightly Review* while still at university), but also in the philosophy of Aristotle and Thomas Aquinas. His isolation in Dublin was mainly due to his idiosyncratic aesthetic ideas, which did not conform to the prevailing mood of literary revival. The scorn and antipathy he felt for the language movement found expression in *Stephen Hero*'s sketches of Irish language classes but also in the stories of *Dubliners*. Joyce sojourned briefly in Paris, where he tried to study medicine but was forced to return to Ireland in 1903 because his mother was dying and because he no longer had the means of supporting himself. On June 10, 1904, he met Nora Barnacle, a Galway girl working in a Dublin hotel as a chambermaid. Their first date was on June 16, and Joyce immortalized that day in his most famous work, *Ulysses* (1922). They left Ireland to live together in Trieste, Italy, where Joyce tried to make ends meet as an English teacher. He had already started working on a book of short stories (three stories had appeared in the *Irish Homestead*, signed by Stephen Daedalus) and in 1905 he sent 12 stories to an English publisher, Grant Richards. Richards agreed to publish the book, which after a horrendously complicated publishing process finally appeared in 1914.

### Dubliners

By the time of publication, Joyce had added three more stories to the book, which now consisted of 15 tales forming a structural and thematic whole. *Dubliners* can be roughly divided into four categories: childhood, adolescence, maturity, and public life. The central thematic concerns are introduced in the first story, "The Sisters," in which words such as paralysis, gnomon (a geometrical figure of incompleteness), and simony (exchange of spiritual values for worldly goods) occur. As the author declared, the stories were written in the style of "scrupulous meanness." That is, Joyce hoped and endeavoured in his writing to be painstakingly realistic and not to embellish the reality of life in Dublin. In a letter to Grant Richards,

Joyce defined his artistic aims as follows: "My intention was to write a chapter of the moral history of my country and I chose Dublin for the scene because that city seemed to me the center of paralysis." From this statement it is apparent that his aim was also to educate real-life Dubliners and, with the surgically sharp knife of his prose, lay bare the heart of the problem and show Dubliners where their problems were hidden. In Joyce's eyes, mental and spiritual paralysis, often caused by the Catholic Church, was the crippling force holding back the citizens of his native town.

The first three stories are told from the perspective of an unnamed narrator; the narrative perspective changes from then onward to the third person. The opening story, "The Sisters," introduces the theme of paralysis by depicting a young boy who learns that the priest he has befriended is dying. The boy hears the word "paralysis," which attracts his lively imagination because of its strange sound, and his inability to comprehend its meaning.

The idea of the incompleteness of meaning is emphasized by the inconclusive ending of all the stories. This is further stressed by the characters' inability to understand the society surrounding them as well as the underlying reasons for their own actions. The inability to change the circumstances they find themselves in exemplifies the overall sense of paralysis in Dublin. Joyce uses an innovative narrative technique in which the omniscient narrator "borrows" the protagonists' words and phrases, thus giving the reader an illusory access to the minds of his Dubliners. This technique is further accentuated by Joyce's unconventional punctuation; he uses dashes instead of inserted commas to designate dialogue, blurring the distinction between dialogue and narration.

The collection ends with a short story called "The Dead," which constitutes a coda to the book and is widely considered one of the greatest short stories in twentieth-century literature. The protagonist, Gabriel Conroy, takes his wife Gretta to the annual party that her old maiden aunts are throwing on the Feast of the Epiphany. Gabriel is a schoolteacher with literary ambitions; he publishes book reviews, travels on the continent, and tries to keep up with cultural events in the world. He attempts to distance himself from the Irish language movement and the nationalist cause, but does not have the moral courage to make a final break with the culture and society he secretly despises. Also, his literary sensibilities are only half-satisfied by his journalistic hackwork. Another party guest, Miss Ivors, calls him a West Briton, half-humorously attacking his reluctance to learn the Irish language. After the dinner Gabriel accidentally spots his wife listening to a song, "The Lass of Aughrim." He discovers later in the evening that the song had reminded Gretta of a long-dead admirer who died of love for her. He realizes that not only is he alienated from society and his own country, but he is also incapable of understanding his own wife. This realization augments his isolation and sense of futility. The story ends with Gabriel watching snow falling, covering all of Ireland—the living and the dead.

On January 7, 1904, Joyce wrote a story called "A Portrait of the Artist as a Young Man." He sent the story to the editors of the review *Dana* who rejected it. Instead, it became the seed of his future novel of the same title—

### *A Portrait of the Artist as a Young Man (1916)*

Centering around Stephen Dedalus and the evolution of his artistic aspirations, this book offers a fascinating portrait of an independent mind struggling to mature in the stultifying Dublin atmosphere. The five chapters present separate incidents from Stephen's life, starting with his childhood. In chapter one he is bullied by other boys at school but manages a heroic feat at the injustice of Father Dolan; in chapter two he grows separate from the political, moral, and literary views of his family and the chapter culminates with his first sexual experience with a prostitute; chapter three portrays his guilt and remorse and finishes with his feelings of liberation after a confession; in chapter four Stephen refuses to choose a religious vocation and starts forming his aesthetic theories—the chapter ends with a chance meeting on a beach with a "bird girl," a vision of mortal beauty; chapter five depicts his life at university, his rejection of Catholicism, and the finalized version of his aesthetic theory; the book ends with Stephen's resolution to go into exile. His artistic credo (frequently taken for Joyce's own) is one of the most celebrated passages in Irish fiction: "I will not serve that in which I no longer believe, whether it call itself my home, my fatherland or my church: and I will try to express myself in some mode of life or art as freely as I can and as wholly as I can, using for my defence the only arms I allow myself to use—silence, exile and cunning" (Joyce, *Portrait* 208).

*Portrait* is a fascinating and frank portrayal of the development of a young artist, but what makes it a truly innovative work of fiction is its unique style. The reader follows Stephen's mental growth, subtly introduced by changes in vocabulary and his evolving ideas. The five chapters follow the structure of "the curve of an emotion," as Joyce called it, whereby each chapter begins with an emotional low point and then gradually ascends. However, since Stephen's story is mainly filtered through a third-person perspective, the narrative maintains a critical and ironic distance. The reader is never quite sure how close the narrator is to Stephen and whether or not he is being ironic about the protagonist, who reappears in Joyce's next novel:

### Ulysses (1922)

In this novel Stephen is again the central character, together with Leopold Bloom and his wife Molly. We learn that Stephen has returned from Paris to attend his mother's funeral and stays on in Dublin, teaching at a local school and arguing and drinking with the Dublin literati at night. *Ulysses* recounts the events of one day (June 16, 1904, the day of Joyce and Nora's meeting) in Dublin and is loosely modeled on episodes from Homer's *Odyssey*. Thus Stephen can be seen as corresponding to the Homeric character Telemachus (Ulysses's son), Leopold Bloom to Ulysses, and Molly to his wife Penelope. However, in addition to the *Odyssey*, Joyce's *Ulysses* borrows from a number of intertexts (among them Shakespeare's *Hamlet*), and refers to other Western literatures as well as Irish literature. Its highly experimental form spirals into technical virtuosity in the later chapters of the book. Joyce makes extensive use of stream-of-consciousness (a technique with whose invention Édouard Dujardin was credited, and which prior to Joyce had already been used by George Moore), parody, pastiche, and a number of other techniques that make *Ulysses* one of the most complex and complicated of modern novels.

Readers follow Stephen and Bloom on a seemingly ordinary day in Dublin. In the first three episodes we see Stephen having breakfast with his housemate Buck Mulligan at the Martello Tower. Their relations are strained and the tension is augmented by the presence of Haines, an Englishman and an enthusiastic student of Irish language and folklore. Stephen leaves the Tower to teach at Mr. Deasy's preparatory school. After giving a history class, he agrees to use his contacts in Dublin literary circles to publish a letter that Mr. Deasy has composed on the subject of the foot and mouth disease that is plaguing Ireland. Thus Stephen, the visionary poet and the self-appointed savior of Ireland, is rather ironically acting as the courier of a "messianic" message contained in Deasy's rather mundane letter.

Episodes 4–6 introduce Leopold Bloom, an advertising canvasser and a family man, who has a deceased son and a teenage daughter, not to mention his adulterous wife. Bloom begins his day by cooking breakfast for his wife Molly. He is still mourning the death of his son Rudy, who passed away some years before the events of *Ulysses*. His daughter Milly has left home and is working as a photographer's assistant in Mullingar. His wife is an amateur singer, admired for her voluptuous beauty and rumored promiscuous lifestyle. Molly is indeed having an affair with the manager of her musical tour, Blazes Boylan, and is expecting her lover's visit at 4 o'clock in the afternoon. Bloom tries to keep himself busy and stays away from their house for most of the day. His meanderings take him to the post office, church (he is Jewish and visits the church only to observe the service, which he does not fully understand), Turkish baths, and a funeral. His wanderings around Dublin, unable to return home, represent the most explicit parallel with *Odyssey*. His thoughts turn constantly to Molly and Boylan, while at the same time he tries to block out from his mind the idea of his wife in bed with another man. Bloom and Stephen finally meet at the maternity hospital, where Bloom inquires after the well-being of a woman in labor, Mrs. Purefoy, and Stephen drinks with the medical students. Stephen goes on to Bella Cohen's brothel. Bloom rescues him from a soldier whom the drunken Stephen has offended and takes him to the cabman's shelter and then to his home on 7 Eccles Street. Stephen refuses to spend the night at Bloom's and disappears; Bloom goes upstairs to bed with his wife. The last chapter of the book is Molly Bloom's unpunctuated monologue in which she reflects on her life, and her relationship with men (Bloom, Boylan, and others). The novel ends with the life-affirming word, "Yes."

The difficulty of *Ulysses* lies not so much in its vast number of characters—occasionally it seems that the entire Dublin of 1904 appears on its pages—but rather its technical virtuosity. The complexity increases through the novel and from chapter nine onward Joyce puts his readers' mental capacities to a fierce test. There is no single "authoritative" narrating voice, and none of this polyphony of voices can be identified as the author's. Indeterminacy is the main characteristic feature of the book, which introduces a multitude of viewpoints and narrative registers, recording numerous different ways of seeing the world around us.

*Ulysses* has become one of the most commented upon works of literature and there is an industry of Joyce scholars working on it. As Joyce predicted himself, the book has kept literary scholars busy ever since its publication. On the level of complexity it is perhaps rivaled only by Joyce's last work, *Finnegans Wake* (1939). The title refers to a ballad about Tim Finnegan, a drunken hod carrier who falls from his ladder to wake up at his own wake. The book's structure reflects Giambattista Vico's division of history and the text is permeated with literary, historical, and mythological allusions, metaphors, and multilingual puns. Joyce described the book as a dream of Fionn mac Cumhaill (an ancient Irish hero), dead and lying next to the river Liffey. Several scholars have called its style "dream-language" and tried to identify the different levels of sleep and wakefulness in it.

Joyce's *oeuvre* also includes some minor works, such as his only surviving play, *Exiles*, and a very early draft of *Ulysses* posthumously published under the title *Giacomo Joyce*, his essays, and poetry, but his monumental position in Irish (and world) literary history is mainly due to *Dubliners*, *A Portrait*, *Ulysses*, and *Finnegans Wake*.

## Samuel Beckett (1906–1989)

> Time passes.
> That is all.
> Make sense who may.
> I switch off (Beckett, *Complete Dramatic Versus* 476).

This is perhaps not the most encouraging way to introduce Samuel Beckett's fiction, but it is nevertheless an apt one. Beckett is frequently compared to Joyce, although their artistic techniques were radically different. However, the level of complexity with which the readers are dealing is the same in Beckett's literary universe.

Born into a Protestant middle-class family, Samuel Beckett was educated at Portroa Royal School and Trinity College Dublin. He taught English at the École Normale Supérieure in Paris between 1928 and 1930, and during this period he met James Joyce and his family. Joyce's daughter Lucia fell in love with Beckett, who frequented their house as a family friend, but also helped Joyce, who by that time was suffering from a partial loss of vision. Beckett contributed an essay, "Dante . . . Bruno . Vico . . Joyce," to a collection entitled *Our Exagmination Round His Factification for Incamination of Work in Progress* (1929), which sought to introduce Joyce's last work, *Finnegans Wake*, prior to its publication. He also wrote a poem, "Whoroscope," which won a competition organized by the Hours Press, and worked on his study *Proust*. He completed a novel entitled *Dream of Fair to Middling Women* around 1932, but chose not to publish it during his lifetime. Forced to return to Dublin, Beckett quickly became bored with its insular atmosphere and the chores of teaching at Trinity. His painful relationship with his domineering mother was another reason prompting him to abandon Dublin and his academic career. During the next five years he lived in Germany, France, and England, returning to Ireland whenever his precariously low funds reached complete zero. In 1934, he published a collection of short stories called *More Pricks than Kicks*. As with Joyce's *Dubliners*, Beckett's collection constituted a thematic whole; in Beckett's case unity was also achieved through the idiosyncratic protagonist Belacqua, who appeared in all of the stories. Belacqua is a student at Trinity studying modern languages (we see him taking an Italian lesson in the first story, "Dante and the Lobster") and the stories give an episodic picture of his life in Dublin and his accidental death during a simple surgical operation that goes badly wrong. Belacqua is named after the slothful Florentine flutemaker in Dante's *Purgatorio*. Beckett's Belacqua is "bogged in indolence," and the stories record his wanderings in and out of Dublin, his affairs with female friends such as Winnie, Alba,

Smeraldina, Lucy, and Thelma (although in these relationships he remains an inactive, passive character). The stories are full of arcane references and learned wit. The young Beckett uses Belacqua not only to show off his recherché vocabulary, but also to demonstrate the exuberant joy that these linguistic somersaults give him. Similarly to Leopold Bloom, Belacqua is an outsider on the streets of Dublin. However, he is not looking for a way to integrate himself into society, rather he enjoys the uniqueness and strangeness of his position. Belacqua's bizarre mental escapades exemplify what was to become the central concern of Beckett's fiction, the duality of mind and body. Belacqua is not concerned with the physical body (he suffers from "ruined feet" like many of Beckett's other characters), and he takes pleasure in his physical sufferings. What matters is his mind, which works unceasingly. The same duality is explored in Beckett's first published novel, *Murphy* (1938). Its eponymous hero is an Irishman living in London. Compared to Belacqua, Murphy's passivity is far more pronounced. He has no job and no interest in acquiring one; luckily, he is supported by his rich uncle in Holland. He falls for a prostitute, Celia, who wants to marry him. When Murphy declares his inability to find a salaried job, Celia leaves him to go back to the streets of London.

In the meantime, a gang of idiosyncratic characters led by Miss Counihan, Murphy's former mistress, is trying to track him down. Murphy meets a character called Ticklepenny and takes over his position as a male nurse in Magdalen Mental Mercyseat Hospital. While Ticklepenny is uncomfortable working with the mentally disabled, Murphy relishes the opportunity to live and work in the lunatic asylum. He becomes obsessed with one of his patients, Mr. Endon, but despite his efforts, Mr. Endon never takes any notice of him. Murphy dies in an accident with a gas fire. Miss Counihan and her cavalcade finally locate Murphy's former flat but they arrive too late. They accompany Celia to the hospital to identify the body. Murphy had stated in his will that his remains were to be discarded from the Abbey Theatre's toilet, but accidentally his mortal remains are dispersed on the floor of a Dublin pub instead.

*Murphy* is a great comic novel, full of ridiculous and farcical incidents. It is also a dazzling linguistic performance. There is a whole chapter explaining the intricacies of the workings of

Murphy's mind—a complex mixture of the ideas of such philosophers as Leibniz and Arnold Geulincx, a little known Belgian
thinker. Murphy's predicament, his inability to achieve harmony, is
due to the fact that he is unable to achieve a total separation of
mind and body. This dualistic split of mind and body remains the
desired but unachievable goal for many of Beckett's other heroes.
Beckett wrote another novel in English, *Watt* (composed between
1942–1944, published in 1953), before reverting to French, first
(and tentatively) with *Mercier and Camier* (written in 1946, published in 1970). The crowning achievement of his prose fiction is
undoubtedly his trilogy, also composed in French, *Molloy* (1951),
*Malone Dies* (1951), and *The Unnamable* (1953). These fragmented
narratives explore such themes as personal identity, the relation
between subject and object, and questions of epistemology and
perception. The publication of *Molloy* by a small Parisian publishing house, Éditions de Minuit, was met with critical acclaim and,
for the first time in his publishing history, Beckett also made a small
profit from the book. His first books had been largely unread and
unsold in Britain and Ireland, where *More Pricks than Kicks* was also
banned by the censors; rather ironically he first became famous as
a French writer. His later fictions become gradually more con-
densed. As he said himself after the publication of *The Unnamable*:
"For some authors writing gets easier the more they write. For me
it gets more and more difficult. For me the area of possibilities gets
smaller and smaller. . . . At the end of my work there's nothing but
dust." This is certainly true of the physical size of his later fiction,
which indicates a definite tendency to drift toward nothingness—
the extreme economy of his writing offers a remarkable contrast
with the verbal exuberance of his early fiction. Although Belacqua
and Murphy are by no means happy characters, the humor and wit
with which their bizarre adventures and mental escapades are
described offers a welcome relief from the rather bleak general outlook that these books proffer. The bleakness and hopelessness of
the human condition reaches its epitome in Beckett's last prose
text, *Worstward Ho* (1983):

> Say a body. Where none. No mind. Where none. That at
> least. A place. Where none. For the body. To be in. Move in.

Out of. Back into. No. No out. No back. Only in. Stay in.
On in. Still (Beckett, *Wortsward Ho* 7).

The immobility, the impossibility of change, stillness, and hopelessness implied in this passage indicate the degree of darkness
which pervaded Beckett's vision in his later fiction. However, the
technical exuberance and intriguing intertextual references combined with the philosophical depth of his work make his *oeuvre* a
well of riches for anyone interested in Irish fiction.

## Flann O'Brien (1911–1966)

Brian O'Nolan (or Brian Ó Nualláin in the Irish version of his name)
was better known as Flann O'Brien and Myles na gCopaleen, his
two most famous pseudonyms. Born into an Irish-speaking family,
he first learned English at school (a Christian Brothers school in
Dublin). He studied at Blackrock College and then at University
College Dublin, after which he joined the civil service as a junior
administrative officer. In 1939, he published his first novel, *At Swim-
Two-Birds*, in the hope of making money (his father's death had left
him as the breadwinner of the family). The novel was well received
by critics but sold only a few copies. Its meager commercial success
is understandable if we consider its complex stories-within-stories
structure. The frame story is narrated by a lazy, nameless UCD student who lives with his uncle (who grudgingly supports him) in
Dublin. The student-narrator offers three possible beginnings for his
future novel, one of which is his own idle life with his uncle, another
his account of old Irish heroes from the legends of Mad Sweeney
and Finn McCool, and the third about a pub-keeper-cum-writer
named Dermot Trellis. Trellis has little or no control over the characters in the book he in turn is writing. While he is asleep his characters decide to wreak revenge upon him and compose a book in
which he, Trellis, is a character. All these subplots merge in the end
when Trellis is saved from his vengeful characters as the narrator
passes his exams, is reconciled with his uncle, and abandons the
book. As *At Swim-Two-Birds* self-consciously declares, a book should
not confine itself, its author, or its characters within a single authorial universe, for each character should be "allowed a private life,

self-determination and decent standard of living." Furthermore, according to the nameless narrator, the characters should be interchangeable between one book and another, and the modern novel should be "largely a work of reference." The critics have seen this as emphatically different from the Joycean world, where the author was seen to exert control over every minute detail. O'Brien is frequently compared to Joyce but his irreverent use of Irish mythology (the verses are translations from Irish used in O'Brien's Master's thesis) is closer to James Stephens. O'Brien himself dismissed his first novel as juvenilia, and when his second novel, *The Third Policeman*, was rejected by every English publisher it was sent to, he gave up hope of ever seeing it published (it appeared posthumously in 1967) and immersed himself in a journalistic career instead. His Irish audience came to know and love him through his thrice-weekly humor column, "Cruiskeen Lawn" in the *Irish Times*. He signed his articles as Myles na gCopaleen (a character immortalized in Gerald Griffith's *The Collegians* and its stage adaptation, *The Colleen Bawn*). These columns ran for more than 25 years and their style varied from humorous commentary on Dublin life to political and social satire. The articles grew increasingly bitter as O'Brien became more disillusioned with life in the Free State. His satirical Irish novel, *An Béal Bocht* (appeared in Irish in 1941 and in English, with the title *The Poor Mouth*, in 1964) attacks the idealized picture of Irish-speaking regions that academics and literary authors had created. O'Brien depicts the fictional community of Corca Dorcha as a backward and poor county, drenched by an incessant downpour of rain. He wrote two more novels, *The Hard Life* (1961) and *The Dalkey Archive* (1964), which did not reach quite the same standard of his first two novels. His second novel, *The Third Policeman*, competes for the title of his funniest work with *At Swim-Two-Birds*. With one John Divney as his accomplice, the unnamed narrator of *The Third Policeman* plans and executes the murder of old Phillip Mathers in order to finance his research on the eccentric philosopher de Selby, whose work concerns questions of time and space and also the interchange of molecules. Two policemen, Sergeants Pluck and MacCruiskeen, pursue the narrator. De Selby never appears in the main text, but the lengthy footnotes document his philosophy extensively and exhaustively. De Selby's philosophy comes in handy when launching a philosophical quest for explanations as to why postmen and bicycles interchange their respective appearance, and the erotic heat that a female schoolteacher's bicycle can exude.

O'Brien's fiction remained suspended between the real everyday world and the fantasy world of de Selby and bicycles. Distrusting the introverted monomaniacal control that he saw in the Joycean universe, O'Brien tried to eke out a satisfactory fictional realm which "should be a self-evident sham to which the reader could regulate at will his degree of credulity."

## Sean O'Faolain (1900–1991)

Sean O'Faolain was christened John Whelan, and later adopted the Irish form of his name. He grew up in Cork city, where his father was a member of the Royal Irish Constabulary and his mother ran a boarding house. Considering that his parents were devoted to the British Empire and aspired to middle-class pious respectability, Sean O'Faolain's life took a very different turn from what his family had planned for him. The future writer and Ireland's grand old man of letters went to University College Cork to study Irish, English, and Italian, but became involved in the IRA and joined the Irish Volunteers (a paramilitary organization). During the Civil War, he was posted as the director of propaganda for the First Southern Division of the IRA but subsequently became disillusioned with the Republican cause, went back to his studies at Cork, and then on to Harvard on a scholarship to do an M.A. in English. By that time he was interested in writing. His early fiction reflects the experiences he accumulated during his adventurous years in Cork. The first collection of short stories, *Midsummer Night Madness and Other Stories* (1932), depicts the romantic attraction and the bitter disappointment that the Republican revolutionary vision inspired in people like O'Faolain. The stories portray a youthful romantic hero and are set during the Civil War and the Anglo-Irish War. The opening story, "Fugue," and the concluding story, "The Patriot," frame the collection and chart the movement from passionate commitment to the eventual rejection of the nationalist cause. An underlying theme of these stories is the young hero's quest for a personal response and ideological stance, his creation of identity, and the outlines of his individual thinking. This collection was followed by three novels: *A Nest of Simple Folk* (1934), *Bird Alone* (1936), and *Come Back to Erin* (1940). In this historical phase of his writing, O'Faolain examined Irish history from the Fenian rising (1798) to the War of Independence through the fictional lens of a family saga. The older family members and their contacts with the Fenian movement and their loyalty to the revolutionary cause turn them into personifications of Irish nationalism, but also icons of national frustration. The younger characters, such as Denis Hussey in *A Nest of Simple Folk* and Corney Crone in *Bird Alone*, are profoundly influenced by their example. However, they do not accept them unquestioningly, but rather remain critical of their relevance and viability in the modern world. This is most poignantly achieved in the third novel of the series, in which O'Faolain analyzes Ireland in the 1930s, depicting his central character's dawning realization that the type of Revolutionary cause he used to be the proponent of is outdated and has no place in modern Ireland. These ideas are further elaborated and explored in O'Faolain's subsequent collections of short stories such as *A Purse of Coppers* (1937), *Teresa and Other Stories* (1947), and *The Man Who Invented Sin* (1949). O'Faolain also wrote a number of non-fiction books, including biographical studies such as *Eamon de Valera* (1933); *Constance Markievicz* (1934); the life of Daniel O'Connell, *The King of the Beggars* (1938); and *The Great O'Neill* (1942), the life of Hugh O'Neill, Earl of Tyrone. In 1940, he founded a literary journal, *The Bell*, which he edited from its foundation until 1946. Under his editorship, *The Bell* became a forum for analysis of the Irish social and political situation, and his editorials gained notoriety for their critical attacks on the oppressively stultifying atmosphere prevalent in the Irish Free State at that time. O'Faolain's attacks on traditionalism as exemplified by Gaelic and Catholic ideal "Irelands" were instrumental for the revisionist historians of the 1970s and 1980s. In Irish literary history he goes down as a major short story writer.

## Frank O'Connor (1903–1966)

Another influential short story writer, O'Conner's real name was Michael O'Donovan, and like O'Faolain, he was born and raised in

Cork and became involved with the Republican cause (O'Connor was interned in Gormanstown prison in 1923). His first collection of short stories, *Guests of the Nation* (1931), records his own experiences and his growing disillusionment with the guerrilla war of Independence. The collection was followed by a novel, *The Saint and Mary Kate*, in 1932, and in the same year he also published a volume of translations from Irish, entitled *The Wild Bird's Nest*. With W. B. Yeats he established the Irish Academy of Letters as a force opposing censorship. O'Connor's own work was banned on several occasions during the 1940s: The Censorship Board condemned as indecent his novel *Dutch Interior* (1940) and two collections of short stories, *The Common Cord* (1947) and *Traveller's Samples* (1951). Both O'Faolain and O'Connor preferred and excelled in short fiction. In this they both attest to the influence of the Irish oral storytelling tradition and the formative influence of Daniel Corkery. Corkey was Professor of English at University College Cork from 1931 to 1947. His thesis, published under the title *Synge and Anglo-Irish Literature* (1931), identified the three forces necessary for the creation of a truly national literature: religion, nationalism, and the land. Although initially heavily influenced by these ideas, O'Faolain and O'Connor both moved away from Corkery's narrow traditionalist and nationalist vision in the later stages of their careers. O'Connor's disappointment in 1940s Ireland grew to such an extent that he resorted to one of the most common but also extreme measures by going into exile. He was invited to give a lecture tour in the States and he stayed there for more than ten years, teaching in various colleges and universities. He returned to Ireland some years before his death in 1966.

O'Connor's reputation and literary fame are based on his short stories. He is one of the most prolific of Irish writers, and stands out as an excellent and sensitive recorder of his native Cork dialogue. He is also celebrated for his accurate depictions of working-class Cork atmosphere. His style is realistic; his technique is a perfect example of traditional storytelling with its roots in the oral tradition, from where O'Connor acquired his liking for the central figure of the storyteller. He was famed for his depiction of the "lonely voice" (the title of his study of the short story as a genre) of the "outlawed figures wandering about the fringes of society." He had a deep dislike of Joycean stylistic experimentation, and felt that Joyce and experimental fiction had betrayed the reader's trust in story and storyteller. His own achievement can be seen in the painstaking rebuilding of that trust in his fiction.

## Liam O'Flaherty (1896–1984)

Liam O'Flaherty was born and grew up on the island of Inismore in the Aran Islands, where he also attended the local elementary school. He went on to study at Rockwell College in County Tipperary, where he became a postulant of the Holy Ghost Fathers, a decision heavily influenced by the free education offered by the Fathers. He refused to take holy orders, but in order not to disappoint his mother, stayed another year at the Dublin diocesan seminary at Clonliffe, where he again rebelled just before taking the oath. For a brief period he attended lectures at University College Dublin, before he joined the Irish Guards Regiment and spent the next three years in the trenches of World War I. He was wounded in 1917 and then discharged. Subsequently, he became involved in the radical political movement, inspired by the angry socialism advocated by James Connolly. His three historical novels examine the events that Connolly considered pivotal in Irish history—*Famine* (1937), *Land* (1946), and *Insurrection* (1950)—respectively depicting the Great Famine, the Land War, and the Easter Rising of 1916. O'Flaherty published seventeen novels altogether and a great number of short stories (a number of these were originally composed in Irish).

His books are uneven, composed and executed in a rapid, passionate manner, his staccato sentences seeking to evoke scenes and characters with photographic exactness. His first reader at Jonathan Cape publishing house, Edward Garnett, introduced him to the great Russian masters such as Fyodor Dostoyevsky and Nikolai Gogol. O'Flaherty was also greatly influenced by Émile Zola's naturalism. His novels can thematically be divided into two groups: those that depict rural life and those that center around city life. Of the latter, the most famous is his novel *The Informer*, published in 1925 (John Ford's film version was released in 1935). The novel conveys O'Flaherty's own sense of alienation in the city of Dublin, having grown up in the rural West of Ireland. Dublin here is not a center of paralysis (as in Joyce's fiction) but rather a site of dehumanization and hostility. Gypo Nolan informs on another revolutionary (in order to receive the reward of twenty pounds he desperately needs) and is forced to flee from the revenge of the "Organization" that pursues him. Before he manages to hide in the Dublin Mountains, he is in turn betrayed by his mistress and is executed. *The Informer* was a huge success (especially after the Hollywood adaptation), and O'Flaherty spent the rest of his life trying to recreate this moment of triumph. *Famine*, his greatest novel, dedicated to John Ford, is more accomplished from a literary point of view. The novel follows the fate of the Kilmartins family. Brian, an old patriarch, is at first suspicious of his young daughter-in-law, Mary, but the terrible sufferings of the Great Famine reconcile the two. The novel offers a convincing portrayal of the incompetence of the officials during the Famine. The younger Kilmartins escape to America and the dying Brian gives them a piece of mortar from their family fireplace to take with them. Sean O'Faolain called the novel "almost Biblical" and referred to it as "the Irish Exodus." Although *Famine* is a historical novel, its main concerns are the same ones that attracted O'Flaherty's attention in his contemporary Ireland: the fight between man and nature, backward rural life, poverty, and emigration. This is a rather bleak view of the world, but the Irish Free State did not inspire O'Flaherty's contemporaries with any happier prospects. The situation of women was especially difficult, and this is most impressively dealt with in the novels of Kate O'Brien.

## Kate O'Brien (1897-1974)

Kate O'Brien was born in Limerick (the daughter of a horse dealer) where she also went to a convent school. She won a scholarship to study at University College Dublin. Having graduated from the university, she worked as a journalist, traveled in the United States and Spain (where she worked as an au-pair), and got married and divorced soon thereafter. After the great success her play, *Distinguished Villa*, enjoyed in London in 1926, she decided to become a full-time writer.

The main subject of her novels is the life of upper-middle-class Catholics, their suddenly prosperous world, the earlier representation of which is familiar from Gerald Griffin's novel *The Collegians*. Both Griffin and O'Brien set their most famous novels in the county of Limerick, which in O'Brien's case is the real-life equivalent of her fictional "Mellick." She is celebrated as one of the best Irish woman novelists. Women form the central subjects of her fiction, which focuses especially on the inner struggles of young women, and the sexual and moral conflicts of their lives.

Her first novel, *Without My Cloak* (1931), depicted the plight of the son of a wealthy Catholic landholder and his hopeless love for a young peasant woman. The novel won the Hawthornden and James Tait Black prizes. O'Brien's next two novels portrayed the conflict that many women at that time confronted: the moral values instilled in girls by the Catholic Church and the desire to explore their sexuality. Agnes Mulqueen in *The Ante-Room* (1933) resists the physical attraction of her sister's husband, whereas Mary in *Mary Lavelle* (1936) follows her nature. The latter novel was banned by the Censorship Board. O'Brien exacted revenge by writing *Pray for the Wanderer* (1938), the story of a writer who is banished by her native country and who composes plays that offend the inhabitants of her native Mellick with their daring subject matter. The next novel, *The Land of Spices* (1941), is O'Brien's masterpiece. The novel centers around the story of two women and the (platonic) relationship they form. Helen Archer, the Mother Superior of an Irish convent is drawn to a student of hers, Anna Murphy. The novel portrays the growth of Anna's artistic sensibilities, and echoes in several occasions Joyce's *A Portrait of the Artist as a Young Man*.

As an Englishwoman living in Ireland, Helen Archer is isolated and yearns for her spiritual home—the cities of Vienna, Turin, Crackow, and Brussels where she studied and worked before coming to Ireland. The setting is the first half of the twentieth century and the upsurge of nationalist feelings in Ireland. Helen fails to comprehend the significance of the events she witnesses and does not fully understand the Irish people surrounding her in the convent. Her outward alienation is emphasized by her mental isolation, as she is trying to repress her childhood grief—having witnessed her adored father "in an embrace of love" with another man, young

Helen decided to bury herself in the convent life. She sees her childhood as a life lived in a lie and decides to wreak revenge on her
father by depriving him of his only child. Upon meeting a young
student called Anna, Helen recognizes herself in her new friend. By
standing over Anna, guarding and protecting her, she learns to transcend her own dilemma, her inability to love another human being.
Anna's obvious literariness, her interest in words, their sound and
meaning, and her curiosity about life are strongly reminiscent of
Stephen Dedalus. O'Brien manages to evoke vividly and masterfully
the coming of age of a an intelligent and creative young woman. *The
Land of Spices* was banned under the Censorship Act because of the
portrayal of a "homosexual act" between Helen's father and his artist
friend. O'Brien wrote another novel, *The Last of Summer* (1943),
after which she published *That Lady* (1946), set in Spain at the time
of Philip II, and also a couple of travel books and a study of the
Spanish saint, *Teresa of Avila* (1951). Together with Elizabeth
Bowen, she remains one of the most interesting Irish woman writers, whose subtle and perceptive studies probe the secrets of human
nature, portraying women awakening to self-knowledge and acknowledging their sensual desires.

## Elizabeth Bowen (1899–1973)

The question of Elizabeth Bowen's Irishness and the difficulty of
"placing" her either in the Irish or British literary canon have been
remarked upon by numerous scholars. Importantly, Bowen's two
best-known novels, *The Heat of the Day* (1949) and *The Last
September* (1929), portray transient characters whose ambivalent
national identity reflects upon their inability to achieve a coherent,
unproblematic self-image. As the young heroine of *The Last
September*, Lois Farquar admits: "I like to be in a pattern. . . . Just to
be is so intransitive, so lonely."

Bowen's own life can be seen as guided by the same quest for a
pattern and the same sense of intransitivity. She was born into an
Anglo-Irish family and spent her childhood years between Dublin
and their ancestral home, Bowen's court, (her book *Bowen's Court
and Seven Winters* [1942] covers this period in her life) until her

father's failing mental health prompted her mother and herself to spend most of their time in seaside resorts of South of England. She studied art in London for a short time, until she married Alan Cameron in 1923 and moved to Oxford and then to London. This was a prolific period for her: two collections of short stories appeared in quick succession, followed by a number of novels. The most important of these was her second novel—

### The Last September

The world evoked in *The Last September* is situated in a clearly defined historical and geographical context. Set in 1920s Ireland, County Cork, the novel centers around a portrayal of Lois Farquar, the orphaned niece of Sir Richard and Lady Naylor, and her pursuit of personal fulfillment during the War of Independence. The titles of the novel's three parts—"The Arrival of Mr. and Mrs. Montmorency," "The Visit of Miss Norton," and "The Departure of Gerald"—indicate the instability inherent in the Anglo-Irish way of living and convey the sense of transitivity and movement. The house, Danielstown, seems to be a site of constant comings and goings; for example, Hugo and Francie Montmorency, who are the first visitors to arrive, have sold their house, thus they have to keep "visiting" their friends in order to keep a constantly changing roof above their heads. The next visitor to arrive, a cosmopolitan lady called Marda Norton, is a professional "house guest."

Lois, on the other hand, indicates an ambivalent attitude toward this intransitivity. She is both looking for adventure and wary of change. Going to the art school in Italy, as suggested by her aunt, or marrying her English suitor Gerald Lesworth both seem to require stepping into a ready-made pattern, a move she would like to make but is frightened of. At the end, Gerald gets killed in an ambush, Lois is sent to France to improve her French, and Danielstown is burnt down by the IRA. The departure of the young people and the burning of a Big House signal the end of an era for the Anglo-Irish Ascendancy.

Elizabeth Bowen composed eight more novels, published several collections of short stories, and wrote criticism, history, and travel writing. Her fiction continued to depict characters like Marda and Lois, accentuating her own conflicting heritage and identity—an Anglo-Irish lady living and writing in England. Ireland frequently figures in her fiction as an occasional backdrop, although her novel *A World of Love* (1955) is the only one to be set solely in Ireland. *The Heat of the Day* (1949), in which Ireland also figures as a secondary geographical location, is widely considered to be her finest novel. It was also adapted for television by Harold Pinter.

### The Heat of the Day

Bowen drew upon her own experiences of living in wartime London when creating the character of Stella Rodney. Like Bowen, Stella is engaged in secret official work (Bowen offered her services to the Ministry of Information and during her wartime visits to Dublin, reported on Irish neutrality and the mood in Ireland toward England) and she also has her deceased husband's family estate in Ireland, which her son inherits. Stella is pursued by an insistent admirer named Harrison, who haunts her flat and plants doubts in her mind about her lover Robert Kelway. Robert turns out to be a traitor, but more than this revelation, the true crux of the story lies in Stella's mind, where doubts, concealment of truth, and the denial of her feelings form a mental landscape paralleled by that of lonely, claustrophobic wartime London, a city of surreal unreality.

## Francis Stuart (1902–2000)

Stuart was born in Australia into a Protestant family originally from Northern Ireland. They returned to live there after his father's suicide. Francis was educated in England. When he was 18 years old he married Maud Gonne's daughter Iseult (Maud Gonne was Yeats's beloved and a pivotal figure in the Irish revival). Stuart fought in the Civil War on the Republican side and was captured and interned in a military prison. He published a collection of poems shortly after his release, but his literary reputation was made in the world of fiction; during his lifetime he published over twenty novels. His novels are uneven but fascinating in their relentless search for an adequate depiction of man's alienation within society and for alternative modes of living and thinking. During this early phase from 1931 to 1939, he published a dozen novels in which he seeks to define the thematic territory to be explored throughout his career. This is primarily the portrayal of anti-social heroes who are indifferent to society's accepted values and traditions. Stuart's characters go through periods of intense (and frequently inhuman) suffering, a necessary stage in order to find personal fulfillment. His early novels, *Pigeon Irish* (1932) and *The Coloured Dome* (1932), are the best examples of his thematic preoccupations at the time. The former presents a pessimistic picture of Ireland's future, in which the country is under attack by a materialistic and scientific civilization. The personal sacrifice of the protagonist Joe Arigho saves his friend Frank Allen, the narrator of the book, from execution, but for society his martyrdom remains pointless. Frank is publicly humiliated and socially ostracized but his sufferings reveal to him the tragic pattern of human existence.

These early novels exemplify Stuart's dissatisfaction with Irish society, which he regarded as commercially oriented and failing to uphold its mystic romantic past. His own personal life was troubled; he was unhappy in his marriage and suffered from severe financial problems. In 1939, he accepted a post at Berlin University as a lecturer in English. The onset of the Second World War did not deter Stuart from moving to Germany. His decision caused hostile reactions in Ireland, which did not subside when, in 1941, he started broadcasting from Germany to Ireland. His talks were mainly concerned with Irish politics and literary matters. He and his female companion, Gertrud Meissner, were arrested and imprisoned by French forces in 1946. After their release, they spent three years in Germany living in abject poverty and near starvation. During this period Stuart wrote a trilogy of novels—*The Pillar of Cloud* (1948), *Redemption* (1949), and *The Flowering Cross* (1950)—which drew upon their experiences. *The Pillar of Cloud* is set in a German concentration camp and depicts its protagonist's relationship with two women. Although Dominic, the protagonist, loves Halka, he marries the consumptive Lisette in order to obtain medical treatment for her. The two women transform Dominic's experience, bringing joy and forgiveness into their horrific existence. Their unorthodox three-way relationship is described as innocent, and the two women

appear as saintly or Christ-like in their ability to forgive their tor-
turers. All these novels subvert accepted moral values and standards
in order to exemplify the need for a radical questioning of social
norms and conventions. The novels chart the movement from the
protagonist's suffering to a better understanding of his predicament,
which illuminates his existence.

In 1952, Stuart moved to England and during the next six years
published another five novels. In 1958, he started composing an
autobiographical work which he completed in 1967. It took him
four years to find a publisher. *Black List, Section H* finally appeared
in 1971. The novel is overtly based on Stuart's life; the characters
appear under their real-life names such as Iseult, W. B. Yeats, and
Maud Gonne. The novel describes his participation in the Civil War,
his marriage to Iseult, his encounters with W. B. Yeats, his travels in
Europe, and finally his move to Germany. The protagonist, H, is
driven by his personal and artistic agenda, according to which a poet
must set himself apart from the rest of society and always remain
an outsider. H's move to Germany is portrayed as a conscious decision to alienate himself from society and court dishonor. His decision is therefore not political but personal and artistic. The
experience of humiliation and rejection is necessary to provide him
with sufferings that make him Christ-like and provide him, like
Christ, with the power to affect the minds of others.

*Black List, Section H* brought Stuart back to the attention of the
critics and the wider reading public. Encouraged by this success, he
produced five more novels, written in the same experimental vein
and intended to shock with their unorthodox treatment of sexual
and religious matters.

## Brian Moore (1921– )

Brian Moore was born in Belfast. His family was Catholic, and his
father was a respected surgeon, his mother a former nurse. Having
studied at St. Malachy's College (he never graduated), Moore joined
the Air Raid Precautions Unit and a few years later the British
Ministry of War Transport. He worked in North Africa, Italy, France,
and Poland. In 1948, he emigrated to Canada, where he first tried to
make ends meet with proofreading and other odd jobs until he

became a reporter on the *Montreal Gazette*. He moved to the United States in 1959 and ended up living in Malibu, California. Moore is a prolific writer; he has published around fifteen novels, a book about Canada, a documentary novel, numerous short stories, and journalistic pieces. His novels have won various literary prizes, for instance, his first "serious" novel (he started out writing thrillers), *Judith Hearne* (1955), won the Author's Club First Novel Award; *Catholics* (1972) won the W. S. Smith Literary Award; and *The Great Victorian Collection* (1975) was awarded the James Tait Black Memorial Prize.

In his first novel, *Judith Hearne* (republished as *The Lonely Passions of Judith Hearne*), Moore provided a powerful picture of his city of childhood, Belfast, and its stultifying atmosphere in the 1950s. The characters are confined and constricted by a multitude of rules; religious, social, educational. The eponymous Judith is a case in point. Coming from a well-to-do Catholic family Judith is now facing difficult times. She has been nursing her old aunt for years, a chore that has prevented her from having a job and a personal life. The novel depicts her growing alienation and disillusionment as she comes to realize that she does not fit into the role that the society expects from her. An unmarried spinster with no proper vocational training or education, she loses her religious faith and succumbs to alcoholism. The picture Moore paints of Belfast is grim, dreary, and hopeless. His anticlericalism is pronounced and ardent.

Moore has been praised for his chameleon-like style; he rarely repeats himself and the fictional terrain his novels cover is impressive in its range. *The Emperor of Ice-Cream* (1965), his other Belfast novel, differs radically in tone and treatment of the city. The novel's protagonist, Gavin Burke, is convinced of his powers to change the world, even if governed by the conservative and Catholic values represented by his father. The central conflict of the story is the confrontation between a father and son. Gavin's father is a lawyer, a controlling, pedantic, and tyrannical figure. Gavin's rebellion is a youthful act of resistance against the kind of life his father had envisioned for him (he would have to become a lawyer and work for his uncle) and, differently from Judith Hearne, he is very far from despair but hopeful of a future. Gavin does achieve success of sorts, but it seems a temporary solution rather than a permanent turning of the tables—for him and for Belfast.

Family and family lineage play a central part in *Mangan Inheritance* (1979), a novel centering around the story of James Mangan, a descendant of the famous nineteenth-century Irish poet, James Clarence Mangan. An Irish-American writer married to a successful film star, James Mangan decides to embark on a quest for his heritage and his own self. As is frequently the case in Moore's fiction, this quest for the past becomes a way for the characters to learn to understand themselves. However, the past does not offer easy answers, as James Mangan will learn, and it does not simply present one with a new identity. Moore's protagonist must learn to live with the family ghosts and his personal skeletons, his failed marriage included, and to accept the deepest secrets of both the past and his own personality.

Instead of the past, *Catholics* looks toward the future. Set in the future (at the time of the novel's publication the end of the twentieth century was still a "future"), the novel depicts a changed Catholic Church, which after a merger with the Protestant Church, is now looking for ways to embrace Buddhism. An even more substantial change is the Church's giving up on miracles. This is a new, "progressive," fervently rational church. One of the central characters in Moore's novel is a young proponent of this new church, Father Kinsella, an American working in Amsterdam. He is sent to the monastery on the Island of Muck on the Irish coast where "old" traditions are still being followed. While on Muck, he meets his opponent, the old Abbot of Muck, who believes in miracles and old traditions and their life-affirming nature. Paradoxically, the Abbot himself has lost his faith but still retains a belief in its importance. He does give in to the orders of the Father General at the end of the novel, but enters "null," the absolute void, petrified by the awareness of God's silence.

*Catholics* attracted considerable attention and praise at the time of its publication. However, critics also noted that Moore's move from an analysis of the contemporary clerical world and its effects on people's lives to a futuristic portrayal of Catholicism is not entirely convincing, the solution offered being too simple and straightforward. Moore returned to this subject, exploring it from a different angle, in his subsequent novels. For instance, his only historical novel, *Black Robe* (1985), set in seventeenth-century Canada, depicts the first Jesuit missions in Canada. The more recent *The Color of Blood* (1987) is again set in a fictional terrain, a fictitious Eastern bloc country, in a futuristic present. If *Judith Hearne* depicts a confrontation between the religious and non-religious worlds, and *Catholics* represents a conflict between different religions, then *The Color of Blood* moves the center of conflict to the social and political sphere. In this, we can see Moore's art going toward depicting not a crisis of faith, but a questioning of the world in which we live with its fundamental social and individual problems.

## William Trevor (1928– )

William Trevor Cox was born in a small town in County Cork into a Protestant middle-class family. He attended St. Columba's College and Trinity College Dublin, after which he spent a couple of years teaching in Ireland and in England. Quite successfully, he tried to sculpt for a couple of years, exhibiting in London, Bath, and Dublin. In 1958, he published his first novel, *A Standard of Behaviour,* and since 1960 he has become one of the most prolific short story writers (over six volumes of short stories) and novelists (more than twelve novels) to have emerged from postwar Ireland. Trevor frequently uses Ireland and England as the setting for his stories. He describes himself as a short story writer who likes writing novels. He is generally admired as one of the finest modern short story writers, and his technically crafted tales have a Checkovian feel, exploring a deep longing in his characters, who attempt to come to terms with the fundamental unchangeability of their lives. His first collection, *The Day We Got Drunk on Cake* (1966), features characters unable to communicate their feelings. Truth is in these stories a form of silence, as it is often inexpressible or impossible to recognize. Trevor creates a series of bizarre characters, vividly evoked in the tragic-comic world of his fiction. The successful evocation of eccentric types became the trademark of his later fiction. His characters frequently hide or search for consolation in the imaginative world of their minds. This is the case in his second volume, *The Ballroom of Romance* (1972). The title story of the collection centers around a middle-aged spinster, Bridie, and her dreary life caring for her crippled father. Bridie draws consolation from thinking about her youth,

dwelling on her memories of village dances, thus making her para-
lyzed present even more poignant. The lost love of her life is an
imaginary affair with Patrick Grady, a young man she used to dance
with and who, she thought, was in love with her, but who married
another girl instead. Realizing the futility of her dreams, Bridie will
eventually come to understand that she will probably have to marry
a man she does not love in order to escape loneliness after her
father's death.

Loveless marriages, entered into because of fear of the Church
or through disillusionment and alienation, are the staple themes of
Trevor's Irish fiction. His evocations of Ireland are frequently bleak
and Joycean, depicting a mental paralysis that cripples the characters' willpower. On the other hand, Trevor also explores historical .
circumstances and their (often deadening or confining) effect on his
characters' lives. This is exemplified in his most technically complex
novel, *Fools of Fortune* (1983). This book belongs to the genre of
Irish Big House novels, depicting the fate of a Protestant Anglo-Irish
Ascendancy family, the Quintons. The central tension in the novel
emerges from the opposition of England and Ireland which com-
plicates the protagonists' personal relationships. History and politics, two powerful forces, make the love affair between Willie
Quinton and his English cousin Marianne Woodcombe difficult if
not impossible. The novel begins with the burning of the Quintons'
Big House in County Cork during the Civil War, a scene which her-
alds the tragic inevitability of Willie's and Marianne's fate. History
is to be blamed for the separation of the two lovers, as Willie feels
compelled to avenge the violent deaths of his two sisters and father
and the burning down of their family home. The decisions he has to
make and his own character are remarkably similar to one of his
ancestors, Anna Quinton, who, during the Great Famine of the
1840s was forced to choose between family loyalties (she was from
the Woodcombe side of the family, coming from England) and Irish
history (she was committed to helping Famine victims). Anna's fate
and her decisions are ever-present in the back of Willie's mind, and
the novel's texture reverberates with this historical parallel. The
novel does not end on a tragic note, for, after having served penance
for their past actions (Willie murders the man whom he thought
was responsible for the burning down of his home), Willie,

Marianne, and their daughter Imelda are reunited in the end. They are unable to enact the future they dreamed they would have, but the lyrical tone with which the book concludes gives the reader a hopeful glimpse of a happier future, despite the entanglements of history.

In his later fiction, Trevor continues to explore the tensions in Irish society and the predicaments that Irish history can force on peoples' lives. His achievement lies in the marvelously evocative depiction of Ireland and its quirky, eccentric inhabitants.

## Edna O'Brien (1930– )

Edna O'Brien made an impressive start to her writing career in the 1960s with a trilogy of novels examining her heroines moving from the rural West of Ireland to Dublin and then to London. *The Country Girls* (1960), *The Lonely Girl* (1962; reprinted under the title *Girl with Green Eyes*), and *Girls in Their Married Bliss* (1964) centered around the lives of two friends, Bridget "Baba" Brennan and Caithleen "Kate" Brady, and their growing up in and breaking away from a restrictive, traditionalist Irish country village. All three novels were banned under the Censorship Act, which made O'Brien's literary debut a sensation in Irish literary history.

Describing Kate and Baba's life in the village, their suffering in the stultifying atmosphere of a convent school, their eventual "flight to freedom" to city life in Dublin, their love lives, marriages and children, divorces and breakups, O'Brien draws a realistic, unflinching picture of the lives of these two Irish women. Kate and Baba exemplify a destiny common to Irish women at the time. These books talk openly about abusive relationships and alcoholism but also about the hypocrisy of convent life and the Catholic Church in general.

In the first novel of the trilogy, *The Country Girls*, the events are narrated by Kate. She is the only child of her parents' loveless marriage, wrecked by her father's alcoholism and abusiveness. The Bradys have to give up their rundown Big House as they are unable to keep up even that ramshackle household with the "head of the family" spending all their money on his frequent drinking sprees. Kate's mother is a deeply disillusioned and yet obedient wife, afraid

of the sexual side of marriage and trying to instill in her daughter
the idea that joining a convent is preferable to matrimony. After her
mother drowns in an accident, Kate goes to live with the well-off
Brennans. Together with Baba she is sent to a convent school (Kate
wins a scholarship while the pretty and headstrong Baba relies on
her family paying her fees). Baba is unhappy in the convent and the
girls contrive to be expelled. They go to Dublin where they desperately try to disassociate themselves from their "country" background. The novel ends with Kate being stood up by her older
admirer, Mr. Gentleman. Exotic, foreign, and enigmatic, Mr.
Gentleman symbolizes the opposite of dreary country life but
remains an elusive, never to be achieved goal—or a dream. The next
two novels of the trilogy follow Kate and Baba's lives in Dublin and
London.

*August is a Wicked Month* (1965) tells the story of an Irish nurse
Ellen, living in London and trying to come to terms with issues such
as loss, death, and despair—her only son dies and Ellen tries to get
over it by throwing herself into a series of casual relationships at a
fashionable holiday resort on the Riviera. It could be said that in
O'Brien's later fiction (she is a prolific writer and has published a
number of short story collections in addition to her impressive output of novels), she has moved from the depiction of girls coming
into maturity to an examination of the different perceptions that
adult women have of themselves, and their relationships with their
off-spring and their husbands or lovers. As exemplified by her novel
*I Hardly Knew You* (1977), loveless marriages, brutal husbands, and
abusive unfulfilling sexual relationships form the staple diet of
O'Brien's fiction. Mothers frequently figure as central characters,
setting the standards against which their daughters value themselves
and often passing on their own fears and insecurities (this is the case
in *The Country Girls* but also in *Time and Tide* [1992]) thus negotiating a powerful (though often in a negative way) position in their
daughters' lives. Significantly, in 1976, O'Brien published *Mother
Ireland*, an autobiographical account of her own childhood, interwoven with an exploration of Irish mythology and history. As
O'Brien said in the opening passage of the book, "Ireland has always
been a woman, a cave, a cow, a Rosaleen, a sow, a harlot, and, of
course, the gaunt Hag of Beare" (O'Brien 11). It is a fitting descrip-

tion from a writer whose own career has consisted of a detailed examination of Irish women, their place in society, and the troubled position that the image of the mother has in society.

## Jennifer Johnston (1930– )

Jennifer Johnston was born into the family of a distinguished playwright, Denis Johnston, and the actress-cum-director Shelah Richards. Although she wrote stories as a girl, literary success arrived at the age of forty-two when she published her first novel, *The Captains and the Kings* (1972). She has now written around ten novels which all deal with a moment of crisis in their protagonists' lives; in her earlier fiction this moment frequently coincides with important events in Irish history. Her novels are short with taut structures. While among her first novels two follow the fate of male protagonists, her subsequent fiction is mainly populated with female characters. *The Captains and the Kings* examines the friendship between Charles Pendergast, an old widower with an Ascendancy background, and a young working-class Catholic boy, Diarmuid Toorish. Their friendship is undermined by other characters, and the connection between the two worlds, Catholic and Protestant, Ascendancy and working class, remains but for a fleeting moment. In *How Many Miles to Babylon?* (1974), Johnston examines a similar situation: the friendship between a young Ascendancy heir and a peasant lad, which leads the two to go to World War I together from which neither returns alive. Johnston has remarked upon her interest in the First World War, which she sees as a locus for the current problems in Northern Ireland. In her historical fiction she often uses war as a metaphor for the Northern crisis of the 1970s and 1980s.

*The Gates* (1973) depicts the fate of the school-girl Minnie, who, upon returning to Ireland from England where she went to school, is confronted with divided family loyalties and has to make sense of her father's complicated past, entangled in Irish history. By marrying a Dublin shopgirl, Minnie's father committed a *faux pas* that his family could neither forgive nor forget. Committed to an independent Ireland, Pat MacMahon fought against the fascists in the Second World War—but in the British army, a choice hard to understand in a determinedly neutral Ireland, where the British army had a decidedly negative, unpatriotic image. Minnie has to disentangle these paradoxical relationships and allegiances to understand her own Anglo-Irish background and its historical implications in Irish society.

Isolation, separation, alienation—Johnston's characters are often recorders, watchers, onlookers. For example, Helen Cuffe in *The Railway Station Man* (1984) had a protected childhood and was well-loved. She is shaken out of her sense of security when her husband is accidentally shot during the Troubles, and the deaths of her son and her lover make her isolation complete. Isolation is also the overpowering force in Stella Glover's life in *The Illusionist* (1995). Stella is in an abusive relationship and incapable of leaving her husband and the father of her child. He has isolated her from the rest of the world but refuses to let her become a part of his own world. He even contrives to take away their daughter from her; by giving Robin gifts and praising her, he manages temporarily to win her over. Family relationships, especially difficult mother-daughter relationships, form the thematic center of *Two Moons* (1998). While examining in a more detailed manner the lives of two women, Mimi and her daughter Grace, this novel spans three generations as it also incorporates Grace's daughter Polly. Facing her own slow demise, Mimi is coming to terms with her past and present. Grace, in her turn, is dealing with a sort of mid-life crisis; as an accomplished actress, she is still ambitious in her career. Her daughter Polly feels neglected by Grace who, as it seems to Polly, has always prioritized her career over her family. These three characters represent the different roles that women have in society, and the possible conflicts and dilemmas they create. Grace's mind and speech are full of echoes from the plays she has been involved in, and as she is in the middle of learning Gertrude's part for Shakespeare's *Hamlet*, the latter plays an important role in the novel. Grace becomes a Gertrude of sorts, acting out the betrayal and the incestuous relationship portrayed in the play by having a brief affair with Polly's fiancé, Paul. Her illicit affair is in its turn an echo of her father's "forbidden" affair—he had married Mimi in order to "cure" himself of his homosexuality, but nevertheless had an affair with another man. All these women must learn to come to terms with their past and present, a goal the success of which is left ambiguous at the end of the novel.

The relationships analyzed in Johnston's fiction frequently remain short term because of the separation imposed by class, creed, or race. Her novels chart the gradual movement toward the crisis in which outer forces have a powerful, frequently destructive, impact on the inner world of her protagonists. The outcome of Johnston's earlier novels is bleak and there is little hope for a better future. Her most recent novels offer more optimistic possibilities for the future, while still aware of the baggage that cannot be forgotten or ignored —the past.

## Roddy Doyle (1958– )

Working as a schoolteacher at the time, Roddy Doyle took out a loan to publish his first book, *The Commitments* (1987), privately. He adapted the novel for the screen and in 1991 Alan Parker's film version was released to great commercial success. Films based on his subsequent novels, *The Snapper* (1990) and *The Van* (1991), established Doyle as a worldwide popular author whose work vividly evokes the working-class environment in his fictional Barrytown, a housing estate north of Dublin. In addition to his commercial success, in 1993 his novel *Paddy Clarke Ha Ha Ha* won the Booker Prize, making Doyle the first and so far only Irish author to have achieved that distinction.

Already in his first novel, Doyle mapped out the idiosyncratic fictional territory he had discovered and which he continued to explore in his later fiction—an apolitical working-class Dublin. The vibrant colloquial Hiberno-English dialogue vividly evokes the youngsters Doyle portrays in their contemporary locality. *The Commitments* traces the "life and times" of an Irish soul band. The culture with which the members of the band are imbued is global pop culture, shaped and defined by television and pop music. In his "Barrytown Trilogy"—*The Commitments, The Snapper,* and *The Van* —the main concerns of his characters lie in the ups and downs of their everyday lives: unwanted pregnancy, unemployment, and single mothers are issues with which Doyle deals. However, none of these problems is tackled on a serious or tragic level, nor does it become the source of family crises or wider political issues. Doyle's novels are detached from political and social commentaries; he explores late twentieth-century Ireland, its changing cultural and social conventions, and the influence of mass culture on society. The comedy and humor of his earlier novels is in *Paddy Clarke Ha Ha Ha* replaced by realism of a bleaker kind. The novel is told from the point of view of ten-year-old Paddy, who relates his story of growing up in Barrytown, the breakdown of his parents' marriage, and his problems at school. Instead of 1980s Barrytown, the readers are in this novel given a picture of 1960s Barrytown in transition; the city is growing and taking over the rural outskirts and fields. Paddy and his friends map their territory among half-finished housing estates and roads, while their mental territory is shaped by American television shows and British football, which are shown to gradually replace Gaelic football, Irish language, and national history in the popular imagination. Paddy, a child of a broken home, is socially stigmatized and experiences the trauma of having to grow up and stand up for himself far too soon. His learning of these adult skills of survival is occasionally comic, but the book is guided by a darker mood which precludes the happy ending of the trilogy preceding it. Similarly, his next novel, *The Woman Who Walked Into Doors* (1996), is guided by this more serious, darker edge. The book depicts family violence and is told through the perspective of Paula Spencer, a wife and mother who suffers under the terror of her physically abusive husband Charlo. Paula has to combat not only physical violence at home but also public opinion, which takes the side of the husband, justifying his behavior and ignoring the problem. The title refers to the common excuse that battered wives give for their bruises and injuries. Doyle is in this book continuing to explore the role of the family in Irish society, concentrating more specifically on the question of women and their status. His next novel, *A Star Called Henry* (1999), is the most somber of his later fictions, depicting the fate of Henry, born in 1901, who at the age of fourteen was involved in James Connolly's Citizen Army (a fierce socialist and nationalist, James Connolly established the Citizen Army to protect workers' rights during the strikes; he participated in the Easter Rising and was executed with the other leaders of the Rising in 1916) and later became one of the ruthless members of

Michael Collins's "Apostles" (an IRA grouping in the Anglo-Irish War of 1919–1921). In this novel Doyle replaces the late twentieth-century suburbs with depictions of the earlier slums of the same city. However, Doyle does not analyze historical events deeply enough; they remain merely a backdrop for the adventures of his protagonist. The language of the novel is still driven by the same energy and vitality familiar from Doyle'c earlier fiction, but it does not become anchored in the convincing background of the 1980s Barrytown and ultimately fails to bring Henry alive.

So far, Doyle's real achievement has been the rich and convincing evocation of his Barrytown characters and the accurate, detailed picture of their daily existence. It is a fascinating, poignant, and humorous chronicle of the Ireland of our time.

## John McGahern (1934– )

McGahern was born in Dublin but grew up in County Cavan, where his father was a local police sergeant. He studied at St. Patrick's Training College and University College Dublin. After graduating from university he worked as a teacher at St. John the Baptist's National School in Clontarf. He published his first novel, *The Barracks*, to great critical acclaim in 1963. His second novel, *The Dark* (1965), was banned under the Censorship Act; McGahern was dismissed from his teaching job without explanation and moved to London (his dismissal was probably also due to his marriage to a divorced woman). Years of travel followed; he lived and worked in Spain and the United States before going back to Ireland to settle down on a farm in County Leitrim, where he still lives today.

McGahern has published six novels and a couple of collections of short stories to date. With very few exceptions, his fiction is set in Ireland. His observations of human nature are rendered with microscopic exactness as he carefully records the minutest details of his characters' inner worlds. Together with John Banville he is considered one of the finest Irish writers at work today.

*The Barracks* takes suffering and mortality as its central subject matter. Following the last days of Elizabeth Reegan, a middle-age woman married to a local police sergeant, the novel depicts her slow death from cancer. Elizabeth's situation is hopeless but what acquires central importance in the novel is her endurance and the tremendous will power with which she faces her inevitable demise. Most of the narrative consists of Elizabeth's inner monologue in which she reminiscences about her life and marriage. Although Elizabeth's story and her voice are of central importance, the narrative embraces the entire village community and Elizabeth's family (her husband's three children from a previous marriage), thus weaving the social and communal voices into the novel's textual fabric. The novel is related in a realistic manner, with painstaking attention to detail and observation, and recording of the characters' minutest changes in mood and word. Elizabeth's questioning and pursuit of metaphysical problems, her attempts to find meaning and significance in the life she is saying good-bye to, raise the novel to a highly poetical and metaphysical plane.

McGahern's second novel, *The Dark*, encountered difficulties with the censors, who objected to the depiction of masturbation in the novel. *The Dark* pictures the childhood and adolescence of the young Mahony, a boy whose first name is never revealed. He grows apart from his domineering, patriarchal father (his mother is dead) while trying to bury himself in his studies and fulfill the promise he has made to his dying mother to become a priest. His plans are wrecked by his awakening sexual feelings, which lead him to frequent masturbation. Unable to find freedom in priesthood or sexuality, he dreams of university as the ultimate freedom. He manages to get one of the few scholarships on offer, but the reality of university life fails to live up to his dreams. Bitterly disappointed, he returns to his childhood home, reconciles with his father and heads off toward Dublin and an unknown future.

While Elizabeth Reegan used her past life as a focus through which to filter her present, young Mahoney is trapped in the present, which provides him with a welter of alternatives. Mahoney is frustrated by being constantly made to conform to the wishes and desires of others. His integrity, and his freedom to make choices are curbed, and yet, the most painful lesson he has to learn is to accept the imperfections of life.

McGahern wrote his next novel, *The Leavetaking*, as a response to the banning of *The Dark*. The protagonist Patrick Moran, a teacher at a Catholic school, is made to quit his job because of his marriage to a divorced American woman. On his last day at school, Patrick looks back over his life and realizes for the first time that his life has been shaped by two leavetakings, the first being his mother's death. Patrick refuses to be chained by the past and finds love to be the redeeming force which can ultimately save him. However, love is only possible outside Ireland, in exile.

Love or its substitutes become the central theme in McGahern's next novel, *The Pornographer* (1979). The nameless narrator is a former teacher who now earns his living by writing for porn magazines. His lonesome existence is interrupted when his aunt is taken to the hospital in Dublin. He visits her and tries to ease her last days. He shows considerably less kindness in his dealings with other women. He becomes involved with an older woman who becomes pregnant by him. Refusing to have an abortion, the woman leaves him and Ireland. As a pornographer, the narrator is living in two separate worlds—or so he tries to convince himself—however, his dilemma is to make moral choices and decisions in a contemporary, immoral world. Should he smuggle whiskey into the hospital for his dying aunt and should he marry the woman who becomes pregnant by him? The choices McGahren's pornographer is faced with make him realize that it is as impossible to stay separate from his writing as it is to remain completely detached from the everyday world.

McGahern's next novel, *Amongst Women*, was short-listed for the prestigious Booker Prize and won the Irish Times-Aer Lingus Irish Literature Prize for Fiction in 1990.

### Amongst Women (1990)

The central character of the novel, Michael Moran, is a veteran of the Anglo-Irish War. He finds it difficult to adjust to the peacetime lifestyle; he is dissatisfied with postwar politics, refuses to collect his pension, and buries himself in the running of his farm and his family. Moran is a typical patriarchal self-appointed head of the family who takes his own frustration and alienation out on his wife and children. Having been given responsibility and status during the war, he finds it difficult to locate the same position of responsibility for himself during peacetime. He attempts to compensate for his frustrations by dominating his home and family. However, in this private sphere, his authority is questioned when his sons, Luke and Michael, refuse to acquiesce to his despotic wishes. Both sons seek freedom outside Ireland, as they both emigrate to England. Moran has to establish his authority "amongst women" (the title refers to a line from the "Hail Mary" prayer, blessed art thou amongst women), but his second wife, Rose, and his daughters turn out to be more man-like, strong, and empowered than he himself. As critics have noted, *Amongst Women* suggests a reversal of traditional gender roles in modern Ireland, a tendency the novel regards with an elegiac nostalgia as it looks back at the days when "women were not like men."

McGahern is well known and admired as a master of short stories, and he has published several collections of stories. His latest publication is another novel: twelve years after *Amongst Women*, in 2002, appeared *That They May Face the Rising Sun* (published in the United States under the title *By the Lake*). The novel is again set in the small, closely knit community of an Irish town. The central characters are Joe and Kate Ruttledge, who have returned to their native Ireland after having gotten married in fashionable London. In marked difference to the usual exodus (young people leaving Ireland to go to the States or England), and fighting "against the tide," this young couple tries to set up home in rural Ireland. The novel brings to life a range of colorful village characters, such as Jamesie, their generous neighbor. It is a convincing evocation of the ordinariness of the daily life in a small rural community where nothing ever happens. McGahern's carefully controlled, understated style celebrates the daily minutiae, giving them a highly poetic quality.

## John Banville (1945– )

When his eighth book, *The Book of Evidence*, appeared in 1989 to great critical acclaim and commercial success, John Banville was finally established as one of the most innovative contemporary Irish writers. Although commercial success eluded him before the publication of *The Book of Evidence*, his earlier novels had received numerous literary awards. *Birchwood* (1973) won its author the Allied Irish Banks prize as well as a Macaulay Fellowship; *Doctor Copernicus* (1976) won the American-Irish Foundation Literary Award and the

James Tait Black Memorial Prize; *Kepler* (1981) won the *Guardian* Fiction Prize; and *The Book of Evidence* was nominated for the Booker Prize and won the Marten Toonder Award in Literature. Despite this impressive list of honors and awards, Banville's route to the status of "established" author was long and arduous. His interest in generic experimentation and the complex intertextual background of his novels made commercial triumph unlikely.

Born in 1945 to lower-middle-class Irish parents, the future writer's family had no connections with the world of literature. Indeed, Banville has implied quite the opposite, recalling how his mother said of James Joyce's *Ulysses*: "I'd put that book at the back of the fire" (Carty 18). Although the beginning of his literary career dates back to the imitations of Joyce's *Dubliners*, which he started to compose at the age of twelve, Banville went to Dublin after Christian Brothers School and St. Peter's College, to take up a place with Aer Lingus as a computer operator. During his subsequent travels and temporary jobs, he disciplined himself to write, and a number of short stories appeared in Irish and American periodicals. In January 1969, Secker & Warburg received the manuscript of *Long Lankin*, which they published in 1970. Already in his first book Banville questioned narrative conventions. Generic experimentation developed in his subsequent novels into a means for exploring what most frequently was to become the subject matter of his fiction—that is the fictionality of writing, the questioning of self-identity, and the inaccessibility of truth. His creative output reflects the depth of his impressive range of interests, as his fiction combines references to such authors as Rainer Maria Rilke, Fyodor Dostoyevsky, and Marcel Proust—to name but a few—but also to such famous scientists and philosophers as Albert Einstein, Sir Arthur Eddington, Arthur Koestler, and Ludwig Wittgenstein.

At first sight, *Long Lankin* appears to be a collection of short stories, however, as its ambiguous subtitle "a work of fiction" signals, it should rather be seen as a product of generic experimentation, a hybrid somewhere between a collection of short stories and a novel. As in James Joyce's *Dubliners*, Banville's book is integrated through structural and thematic elements (themes of betrayal and blood imagery run through the book) that make it a coherent whole. His next book, *Nightspawn* (1971), was a metaphysical thriller set in Greece, but his breakthrough (according to the critics but not sales-wise) came with his third book, *Birchwood*, in 1973.

## Birchwood

*Birchwood* is a history of the Godkin family, and the first part of the novel, "The Book of the Dead," depicts the fall of an Irish Big House. The Lawless' estate is taken over by Gabriel Godkin's great-great-grandfather who incidentally is also his namesake, and who marries a daughter of the Lawless family, Beatrice. The house, however, is the site of madness and violence, and the narrative depicts its rapid decline.

The past is evoked in the present, when the narrator's father Joseph in his turn marries a Lawless girl, Beatrice. Her role in the household remains symbolic, as she has to mother a child born from an incestuous relationship between Joseph and his sister Martha. Joseph's plan to leave Birchwood to a true Godkin suffers an unexpected setback when his sister gives birth to twins. Having sent Martha away with one of the twins, Joseph then raises Gabriel as the son of the house. In exchange Michael, the other child, is to inherit the estate, but out of sheer mischief Joseph decides to deceive Martha and makes Gabriel his sole inheritor. Martha, suspecting foul play, returns to Birchwood with Michael and conspires against Gabriel. At the same time Birchwood's state becomes more precarious as Joseph has unsuspectingly sold a substantial part of the estate to the Lawlesses. Financial problems and a peasant rebellion (the Molly Maguires' movement) hasten Birchwood's disintegration, and chaos and havoc accumulate in a spectacular manner: Granny Godkin dies of spontaneous combustion, which may have been caused by the house itself, Aunt Martha goes up in flames, and Grandad Godkin is found dead in the birch wood.

Unaware that he was conceived to be a "true Godkin," that is, ignorant of his real parentage, Gabriel sets out on a quest to locate his missing counterpart. He is determined that he has a mysteriously vanished twin sister, an idea first suggested by his "Aunt Martha," and the second part of the novel, "Air and Angels," relates his travels around the country with Silas and Prospero's Magic Circus. Famine and unrest infect the whole community and violence affects even the timeless world of the circus: Ida, one of the acrobats, is beaten to death, and Sophie, the child of the other acrobat, gets lost. Gabriel's circular journey is completed when he arrives back in Birchwood to find the estate being taken over by the Lawlesses. In Part Three, entitled "Mercury," he witnesses the final battle between the Lawlesses and the Molly Maguires, in which the Circus joins forces with the latter. Finally the Molly Maguires attack what is left of Birchwood, already ruined by the greed and hatred of the Godkins. Gabriel, who does not participate in the bloodshed, confronts Michael, who has been fighting with the Molly Maguires, but is not able to harm him. At last he realizes that Michael is in fact his "lost" counterpart—that is his twin brother. Michael subsequently leaves Birchwood, together with the Molly Maguires, and the estate reverts to Gabriel, who inherits only memories of the old life.

After *Birchwood*, Banville's interest turned to science; he published a tetralogy on science and scientists—*Doctor Copernicus* (1976), *Kepler* (1981), *The Newton Letter* (1984), and *Mefisto* (1986). In 1989, *The Book of Evidence* appeared, his most successful novel to date; nominated for the Booker Prize and acclaimed by the critics, the novel was also a commercial success. Freddie Montgomery, the protagonist, is on trial for murder. Having tried to steal a painting (which he claims to have belonged to his family), he abducts and brutally murders the servant girl who happens to witness his crime. Banville went on to publish a sequel of two books to *The Book of Evidence—Ghosts* (1993) and *Athena* (1995)—in which he explored further the themes of unstable identity and the ultimate unknowability of all knowledge. These themes also form the thematic center of his subsequent novels, *The Untouchable* (1997), *Eclipse* (2000), and *Shroud* (2002). *The Untouchable* traces the life of Victor Maskell, who led a double life as the curator of the Queen's pictures and a communist spy. Doubles are a prominent theme in *Eclipse*, the story of Alexander Cleave, who looks back at his life as an actor after his breakdown, and in *Shroud* where Axel Vander, a famous literary scholar, comes to realize that the secret of his "borrowed" identity has finally been revealed.

## Eoin McNamee (1961– )

Eoin McNamee was born and brought up in Northern Ireland, a place to which he frequently returns in his fiction. After graduating from Trinity College Dublin, McNamee spent a year in New York working as a waiter. He then returned to Dublin to start writing full-time. His first published works were the novella *The Last of Deeds* and three short stories in 1989 (he rewrote one of the stories, "Love in History," and reprinted it in 1992 with "The Last of Deeds" under that title). He came to fame in 1994 with his first novel, *Resurrection Man*. Set in Belfast, the novel depicts a series of brutal killings by the so-called Resurrection Men, a Protestant paramilitary gang. McNamee's narrative technique is cinematic, as his main character, Victor Kelly, fashions his self-image according to a Hollywood-style gangster movie. Frequent references to cinema, such as the "silence of a horror film" or *The Godfather*, also evoke the detached air of a *film noir*, which anesthetizes with chilling calm the horrific crimes of the Resurrection Men. The narrative centers around Victor Kelly, the leader of the gang, who, having been bullied in his youth because of his Catholic-sounding name, now wreaks revenge upon the city and its inhabitants. It seems that the city itself both oozes violence and scripts the blood-curdling roles for Kelly and his gang. Rather than looking for the historical roots of sectarian violence in the North, McNamee brings the insipient violence, hidden in the modern city, into the open. The Belfast of *Resurrection Men* becomes both real and mythical, as the novel turns its knife-sharp analytical eye on the heart of the city and the human soul.

McNamee's second novel, *The Blue Tango* (2001), again treads a dangerous path between fact and fiction. Set in a small town—Whiteabbey—in 1952 pre-Troubles Northern Ireland, *The Blue Tango* attempts to unravel the mystery surrounding the murder of Patricia Curran, the nineteen-year-old daughter of Judge Lance Curran, a former Northern Ireland attorney general.

McNamee's intention here is not to establish the true circumstances of Patricia's death (although the novel does produce a believable account of events), but to explore Patricia's identity and to write about the atmosphere surrounding the case. However, in addition to attempting to dispel the mystery that clouds the last hours of

Patricia's life, the novel exemplifies its author's concern with the origins and mechanics of the making of a public image—or myth.

McNamee's novel centers around an exploration of the (narrative) drive that impelled the Curran drama toward its tragic conclusion and toward the wrongful conviction of an innocent man. The book consists of thirty short chapters, a series of flashbacks and flash-forwards, which produce the effect of a snapshot album. *The Blue Tango* oscillates between fact and fiction, cause and effect, the haunted image reprinted on the front page of national newspapers and the impossibility of knowing the real Patricia. Although the narrator's knowing tone suggests there is more to her than the popular image of a "death-courting coquette," she remains stubbornly elusive, a shadowy figure whose tragic fate haunts and controls the narrative.

The novel presents a gallery of witnesses, testimonies, reports, rumors, yet Patricia herself remains curiously undeveloped, as two-dimensional as a photograph. Despite the quantity of factual information about her, the reader is ultimately left with her "public" image.

*Resurrection Man* hinted that ordinary language is an inadequate tool for conveying the violence depicted in the novel. More than an investigation of an unexplained murder mystery or miscarriage of justice, *The Blue Tango* represents an exploration of the linguistic tools deployed for creating and disseminating fictions. McNamee's novel exposes a dangerous tangle of fiction and fact, reality and representation, myth and history. Instead of the "classic" clarity arriving at the end of a traditional "whodunit"—the murderer exposed and the mystery explained—McNamee's novel presents reality as a double image, as if "the negative of the photograph had been printed and . . . the actual photograph was still awaiting print." McNamee has rooted his novel in the no-man's-land between dream and reality, life and fiction. It is a compelling and poetic investigation, haunting but also haunted by an image, still awaiting development.

## Colm Tóibín (1955– )

Tóibín has published several novels, a couple of travel books, and a selection of journalistic writing. His first novel, *The South* (1990), was set in Spain, where the central character, Katherine Proctor, tries to shake off her Big House inheritance and forge her career as a painter. She falls in love with Miguel, who is involved in the Spanish Civil War on the Republican side. Katherine loses Miguel and their daughter in the war, and returns to her birthplace in Wexford, where she is finally able to find an artistic expression to accommodate the world around her. Tóibín won the Irish Times/Aer Lingus Literature Prize for his first novel, which was followed by *The Heather Blazing*, published in 1993, which won the Encore Award for the best novel of the year. The protagonist Eamon Redmond is a judge in Four Courts in Dublin. The novel moves between two timelines, Eamon's present in Dublin and holidays in the village called Cush, and his childhood in Enniscorthy. As Eamon is a judge, he sees life and society as regulated by and around laws and, above all, the Constitution. He is confident when he has the law to guide him, and when talking about the law (for instance, when he has to deliver his judgments). However, he is considerably less comfortable with everyday human interaction. Both his wife and his father are left suffering from speech impediments after strokes. Eamon, who has not been able to communicate with his wife (or father) for years, is particularly troubled by his wife's insistent attempts to render her frustrations and wishes. Eamon's law is a constraining, silencing force for the other characters and cuts him off from the present-day world he inhabits. For instance, when his daughter Niamh becomes pregnant and considers an abortion, Eamon is incapable of talking about it with his wife. The overwhelming and deadening power of the law is at the end of the novel shown as relenting its grip on Eamon and Ireland, as the novel ends on a hopeful note, depicting Eamon finally being able to form a bond with his grandson Michael.

Family conflicts and inter-generational problems are at the heart of Tóibín's next novel, *The Blackwater Lightship* (1999), set in the Ireland of the 1990s and depicting three generations of women of the Deveraux family trying to come to terms with the fact that their son/grandson/brother is dying of AIDS. Here Tóibín explores the familiar thematic territory of family strife, reconciliation, and re-evaluation of values and traditions in modern society. In the novel *The Story of the Night* (1996), set in 1980s Argentina, he examines the troubles of a young man, Richard Garay, coming to terms with his homosexuality. Political events, the Falklands War, and the collapse of the repressive rule of the Generals mirror Richard's quest toward finding the way to live his life openly. Tóibín is also the author of *Love in a Dark Time: Gay Lives from Wilde to Almodovar* (2002), and in 1999 he edited the *Penguin Book of Irish Fiction*.

## Anne Enright (1962– )

Enright has published three novels and a collection of short stories to date. She is widely thought to be one of the most interesting fiction writers to have appeared on the Irish literary scene in the 1990s. Her first book, *The Portable Virgin*, was published in 1991 to great critical acclaim and won the Rooney Prize for Irish Literature. The stories in this collection exemplify Enright's distinctive, postmodern style; she incorporates frequent intertextual references to other authors (most notably to James Joyce's *A Portrait of the Artist as a Young Man* and *Ulysses*) and uses a combination of historical and journalistic styles in order to explore her characters' past. Her first novel, published in 1995, *The Wig My Father Wore*, is written in the same humorous vein, dark and quirky at the same time. The novel has multiple plots that all center around the life of the protagonist, Grace/Grainne, and offer different perspectives of her story. It is a kaleidoscopic image of modern urban reality and the unreality of contemporary lives.

Grace works on a television game show the "Love Quiz," where she meets an angel who appears on her show, and eventually gets pregnant by him. Different plotlines are in constant flux, producing a televisual effect of channel-hopping. The outcome is a humorous, occasionally satirical portrayal of the perils of modern life and identity. While the rest of the characters are rendered as victims of the neurotic modern era, Grace's relationship with Stephen, the angel, is characterized by their mutually fulfilling love and eroticism.

Love, especially motherly love, is the central concern in Enright's next novel, *What Are You Like?* (2000). As the author herself proclaimed in interviews, she was trying to explore the iconic image of the "dead mother" in Irish culture. The protagonists of the novel, a pair of twins, get separated at birth after their mother's death (according to Catholic policy, saving children's lives was considered more important than saving the mother's). The Church arranges the adoption of one of the twins, Rose, who grows up in England. Maria, the other twin, stays with her natural father and stepmother in Dublin, but emigrates to the United States later on. Thus both girls experience the separation and loss that accompany any immigrant experience. They try to recover the lost stories of women, such as their mother's, in order to fill in the gaps in their own personal history and also in the history of their country and the global community, where women's tales are those most vulnerable to loss, distortion, and forceful silencing.

Enright's last novel to date, *The Pleasure of Eliza Lynch* (2002), shows the author exploring a thematic territory very different from that of her earlier novels. In this book Enright tells the story of Eliza Lynch who in the 1860s briefly became the richest woman in the world. Irish herself, Eliza, while in Paris, has an affair with a Paraguayan heir, Francisco Solano Lopez, and travels across the Atlantic to discover the magnificent riches waiting for her in Asunción. The novel is historical but, as ever, Enright resorts to magic realism to evoke the rich and lushly beautiful world awaiting to be discovered by Eliza Lynch.

A talented young novelist, Anne Enright is worth serious consideration as an heir to Ireland's wealthy tradition of experimental novelists.

## Emma Donoghue (1969– )

Emma Donoghue emerged on the Irish literary scene in the 1990s. Her family background is literary; her father is Denis Donoghue, a distinguished literary critic and professor of literature and her mother is an English teacher at a secondary school. Emma Donoghue herself has a strong academic background; she is a graduate of University College Dublin and she completed her doctorate at Cambridge University. She started her first novel while still at UCD. *Stir-fry* was published in 1994. This novel could be seen as yet another coming-of-age story centered around a young female student, but Donoghue makes *Stir-fry* more complex by analyzing not only her protagonist's sexual awakening but also her discovery of her true sexuality; *Stir-fry* is a campus novel with a lesbian twist. The young college student Maria answers an ad and ends up sharing a student apartment with two "mature" college students, Jael and Ruth. Gradually Maria realizes that the two girls are not only friends but also lovers. She becomes fascinated by their relationship, which reveals a different world from that of her traditional Irish background.

Donoghue's second novel, *Hood* (1995), was awarded the Gay, Lesbian, and Bisexual Book Award for Literature by the American Library Association. The novel centers around the depiction of the lesbian relationship between Pen and Cara, who live with Cara's separated father. At the beginning of the novel Cara dies in a car accident, and the narrative charts Pen's gradual coming to terms with her own sexuality to the degree that she is finally able to "come out" of her hood. The novel is as much about lesbian (sexual) identity as it is about Irish (national) identity. Pen and Cara are both products of an Irish Catholic childhood, upbringing, and education. The same prejudices have shaped their lives. While Cara unashamedly acknowledged and announced her sexual orientation, Pen thinks of it solely in terms of her relationship with Cara. She is also very concerned about her national identity, as being Irish and living in Ireland is clearly of major importance to her. Emigration is not an option; she is Irish born and bred and has to continue living in Ireland in order to feel herself to be a "real" Irish person.

Donoghue's collection of "revisionist" fairy tales, *Kissing the Witch* (1997), is based on the rewriting of well-known European fairy tales. Although other writers, most notably Angela Carter, have explored the same ground of fairy-tale-dom, Donoghue manages to give her book a unique touch. Her stories feature relationships between women, and she examines how female characters, by forming such strong relationships, learn to overcome the troubles and mishaps they encounter. In her stories women learn to depend on other women, thus forming a community of female trust and interdependence. This community inspires and encourages her characters to rewrite the stereotypes and myths that have governed society thus far.

Donoghue's third novel, *Slammerkin* (2000), is a fictional account of the life of Mary Saunders, a prostitute in eighteenth-century London who murdered her mistress. *Slammerkin* is darker and more pessimistic than Donoghue's earlier fiction. She used the few surviving facts of the real-life Mary Saunders's life to build her story. Her book is fictional, though thoroughly researched. History is Donoghue's central concern in her next book, a collection of short stories entitled *The Woman Who Gave Birth to Rabbits* (2002). The stories center around events from Irish and British history, as Donoghue is determined to save fascinating but neglected or forgotten characters from the dustbin of history.

Donoghue is frequently pigeonholed as a lesbian writer. True, in her fiction she does examine lesbian relationships, but more often she analyzes the ways in which women can offer each other support in understanding, mutually nurturing, and caring relationships. Reactions to her novels (but more often to her own sexual orientation) vary; as she said herself: "It is a time of transition and confusingly rapid change, a time in which it has been immensely exciting to be out as an Irish lesbian writer. Reactions have varied from great warmth, through naïve surprise, to pulpit-thumping (my sister went to Mass the day after I appeared on television, and heard me denounced from the altar as a danger in this age of AIDS)" (Donoghue 87). The work by this fiercely intelligent and fascinating author is worth watching out for.

---

## Notes

1. All factual information regarding the lives of the authors discussed in this chapter is derived from the following studies: James M. Cahalan, *The Irish Novel: A Critical History* (Dublin: Gill & Macmillan, 1988); Robert Welch, ed., *The Oxford Companion to Irish Literature* (Oxford: Clarendon Press, 1996); Seamus Deane, *A Short History of Irish Literature* (London: Hutchinson, 1986).

2. For a reprint of Gavan Duffy's (a nationalist journalist and politician) attack on Lever, first published as "Mr. Lever's 'Irish' Novels," in *The Nation*, 1843, see *Field Day Anthology*, Vol.1 (Derry: Field Day Publications, 1991) pp. 1255–1269.

# Chapter Five

# Major Themes, Movements, and Issues

## The National Tale

The national tale as a genre was developed in Ireland, primarily by women writers, over the decade preceding the publication of Walter Scott's *Waverley* (1814). Having emerged from the novels published around the 1790s, the national tale in its turn gave birth to the historical novel around the 1810s.[1] The two genres are almost identical in terms of plot and characterization, but differ radically in their respective narrative strategies and political implications. While the national tale is firmly grounded on the geographical locale and dependent on the vivid evocation of a specific (Irish) place, the historical novel is more concerned with plot and the demonstration of the linear process of growth through historical change. At their early stages of development the national tale and the historical novel frequently borrowed each other's features. After Scott's *Waverley*, the national tale incorporated Gothic elements and discovered new models for representing historical developments, continuing to offer an alternative to the historical fiction. The national tales enjoyed a wide popularity at the time of their publication and the recent Irish criticism has lately witnessed an upsurge of interest in the genre.

Ireland and its complicated political situation between the 1790s and 1810s offered especially fertile ground for the flourishing of such genre as the national tale, the examples of which were often politically radical. The year of the Union, 1800, was immediately preceded by the United Irishmen rebellion in 1798, the violence of which was still acutely present in the public consciousness, and the everyday presence of the English army in Ireland had very obvious political implications. Contrary to promises, the Union did not grant political and civic rights to the Catholic population in Ireland. Catholics were not only unable to vote, but restrictions also applied to their right to educate their children; to carry arms; to inherit, own, lease, and work land; to trade and employ; and to enter the major professions. Furthermore, the Union also saw opposition among the Protestant Ascendancy, who did not like to see their local position of power shifting away to London and Westminster. For the English, the Union represented a security measure against France (significantly, the United Irishmen rebellion had been supported by the French) but it also constituted a means to abolish the "corrupt" Protestant Parliament. The failure to grant Catholic emancipation meant that the Union remained incomplete and unstable, both on the factual and conceptual level. In some sense, the authors of the national tale sought to fill in the gap and solidify the Union in fiction.

It can be argued that the national tale had already emerged in the eighteenth century, but Sydney Owenson's subtitles—such as "A National Tale" or "An Irish Tale"—helped to define the genre in the early nineteenth century. This label seemed to be convenient and catchy enough for the publishers for whole series of novels appeared under headings like "Irish National Tales," "Today in Ireland," and "Yesterday in Ireland." Lady Morgan's pioneering work, *The Wild Irish Girl: A National Tale* (1806), along with Maria Edgeworth's *Ennui* (1809) and *The Absentee* (1812), formed and shaped the genre. Deploying the plot of a romance and picturing an encounter of a traveling stranger and a romantic, mystical native, the radical innovation that the national tale offered was the portrayal of the dislocation that affected both the traveler and the native, forcing them to reevaluate their personal and national identities. The fictional project that these authors endeavored to achieve was summed up by Walter Scott when he declared that Maria Edgeworth's novels had had a major impact toward the completion of the Union. As Scott said in his "General Preface" to the 1829 edition of *Waverley*, Edgeworth's Irish characters "have gone so far to make the English familiar with the character of their gay and kind-hearted neighbours of Ireland, that she may truly said to have done more towards completing the Union, than perhaps all the legislative enactments by which it has been followed up" (Scott 352). It is important to emphasize that while the Catholics felt themselves to be a minority (in political terms), the Protestant Ascendancy members were claiming that the Union left them in the position of an "embattled minority." Authors such as Lady Morgan and Charles Robert Maturin evoke and explore the effect that these feelings had on the Protestant imagination and the formation of the Anglo-Irish minority identity in Ireland and Britain.

The national tales chart the changes in political and national consciousness, portraying the changing meanings of the Union (for Catholics and Protestants) and the parliament (although the Irish parliament had effectively consisted only of Protestants, in the popular post-Union imagination it became known as "our parliament"), and also the different models of Irishness. While in *The Wild Irish Girl* Glorvina personified an unproblematic Irishness, in Lady Morgan's later novels national identity is not so unequivocally located but, rather, problematized as a shifting and fluctuating entity. Morgan's later novels exemplify very different heroines, such as Beavoin O'Flaherty in *The O'Briens and the O'Flahertys* (1827), a half-Italian and half-Irish nun who knows Ireland as well as Glorvina does, but who travels across Europe and Ireland with a remarkable ease, shifting disguises. Beavoin is a clever woman, very different from the pure and childlike Glorvina. Also the Ireland and the various types of Irishness its inhabitants possess and profess in *The O'Briens and the O'Flahertys* offer a view different from that unified, ancient Ireland that Mortimer discovers with Glorvina's help in *The Wild Irish Girl*.

The problematic evolution of national identity is reflected by Charles Robert Maturin's fictional output. His *Milesian Chief* (1812), for instance, takes the plot that Morgan's *The Wild Irish Girl* had established for the national tale and rewrites it so that it becomes one of the first examples of Irish Gothic. The protagonist of the novel, a young female artist called Armida Fitzalban, is brought up in Italy, from where he moves to Ireland. Whilst in Ireland, Armida meets a young Irish patriot, Connal O'Morven, with whom she falls passionately in love, forgetting her good manners and her engagement to an English army officer. The leader of a few desperados, Connal and his patriotic group go on to a hopeless rebellion against the English hegemony. The rebellion is disastrously unsuccessful, Connal is executed, and Armida drinks poison and dies while holding Connal's body in her arms. Instead of a happy marriage between Irish Glorvina and her English suitor, *Milesian Chief* indicates a more somber outcome, exemplified by Armida and Connal's union, which emphasizes the overall sense of hopelessness and despair.

If *The Wild Irish Girl* romantized its setting, locating its geographical heart in the ancient Ireland and its present-day natural wilderness, then Maria Edgeworth's novels were mostly situated in the drawing-rooms of country houses and castles. Thus between these authors emerges a polarized picture of the Irish "reality"—the drawing room and the wilderness of countryside. Maturin, but also Morgan in her later fiction, seeks to incorporate both realities in his novels, which makes them an apt representation of the post-Union stratified situation. Significantly, the protagonists of these novels, such as Maturin's Armida and Morgan's Beavoin, personify this polarization in their own hybrid national identity. While Glorvina was "pure" but also pureblooded Irish, Morgan's later characters and Maturin's Armida are cosmopolitan Irish patriots. This is also the case in Charles Lever's *Lord Kilgobbin* (1872), which is polarized both in setting and characterization, for Lever's heroine, Nina Kostalergi, is half-Irish, half-Greek, and brought up in Italy, and the novel's setting incorporates Turkey, Greece, London, and the Irish Bog of Allen.

Lever, Maturin, and Morgan portray an Ireland that (frequently) brings about a violent transformation in their protagonists' lives. Maria Edgeworth's novels have traditionally been seen as more moderate in their political content. However, while attempting to make Ireland understandable for the English and representing the country realistically in order to introduce the historical conditions that have shaped its present, Edgeworth's fiction not only portrays but also analyzes the Irish situation, explaining the deep political, linguistic, and social roots of the "Irish question." Owenson and Maturin's novels, although inspired by Edgeworth's example, are more vividly militant and overly political in their ambition, yet, Edgeworth's later tales show her subtle growth toward embracing a nationalist standpoint.

## The Big House

The Big House is a recurrent and popular motif in Irish literature.[2] Referring to the Ascendancy mansions, the authors examine the life of the Protestant landholders from the late eighteenth century to the founding of the Irish Free State. Frequently the house (often dilapidated or under attack) becomes the symbol of the anxieties and uncertainties that governed the life of Protestant Ascendancy. While the Big Houses remained culturally and politically isolated from Irish culture, at the same time their fictional representations evoke nostalgia for the class and the cultural wholeness that is reflected in these elegiac pictures of the lost days of aristocratic grandeur and spirit. The Big House theme continued to inspire postwar Irish writers, such as Jennifer Johnston and William Trevor, who explored and analyzed the Big House phenomenon in Irish culture. Finally, the Big House theme was given a postmodern makeover by contemporary Irish writers such as John Banville and Aidan Higgins.

Maria Edgeworth's *Castle Rackrent* (1800) is traditionally seen as inaugurating this trend in the Anglo-Irish literature. Here Edgeworth introduced what were to become the staple ingredients of Big House fiction: the dilapidated house, the rise and fall of the gentrified family, the irresponsible absentee landlords, and the rise of the (frequently militant, and therefore threatening) peasant class. The fears of the Anglo-Irish Protestant Ascendancy were heightened to a paranoiac extreme in the Gothic treatment of Big House in the novels by Charles Robert Maturin and Sheridan Le Fanu. Covering an impressive geographical territory (the novel's multiple plotlines are set in continental Europe, India, and Ireland), Maturin's *Melmoth the Wanderer* (1820) is framed by the story of the young John Melmoth, the last descendant of his family, and his coming to the inheritance of his uncle's ruined Big House in County Wicklow. His dying uncle is the exemplar of the suspicions grown into obsessions, governing the lives of Protestant landholders. Old Melmoth's paranoia about his servants taking over his house and his imminent destitution have been interpreted by critics as a convincing and realistic evocation of the feelings of Protestant Ascendancy, whereby the landlords' guilt is intertwined with their fear at the rise of Catholicism.

Sheridan Le Fanu's *Uncle Silas* (1864) represents another Gothic investigation of Protestant guilt. Although the novel is set in England and at first sight does not have any links with the Anglo-Irish landlords and their problems, critics have persuasively argued that the social and political concerns prevalent in Ireland at the time reverberate in its textual fabric. Furthermore, it has been established that Le Fanu placed his story in the English context at the demands of his English publishers. He situated his protagonist, the haunted and terrorized Maud, first in her isolated childhood home at Knowl and later in her uncle's crumbling manor house in Derbyshire. Maud is never safe under the roofs of these houses. While in Edgeworth's fiction the threat came from outside (the peasants), in Le Fanu and Maturin's fiction the horror is growing from within—the family secrets are too violent and too real to be contained, and they explode the safety net of a secure and familiar-looking Big House structure.

Charles Lever's *Lord Kilgobbin* (1872) represents a transitional treatment of the Big House theme. Lever situates his manor on a no-man's land between the Bog of Allen and the firm Irish/international soil. The shifting sense of certainties is reflected in the questionable validity of Lord Kilgobbin's title and his doubtful aristocratic lineage. If Lever's Kilgobbin is the site of uncertainty and change, Elizabeth Bowen's *The Last September* (1929) records an already irrevocably changed Big House world. In Bowen's novel the house called Danielstown is nearing its inevitable destruction and the author's elegiac tone registers the melancholic beauty and the grandeur of its last days. The burning of Danielstown at the end of the novel symbolizes the end of an era, the inevitable demise of the carefree days of tea and tennis parties. Significantly, the owners of Danielstown, Lady Naylor and Sir Richard, have no children of their own and their house witnesses the constant comings and goings of numerous visitors and relatives. The heirless Danielstown is isolated from the rest of the country—a random newspaper or magazine that the house guests have picked up on their way to Danielstown are the only intrusions of the outside world—but this seeming tranquility is illusionary, for the mansion's quietness is violently disrupted by the events of the Civil War, which finally break in the demesne walls.

The demise of the Big House world is the main subject of Somerville and Ross. Their realist portraits of the crumbling order of the Big House culture depict the decline and destruction of the houses, not by the hands of outside invaders but through the irresponsible and reckless mismanagement of their owners. *The Big House of Inver* (1925) is a case in point here. The novel is a twentieth-century retelling of *Castle Rackrent*, depicting the decline and fall of the Prendeville family. Shibby Prendeville, an illegitimate daughter and the last of the Prendeville line, harbors dreams of Big House grandeur, but her illusions are violently shattered as she has to come to terms with the inevitable end of the Big House era and her own colonial dreams.

Although until the 1920s Anglo-Irish manor houses were part of the actual reality of the everyday life in Ireland, Big House continued to be a vibrant and oft-used theme in the Irish Free State. In these evocations of Ascendancy life, Big House continues to embody ambivalent functions, as a reminder of past violence and oppression, but it is also the site of elegiac nostalgia for the lost past. The Big House appears in a number of works, such as Sean O'Faolain's short stories; Joyce Cary's *Castle Corner* (1938) and *A House of Children* (1941); Mervyn Wall's *Leaves for a Burning* (1952); Julia O'Faolain's *No Country for Young Men* (1980); Jennifer Johnston's *The Captains and the Kings* (1972), *The Gates* (1973), *How Many Miles to Babylon?* (1974), and *Fool's Sanctuary* (1987); William Trevor's short stories and novels, most importantly his novel *Fools of Fortune* (1983); John McGahern's short fiction; and Molly Keane's *Good Behaviour* (1982), *Time After Time* (1983), and *Loving and Giving* (1988).

The Big House novel was recently revitalized by two experimental Irish novelists, Aidan Higgins and John Banville. The rundown Springfield House in Higgins's *Langrishe, Go Down* (1966) achieves a universal symbolic significance as the novel intertwines the theme of the declining Anglo-Irish culture with the decline of Western civilization, portraying the Ireland of the 1930s with the escalating events in war-torn Europe as a backdrop. *Langrishe* portrays the lives of two sisters, Helen and Imogen, who lead their idle and infertile existence in the derelict Springfield House. Although Imogen is trying to break the deadening paralysis of their life by

embarking on an affair with Otto, a visiting German student of folklore, her fling is doomed from the beginning. Different from the traditional Big House novel, Otto does not seek to possess the
Springfield House but to dominate Imogen. His ill treatment of
Imogen foreshadows the arrival of the new era of violence (the
novel is set during the rise of Nazism in Germany). Imogen and
Helen are surrounded by reminders and memories of death and
dying. Indeed, as critics have noted, Higgins describes the two
Langrishe sisters as if buried alive under the mementoes of a dead
or dying culture. Yet these mementoes do not manage to conjure up
a picture of cultural wholeness, or even the (hi)story of Springfield
House. Helen and Imogen remain isolated from their (historical)
past and live in alienation from the rest of the society. Otto's
research does not unearth a living history. On the contrary, as his
method is to explain "the unknown by still less known," his fascina-
tion with recondite facts and anecdotal stories about Ireland's past
transform Ireland's history into an "old curiosity shop" that has little relevance to the present. Imogen's stillborn baby, the outcome
of their affair, symbolizes the death of the culture from which the
Langrishes originate.

The challenge of conventional history is taken further in John
Banville's novel *Birchwood* (1973), which questions the validity of
historiography as such. Banville's protagonist Gabriel Godkin is
attempting to tell the story of the "fall and rise of Birchwood," the
temporal topsy-turvydom of which is exemplified in the playful
inversion of the usual "rise and fall." In order to do this, Gabriel has
first to find a suitable structure for organizing his memories into a
coherent whole. However, while at the beginning of his story he has
a seemingly unshakeable faith in the potential meaningfulness of
such moments—"They must mean something, these extraordinary
moments when the pig finds the truffle embedded in the muck"—
during the course of his narrative Gabriel comes to accept that due
to the process through which his existence is to be fixed, the rendering of his story and the history of Birchwood remain either
ambiguous or unstable. As the objective of his quest is his identity,
Birchwood seems to offer Gabriel a structural and thematic frame,
that is, his relationship with the house and its history seems to provide him with both a spatial and a temporal center. However—and

here lies *Birchwood*'s main difference from the typical Big House novel—instead of wallowing in his nostalgia for the past, Banville's narrator is constantly forced to acknowledge the impossibility of retrieving his past and has therefore to invent or create the history of Birchwood. Instead of expressing nostalgia for a class, a way of life, or the grandeur of the past, as in a traditional Big House novel, *Birchwood* depicts the isolation of a quest for identity, a narrating voice, and self-realization. By bringing Gabriel's quest to such a philosophical and metaphysical complexity, Banville subverts the Big House novel to challenge the conventional concepts of history and self-identity. Through Birchwood's topsy-turvydom are reflected the problems that continue to enhance and enchain the imagination of contemporary fiction writers.

## The City

Traditionally, the city has occupied a polarized position in the literary imagination; on the one hand it has been viewed as the site where culture and arts are nurtured, on the other hand it is frequently represented as the source of corruption and decay. Irish fiction has long been characterized by the great emphasis it places on the rural setting—from the romantic wilderness of Glorvina's castle in Lady Morgan's *The Wild Irish Girl* (1806) to the debilitating constraints that the village life enforced upon the characters in Edna O'Brien's *The Country Girls* (1960). Indeed, an idealized pastoral version of nationalist past has traditionally treated countryside as the authentic locus of Ireland's identity, the source of Irishness. Yet, the principal cities, such as Dublin in the South and Belfast in the North, have become the most popular settings in modern Irish fiction. Within the city structure, its geographical and imagined boundaries are played out through the ongoing cultural and political debates in society.[3]

James Joyce's representation of Dublin towers over every attempt to discuss the city in modern Irish literature. Joyce famously declared having wanted to give a picture of Dublin so complete that if the city one day suddenly disappeared from the earth it could be reconstructed out of his book, *Ulysses*. His feelings about Dublin changed over the time; he once saw the city as infected by the "hemiplegia of the will" (Joyce, *Letters I* 55), yet remained faithful to the imaginary and geographical center of his fictional universe throughout his career, saying, "I always write about Dublin, because if I can get to the heart of Dublin I can get to the heart of all the cities of the world" (Power 65–66).

Dublin contains multiple layers of history, from Vikings to the Georgian era and onward. Maria Edgeworth and Lady Morgan depicted Dublin after the city had been deprived of its parliamentary power and the more fashionable citizens had left it for London. John Banim in *The Anglo-Irish of the Nineteenth Century* (1828) describes a scene in which his protagonist, Gerald Blount, a son of an absentee landlord, is wandering around Dublin. Gerald is despite himself forced to admit that the cityscape he is admiring could well be the most beautiful city-picture in the world. Joyce is generally thought to be the first author to have tried to depict the city in its multifarious presence, its state of continuous change and movement —the city as a living entity. However, the portrayal of the suburban village of Chapelizod in Sheridan Le Fanu's *The House by the Churchyard* (1863) indicates a similar intention to capture the interconnectedness and interdependence of the multitude of characters that constitute the city or a suburb. The Chapelizod community is not construed out of the sum total of all the characters but rather, by the spacial construct of the village, is created by its inhabitants' activities, interdependent plotlines, and the sounds and smells of Chapelizod. The collective character of Le Fanu's community is humorously captured by the following quotation:

> . . . society resembles a pyramid of potatoes, in which you cannot stir one without setting others, in unexpected places, also in motion. Thus it was, upon very slight motives, the relations of people in the little world of Chapelizod began to shift and change considerably, and very few persons made a decided move of any sort without affecting or upsetting one or more of his neighbours (Le Fanu 158).

Le Fanu's intricately interwoven plotlines reflect the stirs, the shifts, and changes that take place in the pyramid-like community of Chapelizod. Similarly to Le Fanu, Joyce's Dublin is constituted by these nuclei (potatoes) of shift and change; however, Joyce includes his two wanderers, Leopold Bloom and Stephen Dedalus, who negotiate their way through the pyramid. While they set some potatoes in motion, their inner and outer eyes—the city of their mind and the city that they witness—create the cityscape of Dublin on June 16, 1904. In Joyce's representation, the city is divested of its moral significance, as it contains both negative and positive sides of its polarized identity. As Bloom reflects, seeing the streets bustling with busy citizens of Dublin: "Cityful passing away, other cityful coming, passing away too: other coming on, passing on. Houses, lines of houses, streets, miles of pavements, piledup bricks, stones. Changing hands. This owner, that"(Joyce, *Ulysses* 156–157). In *Ulysses*, the living and the dead, the constant comings and goings of the inhabitants of Dublin, constitute a living and lively town, where the beauty of such landmarks as Trinity College is juxtaposed with the sordidness and poverty of the alleyways.

Joyce's overwhelming influence has left the Irish writers grappling with his monumental legacy. His Dublin overshadowed the imaginative realist squalor of Dublin in James Stephen's *The Charwoman's Daughter* (1912) and Liam O'Flaherty's hostile, dehumanized Dublin in *The Informer* (1925). The city encountered in Joyce's writing is no longer the contemporary city reality. Changes in society and in urban living experience have demanded a new and different kind of representations of Dublin. This is achieved in Roddy Doyle and Dermot Bolger's fiction, the best examples of "Northside realism" that emerged onto the literary scene in the 1980s. Doyle's Barrytown is a fictional suburb situated on the north side of the river Liffey. Doyle's characters exemplify the transition from the type of interconnected and interdependent community as depicted in Le Fanu's and in Joyce's fiction (the Dublin depicted in *Ulysses* is far from a modern urban jungle, as Joyce's characters seem all to know each other) into the hostile and alien reality of the late twentieth-century cityscape. As critics have shown, Barrytown is a suburb, itself a transitional space between the city and countryside, and witnesses an increasing amount of alien intrusions into its domesticated space—strangers passing through Barrytown remind Doyle's characters of the unknown that lies outside their territory. The modern city reality is vividly evoked in Dermot Bolger's novel *The Journey Home* (1990), where the bleak-

ness of its "mean streets" pervades the city. Bolger's streetwise characters are forced to leave Dublin, yet their "journey home" does not
become a well-rehearsed journey back to the pure and uncontaminated countryside, as instead "home" becomes a mythical concept
that cannot be found in urban or in rural Ireland.

While every literary attempt to represent Dublin is overshadowed by Joyce's example, the image of Belfast is complicated by the
sectarian divide. Founded as a Protestant settlement, Belfast continued to attract Protestant population and became a Protestant
stronghold in the middle of a largely Catholic countryside. Although
Belfast's Catholic minority has been growing over the last century,
the Catholic population seems to remain painfully aware of the
city's Protestant umbilical cord. Catholics were long excluded from
Belfast's industrial achievements, yet the city never quite realized
its potential, and Northern writers bitterly reflect a sense of disappointment in seeing their city often in the shadow of Dublin or
London. During the years of industrial revolution, Belfast's population grew suddenly, as the Great Famine and the upsurge in trade
instigated by the American War of Independence caused an influx
of labor. From 1951 onward, the population has started to fall and
continues to do so. Belfast is frequently examined in terms of history, a trend that exemplifies the continuous need to search for the
roots of its troubles and the original cause of its problems.

The polarized view of the city and the countryside, the opposition of the hellish city and the edenic rural life, is in Michael
McLaverty's *Call My Brother Back* (1939) reflected through the
opposition of the life in Rathlin Island and sectarian Belfast.
Depicting Belfast during the Civil War, McLaverty portrays the city
as a prison-house from which there is no escape. Although Brian
Moore also sees Belfast as a cage, his fiction centers on the need to
escape the confines of the city. The Belfast depicted in *Judith Hearne*
(1955) and *The Emperor of Ice-Cream* (1965) is noticeably bleak,
provincial, run-down, gray, and ugly. While the eponymous Judith
Hearne is entrapped by the need to follow society's guidelines and,
above all, the rituals of Catholic Church, Gavin Burke, the protagonist of *The Emperor of Ice-Cream*, attempts to locate a no-man zone
between his father's vision (Catholicism combined with United
Irelandism) and the Ulster Protestantism with which he comes into

contact during the Belfast blitz. The novel centers around the portrayal of Gavin's adolescence and his experiences of growing up in Belfast during the Second World War. Gavin is happy to observe the bombing of his hometown and his imagination takes the destruction further, to achieve a total anarchic freedom from the confines of Belfast.

The outbreak of "Troubles" in the late 1960s gave a renewed emphasis to Belfast's image as the site of sectarian strife and guerilla war. Novels such as Maurice Power's *The Killing of Yesterday's Children* (1985), *A Darkness in the Eye* (1987), and *Lonely the Man Without Heroes* (1987); Maurice Leitch's *Silver's City* (1981); and Daniel Mornin's *All Our Fault* (1991) developed a picture of despair and desolation of the patrolled streets, barricades, broken windows, vandalized houses, shootings, and knee-cappings. The image of a rain-soaked city buried in darkness, violence, and despair was so powerful that the recent Northern fiction has witnessed the need to state the return to normal life, subtly emphasizing the achievement of the peace process. Authors such as Glenn Patterson, Robert McLiam Wilson, Colin Bateman, and Deirdre Madden portray a Belfast that has finally been freed from the actual warfare and is now feeding the needs of the growing tourist industry, hungering for the sites of terror and violence. Like the nineteenth-century authors of the "national tale," Patterson's *Fat Lad* (1992) and Madden's *One by One in the Darkness* (1996) utilize the figure of an outsider, a tourist whose encounter with the city brings about a qualitative change in his/her thinking. Instead of giving their tourist-characters the "horror tour" they clamored for, these authors let their protagonists introduce the new, normal, and stable city where the few remaining monuments of the Troubles attest to the fact that war and violence are firmly the matter of the past and have no practical relevance to the present. For example, Robert McLiam Wilson's *Eureka Street* (1996)—while not letting the reader forget that the novel is set in Belfast, which only a few years ago had been the site of bombings and shootings—strives to render a picture of "normal" Belfast. In fact, the novel invites the readers to suspend their disbelief by taking normalcy to the extreme; the "mean streets" of Belfast have become the "love streets" where not only Protestant and Catholic couples, but also Muslim and Jewish couples can walk hand in hand. Yet Wilson does not let his reader forget that violence and death are integral parts of the modern urban experience. The bomb that cuts short the story of a secondary character also awakens the reader to the shock of realization that Wilson's novel is after all set in Belfast, and that bombs are an inevitable part of the imaginative texture of the city.

Belfast has cleansed its (fictional) image of the violence of its nightmarish past. By doing so it seems to have accomplished a full circle returning to the Joycean concept of the city of polarized opposites. However, this is not a modernist reaction to the nationalist romanticized view of the country, but rather an attempt to come to terms with the urban reality of modern life.

## Fictionalizing the Troubles

The outbreak of sectarian violence in 1969 in Northern Ireland and the consequent events (such as the intervention of the British Army, a curtailing of civil liberties which allowed internment without trial and house search without warrant) turned the following twenty years into the most violent period in the history of the North. Curfews, police patrols, bombings, and shootings became part of the everyday life of the community of 1.5 million people torn apart by the sectarian strife. In the literary field, this period opened up a fertile ground for the type of writers who saw the guerilla war as a suitable background for sensational fiction.[4] Tom Clancy (*Patriot Games* [1987]) and Jack Higgins (*A Prayer for the Dying* [1975]) situated their thrillers in the time period and/or geographical context of the Troubles. As the critic Eve Patten argued, for Irish writers there seemed to be two different ways of incorporating the reality of war into their fiction and for examining how the political and social issues impacted the formation of modern Irish identity (Patten 128–130). First, realist writers, placing themselves in a decided opposition to sensational fiction, attempted to achieve an authentic representation of the Northern crisis. This trend is detectable in novels such as Menna Gaillie's *You're Welcome to Ulster* (1970) and Mary Beckett's *Give Them Stones* (1987). Second, writers endeavored to offer a consensual liberal humanist comment on the situation, which usually involved a portrayal of relations between the personal and the political, and a frequent use of the "love-across-the barricades" type of conflict. A well-known example of the second type is Bernard MacLaverty's *Cal* (1983). However, critics have detected in recent fiction a new trend that seeks to challenge stereotypical ways of representing the Troubles, and to shift the focus to a re-examination of the terms of representation. As Gerry Smyth noted, one of the means to achieve this aim was to create a distance, either physical or discursive, in the novelistic vision (Smyth 116).

Robert McLiam Wilson's debut novel, *Ripley Bogle* (1989), is set in London in the late 1980s and follows the eponymous protagonist Ripley over four days in June. Ripley recalls his childhood in the Republican area of Belfast where he was born into an Irish-Welsh Catholic family. Calling himself "Ripley Irish British Bogle," Wilson's protagonist highlights his problematic national identity, and the attempt to embody the constituent parts of the community of Northern Ireland. While Declan Kiberd saw the Anglo-Irish living on the hyphen between the two words, "Anglo" and "Irish," Ripley is deprived even of the life-giving hyphen. Having failed to live his composite identity in Ireland, he emigrates to England. However, emigration and exile do not provide him with adequate answers. Ripley does not find England or the English in any way more authentic than his own problematic hybridity. His search for personal identity is paralleled on the structural level of the novel by the search for an adequate fictional mould that could contain this double quest motif. Ripley's failure to embody his national hybridity is mirrored by the novel's "failure" to accommodate such standard features of the Troubles novel as the thriller element and the "love-across-the barricades" motif. *Ripley Bogle* self-consciously and openly parodies the staple features of the Troubles fiction. Wilson's achievement in *Ripley Bogle* lies in his depiction of Ripley's ironic inability to live the stereotypical options that dominate (Northern) Irish fiction and political and social discourses. By demonstrating the fictional and social anorexia of the staple Troubles diet, Wilson implies the very constructedness of Ripley's national and personal identity. Gleeful Ripley openly acknowledges playing with the reader's/viewer's expectations, as he comes equipped and armored to capture his (English) audience: "The Northern Irish conflict certainly did its bit for the decoration of my early years. I made damned sure I got a good seat. I needed the material and it came to me early and gratis (mostly)" (Wilson, *Ripley Bogle* 26).

The Northern Irish conflict provided material for Eoin McNamee's *Resurrection Man* (1994), which utilizes the thriller genre in order to question the origins of violence as well as the means of representing it. Generally, the thriller is an exciting, tautly plotted sensational type of novel in which a considerable part is played by sex and violence (Cudden 971). *Resurrection Man* does not seek historical explanations for the Troubles; on the contrary, it depicts violence so as to question its provenance, while radically challenging the standard explanations, which treat it either in historical, political, or social terms.

McNamee's protagonist Victor Kelly is the leader of a unionist paramilitary gang called the "Resurrection Men." Kelly, having been bullied at school because of his Catholic-sounding last name and coming from a dysfunctional Protestant family, seeks to adopt a different identity, familiar from Hollywood gangster movies. He and his gang terrorize the streets of Belfast, which have turned into a "technology of ruin," a city of death. Cinematic and televisual imagery emphasizes Kelly's self-generated, Hollywood-inspired image of a glamorized gangster. "The distorted, uneasy silence of horror films" accompanies the chilling preciseness and calm with which McNamee portrays the ritualistic violence of Kelly's gang. The journalists Ryan and Coppinger who cover the murder stories notice that Kelly's murders differ from the usual sectarian killings. Commenting upon the severed tongue of one of his victims, Ryan reflects that "new languages would have to be invented"; a new discourse is needed in order to describe such violence but also to contain characters such as Victor. He is the product of the Troubles and made possible by the Troubles, however, McNamee's novel depicts him as rootless, detached, and alienated from the community that gave birth to him. Behind the cinematic glamour, Victor Kelly is depthless and weightless. He is "scripted" by the city, brought into being by the violence that constitutes his surroundings, and he embodies his geographical locus without taking on its political implications. The journalists note that standard journalese and traditional historical discourse turn out to be inadequate mechanisms for capturing

Kelly's ephemeral image. Kelly's self-image resists capture similarly to Kelly himself, who escapes being arrested by the police.

McNamee and Wilson are the best contemporary examples of representing the Troubles in Northern Ireland. Challenging and deflating the traditional features of the Troubles fiction, these authors call attention to the problems that complicate the construction of Irish identity in the late twentieth century.

## Irish Gothic

The first novel to have self-consciously labeled itself "A Gothic Story" was composed by an English author, Horace Walpole (1717–1797). His *Castle of Otranto*, published in 1764, inaugurated the trend that in the 1790s exploded into a full-scale literary boom of Gothic novels and dramas. Gothic fiction frequently borrows features from other genres, but its most distinctive trademarks are its setting (usually an antiquated place such as a castle, abbey, prison, crypt, cemetery, old house, or theatre) and characterization (the characters are haunted or terrorized physically, sexually, or psychologically).[5] These hauntings frequently take the form of ghosts or monsters that either emerge from the antiquated space or invade it, unearthing the secrets and unresolved conflicts that can no longer be contained or silenced. Wills or testaments (the ownership of these antiquated spaces) are of central importance, as Gothic fiction often centers around problematic family lineages, the discovery of one's true identity, and restoring one's lost property. Gothic narratives are concerned with textual evidence; frequently the authenticity of wills and testaments is questioned or challenged. The universal becomes personal as instead of national history, characters are obsessed with their personal past or family history, which usually hides some dark secrets. This extreme concern with personal past and the haunting of the unconscious are among the main reasons why Gothic fiction is often characterized as claustrophobic, and the genre lends itself easily to psychoanalytic reading; by evoking the repressed desires, the Gothic questions the boundaries set by society and opens up the sources of anxieties that are close to the heart of the era and each individual.

Many Gothic novels produced at the height of its popularity were set in the Catholic Mediterranean countries such as Italy, Spain, or France. In these novels, Catholicism was mainly characterized by excess, and the glittering façade of its pompous ceremonies did not cover up the hypocrisy of institutions such as monasteries and convents. Ireland's dark and troubled history, its mainly Catholic population, and its romantic scenery offered an irresistible terrain for Gothic writers. Colonial history always remains conscious of the threat of insurrection, which creates the perfect setting for an intrusion of fear and darkness. Protestant Anglo-Irish families, having erected their Big Houses in the midst of Catholic Ireland, could never feel entirely secure in the land they had colonized. The 1789 United Irishmen rebellion was just one example of the readiness of the Irish to fight their colonizers. The following examples will demonstrate that Irish writers were unable to draw a clear demarcation line between past and present political situations. In other words, the heightened sensibilities depicted by the Gothic writers were not the matter of history but were of contemporary relevance.

Although the Irish Gothic emerges most forcefully on the literary scene with Charles Robert Maturin, its earliest example can be dated back to the year 1729, when Jonathan Swift's pamphlet "A Modest Proposal" appeared. As critics have noted, in this pamphlet Swift offered a successful template for Gothic texts to come. At first sight, this famous pamphlet appears as an appeal, proposing a scheme to solve the economic problems of famine-ridden Ireland. The poverty of the lower classes and the corruption of the upper classes had reached such a level that Swift could not see a political solution for the disastrous situation. The satiric response that the pamphlet offers is monstrous and barbaric: essentially, the cannibalization of Irish children. The proposal is presented and argued through with chilling calm and persuasiveness, as the pamphlet describes the advantages and the economic possibilities that would open up by feeding Irish children to the "Persons of Quality and Fortune through the Kingdom." "A Modest Proposal" is a disturbing essay that exemplifies the cruelty of the colonial system and how it transforms the social, familial, and economic patterns of the colonized land. By choosing children and family relations as the potential best-selling commodity, Swift locates his argument within a well-known Gothic trope—family history.

Swift's black satire was prompted by his everyday experience of living in Ireland, where the suffering of the poor and the affluence of the rich produced a tragically incongruous situation. Writing a hundred years later, Charles Robert Maturin attested to the continuous existence of these extremes, saying that Ireland was "the only country on earth, where, from the strange existing opposition of religion, politics, and manners, the extremes of refinement and barbarism are united, and the most wild and incredible situations of romantic story are hourly passing before modern eyes" (Moynahan 111). These stubbornly thriving oppositions fed the imagination of Irish writers and continued to provide the subject matter and themes for the flourishing of Gothic fiction. Maturin is usually credited with inaugurating the Gothic in Ireland with his *Melmoth the Wanderer* (1820). However, his less well-known *The Milesian Chief* (1812), preceding *Melmoth* by eighteen years, competes with the latter for the honor of the pioneering Gothic piece. Maturin is celebrated for his evocation of emotionally heightened and passionate scenes. He situates his characters in claustrophobic conditions where they are trapped between impossible circumstances (Protestant versus Catholic, secular versus religious). Importantly, his own alienation from Irish Catholic culture feeds much of the darkness and passion in his fiction. His complex plotlines exemplify the entanglements of history, its openness, and the absence of (historical) closure and straightforward, unproblematic linear narrative. Like Sheridan Le Fanu, he evokes and explores the alienation and displacement acutely felt by the Protestant Ascendancy representatives.

Le Fanu's fiction offers a fascinating picture of the Anglo-Irish situation in which the minority power, seemingly in control, is haunted by the Catholic majority that constantly watches over its shoulder. In *Uncle Silas* (1864), the insecurities of the Protestant Ascendancy are vividly represented by the fears that infest Maud Ruthyn's existence in the house of her Uncle Silas. Instead of everyday politics, the novel draws a convincing picture of the intricate psychological politics that governed lives in isolated manor houses. Maud is the heiress to her father's fortune, and thus her father's will (her inheritance) becomes the source of her troubles, as her uncle

wants to eliminate her in order to become the sole beneficiary of
the will. Austin Ruthyn's determination to demonstrate his trust in
his slandered brother by placing his daughter under his guardianship makes family lineage and the dark secrets that the family
history contains (Silas's past) active participants in Maud's entrapment. Le Fanu emphasizes the theme of entrapment by carefully
arranged parallels between the two parts of the novel. Symmetries
of action, characterization, and location help to create the overall
pattern of correspondences and emphasize the novel's central
theme—Uncle Silas replaces Austin Ruthyn after the latter's death,
and by taking over the role of his dead brother, he connects the
worlds of the living and the dead.

The same thematic and structural devices are successfully
deployed in Le Fanu's best-known short story, "Carmilla" (1872).
The story consists of two tales: the primary narrator, Laura, relates
her encounter with a seductive aristocratic vampire Carmilla, but
her story is interrupted by the tale of General Spielsdorf, whom
Laura meets during a short journey with her father. Laura is
shocked, discovering how closely the tragic story of Spieldorf's ward
recalls her own experiences. She is confronted with what would
essentially have been the sad end of her own story (having taken in
a mysterious young lady, the General's ward died soon after; their
visitor, Millarca turned out to have been the vampire who now stays
with Laura and her father), had she not met the General. Carmilla-
Millarca turns out to have lived in a distant past as Mircalla,
Countess Karstein. Laura is related to the Karsteins, thus Mircalla
(and vampires in general) acts as a monstrous testimonial of survival, an active agent of the undead past that invades and disrupts
the present. As Carmilla/Mircalla/Millarca tells her, even if Laura
dies, she would still continue living in Carmilla. Hence, death
becomes a way of living. This unnatural way of achieving immor-
tality is, in Le Fanu's fiction, presented as abhorrent as Swift's sug-
gestion of consuming Irish children in order to further the country's
economy. Unlike Swift, Laura is horrified but also fascinated by
Carmilla and admits on several occasions to being attracted to the
seductive vampire. In *Uncle Silas* the terror is not only psychological but also physical (Silas and his Dudley conspire toward Maud's
death) and sexual (Dudley constitutes the sexual threat). In

"Carmilla," however, the psychological threat is replaced by the physical and sexual. Here lies one of the crucial differences between a ghost story and a vampire tale: unlike ghosts, a vampire can represent a combination of physical, psychological, and sexual threats. This fusion of fears is most successfully recreated in Bram Stoker's *Dracula* (1897), commercially the most successful follower of "Carmilla," with its exotic setting and vampire motif. Stoker (1847–1911) made an absentee landlord the protagonist, while raising the question of land and ownership in the novel. Indeed, Count Dracula's existence depends on maintaining a link with the soil of Transylvania. Forced to coffin himself in before the break of dawn, the mysterious Count carries with him a coffin with his native soil. Blood and soil are the two substances on which Dracula thrives. As critics have noted, he personifies the most common fears of the Victorian English middle class—decadent aristocratism combined with extremely low-class animalism and sexual deviance. Stoker's *Dracula* takes these fears to an extreme. The novel deploys the common trait of Gothic fiction, to confront the extremes and blur the different levels of discourse. By haunting the hinterlands of life and death, natural and supernatural, ancient and modern, unconscious and conscious, Dracula exemplifies a seamless and effortless crossing of the boundaries that traditionally protected the social and political status quo of the Victorian era. As Dracula and his fellow vampires take such a pleasure from sucking blood out of their victims, the threat they are posing to middle-class security appears sexual. Jonathan Harker, who visits his castle in Transylvania, is both horrified and sexually aroused by the female vampires. Vampires embody the combination of death and sexuality, thus linking one of the major public concerns (death and funerals) of the nineteenth century with the era's secret preoccupation (sex and sexuality). Gender-crossing and sexual promiscuity, and also homosexuality, are in Gothic fiction both secretly desired and abhorred, as everything that is considered abnormal by society is exposed as dangerously alive, not as a safely buried family secret. For instance, Le Fanu's Carmilla is during the day a typical nineteenth-century heroine, languid and fragile, "the prettiest creature," a girl "so gentle and nice," but during her nocturnal escapades she turns into an aggressive woman who preys on both sexes. Carmilla and Dracula's victims become vampires whose sexual aggressiveness toward males constitutes a serious overstepping of nineteenth-century decorum, but whose lesbian tendencies were even more of a threat. Women attacking men was a violation serious enough, but women being attracted to other women could only be considered under the safety net of fiction. Gothic finds its subject in the fears common to society, as it tends to compulsively return to the fixations and obsessions that characterize the era it inhabits. Twentieth-century Irish literature attests to the persistence of Gothic traits and themes, most prominently in Elizabeth Bowen's fiction, and in John Banville's *Birchwood* (1973).

Ghost stories are seen as a special category of Gothic, character-ized by the appearance of supernatural elements that remain unex-plained (Briggs 122–131). In Gothic fiction, the supernatural might find a rational explanation; for instance when Maud finally starts believing that Silas is after her life, she realizes that the evil does not emanate from the house but has a rational explanation, and the seemingly supernatural is administered by actual persons with real-istic (monetary) motives. Ghost stories commonly situate cause and effect on an alternative plane of reality, which operates on different premises. Instead of rationalizing the supernatural, ghost stories provide another type of logic whereby events (hauntings) can be activated by an unburied body or an innocent victim of an unre-solved crime. Concepts of normality in war undergo a serious chal-lenge, including an altered perception of time. This, according to William McCormack, is one explanation for the renewed interest in ghost stories during the First and Second World War (McCormack, *Irish Gothic* 831).

Elizabeth Bowen, another representative of Anglo-Irish Ascendancy and a great admirer of Sheridan Le Fanu, took to writ-ing ghost stories during the Second World War. Her book, *The Demon Lover and Other Stories*, was first published in 1945. Set in the 1940s London or Ireland, these stories depict the overall uncer-tainty of wartime life. When the present (and the future) are under the threat of annihilation, ghosts fill an emptiness left by the ero-sion of the normal temporal structure. As Bowen herself said in the "Preface" to her stories, it is "the 'I' that is sought—and retrieved at the cost of no little pain. And the ghosts . . . they are the certain-ties . . . hostile or not, they rally, they fill the vacuum for the uncer-tain 'I'" (Lee 155). In the stories, such as "The Demon Lover," the ghosts fill the vacuum of Blitz-time London from where most of the population has been evacuated. In "The Demon Lover," a Mrs. Drover is paying a brief visit to her locked-up house in London, where she is confronted with a ghostly letter from her lover who had been killed in the First World War. Everything that previously composed her surroundings has been removed or changed, and, a stranger in her hometown, Mrs. Drover becomes a stranger in her own house. Reassuring memories of the familiar past have evaporated, exposing her to the threat of the vacuum of the uncertain "I." Every space seems to enclose upon Mrs. Drover—the city itself, the house, and even a taxi. Her self-image, the secure and known idea of herself, is consumed by the undead past. Thinking that by leaving the house she can avoid meeting her "demon lover," Mrs. Drover rushes to the street and gets into a taxi only to find that she has exchanged one form of entrapment for another. Although the reader never finds out for sure, Mrs. Drover's reaction—her screams and failed attempts to escape—betrays that the driver is the demon lover she had been trying to flee from. By making her protagonist confront the skeletons from her past, Bowen's fiction treads the familiar Gothic ground of family history.

Like Bowen, John Banville exemplifies the usefulness of Gothic tropes when exploring an open, unresolved past that resists the secure closure traditionally offered by history. His novel *Birchwood* is a prime example of postmodern Irish Gothic. By situating his protagonist in a run-down mansion named Birchwood, Banville makes use of the common Gothic trope (a family home, a dilapidated house as the site of family feuds) while deploying the traditional feature of Anglo-Irish Ascendancy culture—the Big House. During his quest for his nonexistent sister, Banville's protagonist Gabriel Godkin has to intrude into the forbidden spaces in his family history. While trying to discover his true identity and parentage, Gabriel unearths Birchwood's incestuous past and murderous present. *Birchwood* examines cultural displacement and alienation, a common Ascendancy feeling. By blurring historical periods (the novel incorporates references to the Famine, the 1920s, and the present day), Banville problematizes conventional historical time. In the course of the novel Gabriel comes to embrace the concept of a constantly shifting and unstable past. *Birchwood* indicates the way in which Gothic can actively contribute to current debates about memory, identity, and history. In this way, Gabriel exemplifies a shift from the nineteenth-century Gothic, where the hauntings from the unquiet past were met with rational explanations; in *Birchwood* the past cannot be explained away, as the lesson Gabriel learns is that existence is limited by linguistic boundaries. Language, the most powerful and unstable medium, conjures up the world (the anti-quated space) we live in and creates the ghosts that fill the vacuum of the uncertain "I."

## History: A Dream or a Nightmare?

" 'History,' Stephen said, 'is a nightmare from which I am trying to awake,' " wrote Joyce in the "Nestor" episode of *Ulysses* (34). The concept of (Irish) history as a nightmare has become a critical com-monplace. Interpretations abound, for Stephen Dedalus's words can be seen as referring to the continuous presence of history, or to his-tory as a survival test. In short, Stephen is implying history's simul-taneous capacity to seem tangible and unreal. Over the centuries, Irish fiction writers have tried to come to terms with the complex-ities of Irish history, which, indeed, can at times be seen as a night-mare or an endurance test.[6]

Inspired by Maria Edgeworth's *Castle Rackrent* (1800)—a work of fiction often seen as inaugurating the Big House motif in Irish fic-tion—Walter Scott composed his own *Waverley, or 'Tis Sixty Years Since* (1814), which effectively became known as the first histori-cal novel in English. Fuelled by the popularity of *Waverley*, Scott became a best-selling author and the type of writer that Irish his-torical novelists sought to emulate. Scott's novels indicate that he was aware of historical perspective; although he was interested in and influenced by the local Scottish lore and legends, he refuted the commonly held view of history as something strange, bewildering, and different. As critics such as James Cahalan have shown, histor-ical process in Scott's model means a replacement of one cultural order by another. His intentions to differ from a romantic tale are already evident in the subtitle he chose for *Waverley*. As Scott explained in the "Introduction" to the novel, he discarded titles like "Waverley, a Tale of other Days," "Waverley, a Romance from the

German," and "A Tale of the Times," and choose " 'Tis Sixty Years Since" in order to signal the "object" of his tale—"throwing the force of my narrative upon the characters and passions of the actors; those passions common to men all stages of society" (Scott 5).

*Waverley* differs from the world of Rackrents as, for the first time, traditional romantic expectations are being replaced by the portrayal of progress and passions "common to men all stages of society." In the Preface to *Castle Rackrent*, Edgeworth goes to great pains to distance her book from "official" history (in contrast to Scott, who used the discourse of history in order to create the sense of authority). Despite the "censure" and "ridicule" of critics, Edgeworth urges her readers to privilege such genres as biography and letters, as the love of truth "necessarily leads to a love of secret memoirs and private anecdotes." It has to be noted that letters and biography were at the time considered a safe domain for women, whereas "history" was seen as a more manly pursuit. The sense of privacy made public, characteristic to a memoir, is emphasized by the footnotes; Edgeworth claims Thady's idiomatic speech to be untranslatable, thus indicating the vital role of the footnotes which make Thady's tale comprehensible for his (English) audience. Although *Castle Rackrent* could be seen as deploying the same traits as Scott's *Waverley*, Edgeworth's novel is an important forerunner of historical fiction and not its fully fledged proponent. It is a realist (for the first time a regional dialect is given such an extensive representation) and comic portrayal of several generations of Rackrents and the mismanagement of their estate. Edgeworth's private and domestic memoir was soon to be taken over by the public and "official" histories produced by the Irish historical novelists.

The honor of the first Irish historical novelist is frequently bestowed upon John Banim. In fact, Banim was preceded by James McHenry, whose *O'Halloran, or The Insurgent Chief: An Historical Tale of 1798*, published in 1824, examined the United Irishmen's rising of 1798 in the North. McHenry tried to mould *O'Halloran* according to the model established by Scott. In the preface he emphasized the distanced and moderate view advocated in the novel. Although clearly sympathetic to the United Irishmen cause, McHenry claims his representation of the rebellion to be impersonal and tolerant of both sides.

Such tolerance is also evident in the artistic agenda for what was to become the most famous Irish historical novel to have emerged from nineteenth-century Ireland, *The Boyne Water*, written by John and Michael Banim in 1826. Whereas Scott treated Scotland's history as the matter of past, subjected to a modern and moderate investigation, the history that the Banim brothers were dealing with, the Jacobite-Williamite War of 1689–91, was problematically open—an unfinished tale of continuous violence between Protestants and Catholics. The Banims tried to analyze a major event in Irish history in order to understand its stratified present and the reasons that caused the religious strife in Ireland. That their aim was not a romanticized picture of Ireland's past is evident in the novel's preface, which, containing an extract from a letter from John to Michael Banim, dated March 13, 1826, presents John Banim's comments on one of their historical characters, General Sarsfield:

> . . . I am convinced you are wrong in one particular, namely, as to your conception of Sarsfield. Your own words condemn you. You say: "Without veritable grounds for my conception of him, I had imagined him almost a hero of romance, and expected his acts and words to fit that character."
>
> This could not be, my dear Michael; he was a plain, mat-ter-of-fact man, devoted, soul and body, and unflinchingly, to his cause, brave, enterprising, vigorous; nothing beyond this. Have you ever seen his portrait? Very unlike in feature and in bearing to a "hero of romance". I was desirous to give Sarsfield without fictitious or imaginative decoration (Banim 567).

John Banim was a great admirer of Scott and from Scott he learned his trade, especially his talent for rendering his characters as flesh-and-blood individuals without "fictitious or imaginative deco-ration." He also followed Scott's example to make extensive use of his knowledge of peasant life and Irish folklore. The protagonist of *The Boyne Water*, Robert Evelyn is carefully drawn as a voice of mod-eration, negotiating his personal quest between the extremes of Catholicism and Protestantism. Having fallen in love with a Catholic, Eva M'Donnell, and participating in the war as an officer of the Williamite army, Robert connects the individual and histori-cal, giving the Banims ample opportunities for discussing different historical perspectives. Describing Robert's difficult process of learning to understand the Catholic cause allows the Banims to explain the intricacies of Irish history to his readers. As opposed to Scott, the Banims did not furnish their novel with a happy ending. Although Robert and Eva survive the battle of Boyne and the siege of Derry, their counterparts, Robert's sister Esther and Eva's brother Edmund, do not fare so well; Esther dies during the siege and the heartbroken Edmund goes into exile. The ambivalence of this ending indicates that the religious strife was not a thing of the past (the novel is set in seventeenth century), but an ongoing problem in the Ireland of 1826.

Irish historical writers, both unionist and nationalist, frequently returned to such subjects as the 1798 rebellion. The rebellion became an especially popular subject at the time of its centennial in 1898, when numerous novels were published, all centering around the United Irishmen insurrection. The nationalists were primarily interested in commemorating the central event of the nationalist narrative, depicting their heroes as martyrs, and portraying the patriotism and bravery of the people who had fought against the English rule. Examples of this kind of interpretation include Randal William McDonnel's *Kathleen Mavourneen: A Memory of the Great Rebellion* (1898), M. L. O'Byrne's *Ill-Won Peerages* (1884), and George A. Birmingham's *The Northern Iron* (1907). The unionist approach generally downplayed the importance and centrality of the rebellion. The insurrection was often portrayed through the eyes of simple Protestant families who had happily coexisted with Catholics until the United Irishmen unearthed the old feuds and tricked the gullible peasants into supporting their bloody insurrection. This approach is evident in novels such as *That Most Distressful Country* (1886) by E. C. Boyse, *Ballinvalley or a Hundred Years Ago* (1898) by George Wynne, and *Corrageen in '98* (1898) by Adela Orpen.[7]

The 1798 insurrection was by no means the only subject open for Irish historical writers. From the 1930s onward, a new wave of historical novels were published that scrutinized the events of the recent past, such as the Easter Rising of 1916 and the foundation of the Irish Free State. These realist fictions sought to understand the conditions that had brought about the birth of the Free State. Instead of concentrating on the romantic side of the battle for inde-

pendence, these novels were concerned with character development, portraying the frustration and alienation of their rebel protagonists. This approach is best exemplified by the novels of Sean
O'Faolain, Liam O'Flaherty, and Francis MacManus. Historical novels became even more popular in the 1970s, with the appearance of
James Plunkett's *Strumpet City* (1969), Eilís Dillon's *Across the
Bitter Sea* (1973) and *Blood Relations* (1977), Thomas Kilroy's *The
Big Chapel* (1971), and Thomas Flanagan's *The Year of the French*
(1979). Seeking to bring about an enhanced understanding of the
past, these works enabled the reader to experience the crucial distance between the past and the present. The nightmare that Joyce's
Stephen spoke of was over, and once the nation had awakened from
it, analytical, interpretive, and explanatory processes could begin.

However, one important aspect of the history lesson in "Nestor"
was still waiting to be attended to. During this episode in *Ulysses*,
Stephen's students are attempting to answer his questions regarding the Battle of Asculum. "There was a battle," offers one of the
boys, Cochrane. Although he remembers the date, Cochrane cannot
recall the place, whereby the Battle of Asculum becomes simply "a
battle" (Joyce, *Ulysses* 124). In this passage, the schoolboy memory
conjures up a universalized history where the nightmare of recalling one battle becomes the nightmare of all battles. In *Ulysses*, universal and individual, mythological and historical become the
composite parts of the novel's texture; the continuous present of
the Joycean awakening becomes a filter through which the past is
processed and subjected to a constant change by individual perception. The instability that characterizes the novel's style and narration—we are never quite sure who is speaking or narrating the
events of *Ulysses*—indicates that history is the matter of human perception and "changes" according to whose nightmare it is and who
is trying to awaken from it.

The question of history writing, time, and memory were
addressed with renewed vigor by the appearance of John Banville's
tetralogy of novels, the first two of which utilized in a strikingly
innovative manner the form of historical novel. *Doctor Copernicus*
(1976) and *Kepler* (1981) were both praised for their accurate
descriptive faculty in vividly evoking the Renaissance era. However,
in these novels Banville continued the generic experimentation that

was characteristic of his earlier fiction. Banville's novels present a mixture of imaginary and historical, fusing the historical facts with fiction. His protagonists, Copernicus and Kepler, are driven by a passionate longing to know and to find a form in which to express their knowledge. Copernicus and Kepler come to realize that "thinking" means "inventing" or fictionalizing. The narrative form of these novels playfully reflects their epistemological and narratological quests: the structure of *Doctor Copernicus*, for instance, reflects the "music of the spheres" that Copernicus is unable to recreate in the novel. According to Banville, the novel was based on musical themes, such as a fugue. The formal properties of *Kepler*, on the other hand, express Kepler's discovery that the movement of the planets is elliptical rather than circular. *Kepler*'s chapters seem to reflect circular movement, as the end of each chapter returns the reader close to the starting point. However, no section comes back exactly to its starting point, thereby forming an ellipse.[8]

Banville's scientists are aware of their inability to explain the world definitively or to give an accurate description of natural phenomena. Copernicus and Kepler die, knowing that they have been engaged in mere "bright beautiful games." However, this is a paradoxical defeat, for, aware of the failure to arrive at accurate representation of reality, Banville's characters learn to inhabit the world they have "invented." Facts, historical accuracy, and the reliability of historical accounts become less important than the power of imagination. More than scientists, Banville's Copernicus and Kepler are artists whose minds need to make "creative leaps" in order to transcend received ideas and seemingly irrefutable facts such as the earth-centered universe. *Doctor Copernicus* and *Kepler* were well received, one could even say that they were too well received, as reviewers tended to take these novels as accurate and reliable depictions of historical truth and not as fictional accounts of historical figures. Banville's convincing description of such artistic feats shows evidence of the great importance of individual perception in history and history writing.

This is the lesson toward which Irish historical fictionists had been striving for almost two hundred years.

## Motherhood

"Her glazing eyes, staring out of death, to shake and bend my soul. On me alone. The ghostcandle to light her agony. Ghostly light on the tortured face. Her hoarse loud breath rattling in horror, while all prayed on their knees. Her eyes on me to strike me down" (Joyce, *Ulysses* 1). In this passage from *Ulysses*, Stephen Dedalus is remembering his mother's death scene while reflecting upon his unwillingness to kneel down and pray at her deathbed. Haunted by guilt, and weighed down by *amor matris*, unconditional motherly love, Stephen wanders through Dublin, trying to block out the painful memories of his mother.[9]

In Irish fiction, the image of mother and the theme of motherhood are complicated by Ireland's symbolic identity as "Mother Ireland" and the alleged "femininity" of the Irish; Matthew Arnold, a nineteenth century English poet and scholar who wrote extensively on the subject of Celtic studies, famously declared the Irish to be a feminine race. The personification of Ireland as a woman became a convenient symbolic image for Ireland's colonizers, as the country was seen as an object to be possessed. Thus both the concept of Mother Ireland and the feminine Irish race have become symbolic straitjackets in which it is convenient to confine the country and its inhabitants. On the other hand, the Irish nationalist iconography has also tended to represent Ireland as a woman—for instance, as Cathleen Ní Houlihan or Dark Rosaleen. These portrayals often remain one-sided political idealizations, removed from reality. Such stereotyping has been one way of subordinating and silencing women's voices.

The representation of motherhood not only exemplifies the different roles that society ascribes to women, but it also helps us to understand the underlying social and political realities that influence and inspire these representations. For instance, the 1937 Irish Constitution stipulated that as full-time mothers and wives, the home was to be every woman's natural place. This statement practically eradicated women's rights for a career outside the home.[10]

Moreover, because of the strong influence of the Catholic tradition, in the late twentieth century Ireland has had to deal with complex issues such as birth control, women's liberation, feminism, and legalizing abortion. These topics (still rather controversial in today's Ireland) are frequently touched upon by contemporary Irish writers, whose work reflects upon the ambiguity with which women's roles have been viewed by society. Influenced by Catholicism, Irish culture has traditionally emphasized the role of virginity and motherhood. This seemingly paradoxical conjunction means that while embodying maternity (the biological function of women), Mary also symbolizes virginity—that is the denial of female desire and the abhorrence of sexuality. Thus the mother becomes a symbol in which the fear of sexuality is intertwined with the ideas of birth and motherhood.

In addition to Christian symbolism, motherhood is one of the most important aspects in psychoanalytical criticism. The feminist psychoanalytic theory puts forward the concept of the phallic or pre-Oedipal mother. According to this concept, initially the child considers the mother as all-powerful, a stage that precedes the child's awareness that the mother belongs to the more powerful father as she lacks (both anatomically and symbolically) the phallus. The all-powerful mother generates fear in the child who is terrified of unmitigated female power.

Gerald Griffin's portrayal of Mrs. Cregan in *The Collegians* (1829) is a case in point here. Mrs. Cregan is the epitome of a character consumed by social ambition. She is manipulating her son Hardress in order to make him marry a rich heiress, Anne Chute. The Cregans are an upper-middle-class Catholic family with upper-class pretensions. The Cregans and their social pretensions cannot be securely rooted in the glory of ancient past and their dubious family crest indicates their upstart pretensions. While the men of the family indulge in dueling and drinking, Mrs. Cregan is trying to concoct a future—through a profitable marriage—that would settle her ambitions for a higher social status on a financially solid ground. Her actions are motivated by her passionate motherly love for her handsome reckless son. She is unaware of the fact that her machinations push Hardress toward his eventual damnation and fall. On the other hand, knowing his mother's social pretensions, Hardress is unable to confess to her that he is already married to the lowly born Eily. By perpetrating her son's eventual downfall, Mrs. Cregan personifies the unconscious fear of an all-powerful mother demanding the sacrifice of her son to gratify her own desires.

The fear of mother fed the modernist representations of women, which frequently depicted masculine impotence and female power. In James Joyce's *A Portrait of the Artist as a Young Man* (1916), Stephen's mother as a character appears only on a few occasions. Yet, it is Mrs. Dedalus with whom Stephen argues and whose religious piety and influence he is trying to "fly by." At the end of *A Portrait*, Stephen leaves Ireland, having decided to leave behind his burdens (family, nationality, religion), but at the beginning of *Ulysses*, Joyce's next novel, we learn that Stephen has returned to the country of his birth, summoned by a telegram notifying him about his mother's approaching death. On his mother's deathbed Stephen refuses to comply with her last wish and make amends with the Catholic Church. *Ulysses* shows how his thoughts are chained to the "agenbite of inwit" (which in Middle English means remorse of conscience), as his guilty conscious returns over and over again to his act of resistance. The figure of Mrs. Dedalus exerts a powerful control over Stephen's thoughts, actions, and dreams in *Ulysses*.

The representation of mothers in literature is frequently polarized; on the one end of the scale there is the all-powerful mother figure, on the other end the passive and submissive female. Edna O'Brien's representation of mothers in her first novel, *The Country Girls* (1960), is a good example of the latter instance. Caithleen Brady's mother, married to an abusive husband with a severe alcohol problem, tries to protect her daughter but fails to offer an adequate solution to her (social) dilemma. Mrs. Brady is still bound by the traditions and customs of mid-century rural Ireland and believes in the need to conform with social norms. According to her mother, Caithleen has two choices, marriage or convent, and it is clear that the mother's preference lies with the latter. Mrs. Brady's own dissatisfaction and her fear of sexuality prompt her to protect Caithleen from sexual relationships, and steer her toward the convent and virginity. Having escaped the stultifying convent atmosphere, Cathleen chooses the city life, but O'Brien does not portray this as an option in any way superior to the harshly regulated convent routine. Society outside the convent walls is governed by equally rigid rules, and Caithleen, in her pursuit of love (as O'Brien's subsequent novels will show), is going to be subjected to the same hopelessly vicious circle of unhappy marriage and failed prospects as her mother.

Examining the intertwined fates of three women, Mary Morrissy's *Mother of Pearl* (1996) explores the problems of motherhood and opens up the painful silences that surround the seemingly unquestionable concept of *amor matris*. Irene Rivers and Rita Golden, the baby snatcher and the biological mother, both use a child in order to cover up their own lack of self-identity. Irene, cured from tuberculosis and "saved" by her marriage from her nursing job at the hospital where she stripped for male patients in order to "ease" their sufferings, finds that her husband, who she barely knows, is impotent. Her embarrassment in front of her noisy neighbors over being a "barren" woman prompts her to lie about being pregnant. When her "dream child" fails to come to life, as Irene is unable to conceive as a virgin, she steals a newborn baby from a hospital. She takes Rita's child in order to fulfill society's expectations and have a "real" family. The desire and the need to believe in the "dream child" envelopes her husband, who also longs for children. While the reality of Pearl (this is the name Irene gives to the baby) is the answer to Irene's dreams, the baby's biological mother, Rita Spain, née Golden, is relieved to find her child absent from her life. An infatuated eighteen-year-old, Rita was impregnated by the object of her schoolgirl dreams. Forced into marriage and motherhood, Rita is unable to accept her pregnancy, a condition that simultaneously abhors and mystifies her. She is secretly happy to find her baby, Hazel Mary, disappeared, yet her "unnatural" relief provokes in her feelings of guilt and self-disgust. When Hazel Mary is restored to Rita, the little girl finds herself unable to forget the ghostly experience of having been someone else, as her existence as Pearl refuses to disappear. Disturbed by her own memories of her life with Irene, Hazel Mary/Pearl invents a fictional double whom she calls Jewel. This dreamt up twin sister is borne out of her disturbing memories, however, her ghostly weight becomes too heavy for a dream-reality. Hazel Mary/Pearl believes in the existence of her double with such intensity that when years later she becomes pregnant, she aborts her baby, unable to accept the reality of the non-ghostly one and over-burdened by the reality of the ghost.

Morrissy's depiction of motherhood is disturbing; she explores the nature of motherhood not as a biological given but as a socially constructed role. While Edna O'Brien in her fiction never questioned motherhood as a constituent part of a woman's identity, Mary Morrissy's portrayal of three women who all subvert the socially accepted picture of a "good mother" draws attention to the skewed way the definition of maternity and women's identity is still regarded in today's society. Irene, Rita, and Hazel Mary/Pearl, a triad of modern women, are all trying to deal with the expectations of society and their own conflicting feelings about motherhood. Paradoxically, the most "natural" mother of them is Irene the baby snatcher, while the two "biological" mothers experience motherhood as a condition forced upon them by society that demands marriage and procreation. The title, *Mother of Pearl*, suggests the beautiful luminescence of "mother of pearl," the lining of an oyster shell; this beauty, however, does not illuminate every experience of motherhood. Issues such as abortion and women who choose not to have children are often treated as taboo subjects in a society that considers motherhood to be women's constitutional duty. Stephen Dedalus's nightmare of motherly love, "the only true thing in life," is in Mary Morrissy's novel portrayed with a contemporary "twist," offering a fascinating picture of the changing social norms in late twentieth-century Ireland.

## Prose Fiction and the Irish Cultural Revival

The period between the 1880s and 1930s is generally identified as the Irish cultural revival, a period distinguished by the literary output of the nation, marked especially by writers such as W. B. Yeats, James Joyce, and the playwright J. M. Synge. The revival years witnessed a series of turbulent events, such as the rise and fall of Charles Stewart Parnell (a nineteenth-century Irish politician and a passionate supporter of the Home Rule), the Home Rule campaign, the founding of the Gaelic Athletic Association and the Gaelic League, the Easter Rising of 1916, the War of Independence, and the Civil War. The period ended with the partition of Ireland and the founding of the Free State and the statelet of Northern Ireland. The revival is variously referred to as the "Gaelic Revival," "Irish Literary Renaissance," or "Celtic Revival." The exact definition, timeline, and cultural and political implications of the cultural revival are still under active debate.[10]

It is generally understood that the most important genres during the Irish cultural revival were drama and poetry. The prose writers did not form a coherent group or tradition, and therefore they are mainly characterized by their more or less pronounced interest in romanticism, cultural nationalism, folklore, and peasant and Gaelic culture. The most prominent writers associated with the revival were W. B. Yeats, J. M. Synge, and Sean O'Casey. The Irish prose writers who were active during that period were writing either to promote or in reaction to the revival.

The revivalists were trying to locate a native literary tradition that would integrate the Gaelic tradition with the new or experimental. That period also saw the emergence of writers like James Joyce, who were not part of the revival but whose texts engaged with the pressing questions of the time. Nationality, self-identity, and cultural nationalism were at the forefront of the interest of Irish intelligentsia. Instead of having a concept of Ireland and the Irish imposed upon them from "outside," the revivalists hoped to locate the "real" Ireland from "inside." Somewhat paradoxically, authenticity was bestowed to the versions of ancient Irish sagas and legends that were modified and authored by the revival authors. While political divisions kept Catholic Home Rulers and Protestant Unionists in different camps, the revivalists hoped that the cultural nationalism espoused by the revival could bring about a united Ireland. An important feature in this "unity of culture" that the revivalists hoped to achieve was language. Douglas Hyde, a Protestant and the founder of the Gaelic League, was inspired by a dream of "using the language as a unifying bond to join all Irishmen together." Another important constitutive factor of unity was folklore. W. B. Yeats, for instance, saw folklore fulfilling a specific function, as it had to activate and empower the communal memory of the nation. Yeats and other revivalists took upon themselves the task of accommodating Irish legends and folklore for the specific needs of the people. The concept of a mythical (past) unity justified these authentication procedures. As Yeats said: "There is a distinct school of Irish literature, which we must foster and protect, and its foundation is sunk in the legend lore of the people and in the National history. The literature of Greece and India had just such a foundation, and as we, like the Greeks and the Indians, are an idealistic people, this foundation is fixed in legend rather than in history" (Yeats, *Uncollected Prose I* 274). Yeats attempted to anchor the Irish literary heritage not only in the "legend lore of the people" but also claimed for it a lineage similar to the one of the literature of ancient Greece and/or India. Paradoxically, he lacked both linguistic and social prerequisites to be a spokesperson of the peasant community: his "national" language, Irish, was not his mother tongue, and as a descendant of the Protestant Ascendancy, his association with mainly Catholic peasantry remained imaginative and rather removed from the reality.

In contrast, Joyce and the novelist George Moore were fiercely anti-clerical in their writing, a tendency that set them apart from Protestant revivalists like Yeats, who tried to work his way around the role of Catholicism in the "Irish" Ireland he was trying to promote. The revival inspired the type of cultural nationalism that became the founding ideology of the Irish Republic—a united Catholic Ireland.

W. B. Yeats, the founding father of the revival, is best known as a poet and dramatist. His fictional output is somewhat scattered, consisting of a volume of fantastic tales, *The Secret Rose* (1897), and a realistic novel or novella, *John Sherman* (1891); between 1896 and 1902 he also worked on a novel, *The Speckled Bird*, but this text exists only in incomplete draft versions. The Red Hanrahan stories were originally part of *The Secret Rose*, but appeared as a separate volume already in 1904. Tending to concentrate on Yeats's three "apocalyptic stories"—"Rosa Alchemica," "The Tables of the Law," and "The Adoration of the Magi"—critics have seen in Yeats's symbolic narratives an anticipation of Joyce and Moore. By contrast, *John Sherman* is often seen as exemplifying the opposition of England and Ireland, a fairly typical subject in nineteenth-century Irish literature.

The three apocalyptic stories were important to the eponymous protagonist of Joyce's *Stephen Hero*, a Romantic artist figure whose concept of artistic consciousness was influenced by his reading of Yeats's tales. Importantly, artistic consciousness became the central thematic and structural concern in the reworked version of *Stephen Hero*, called *A Portrait of the Artist as a Young Man* and published in 1916. Joyce's texts constitute an ironic take on the Yeatsian concept of a romantic artist figure and the revivalist Ireland. However, Joyce was critical of both the revivalist Ireland and the Catholic Ireland. Having already indicated his negative attitude in the *Dubliners* stories (for instance in "A Mother" and "Ivy Day in the Committee Room"), in *Ulysses* he satirizes all versions of Irish nationalism, including the cultural revival. The virulently nationalist Citizen in the "Cyclops" episode of *Ulysses* is the best example of Joyce's deep dislike of the revival ideas. Joyce was also adamantly anti-clerical. Despite this, the Catholic cultural tradition forms an important part of the philosophical and cultural background of Joyce's texts.

Moore, on the other hand, saw Catholicism as the source of Ireland's problems. In his collection of short stories, *The Untilled Field* (1903) and the novel *The Lake* (1905), he offered a bitter portrayal of the demise of Irish vitality under the overwhelming and paralyzing influence of Catholicism. *The Untilled Field* constituted his contribution to the Gaelic League movement; having composed the stories in English, Moore had them translated into Irish and then back into English, "much improved," as the author declared. Moore's association with the revival was to remain a brief one. His impact was greater on the realist tradition, for critics have concluded that despite Joyce's harsh criticism of Moore, Joyce was profoundly influenced by him—particularly by Moore's use of epiphany and themes such as flight and paralysis, but also his oppositions between priest and artist figures. Joyce's *Dubliners* and Moore's *The Untilled Field* added to the tradition of realist short stories, which became increasingly popular during the revival, including other authors such as Seumas O'Kelly and Daniel Corkery. Unlike Joyce and Moore, O'Kelly and Corkery were staunch nationalists and identified themselves closely with rural Ireland.

Seumas O'Kelly (1878–1918) published his first volume of short stories in 1906. His stories and sketches were characterized by active nationalism and deep sentimentality about rural Ireland and peasant culture. O'Kelly's fiction, thematically very different from

Joyce, centered around depiction of rural Ireland where in the peasant community traditional values were carried on and where fishermen could still recite Gaelic songs. His finest work is usually considered to be the short story called "The Weaver's Grave."

Daniel Corkery (1878–1964) is probably best known as the author of a controversial study of Gaelic Ireland, *The Hidden Ireland* (1925), and his equally provocative reading of Anglo-Irish literature, *Synge and Anglo-Irish Literature* (1931). In his literary criticism Corkery saw religion, nationalism, and the land as the most important features that constituted Irish consciousness. His fictional output testifies his adherence to these values, as his novel, *Threshold of Quiet* (1917), and his numerous short stories depicted rural life from a strongly nationalist point of view.

James Stephens, whose first two novels appeared in 1912, exemplified the fusion of mystical themes and the realist mode. *The Crock of Gold* and *The Charwoman's Daughter* were strikingly different works; the former is a humorous take on mythical and folk material, which nevertheless manages to render a realist picture of contemporary society, whereas the latter is a class drama set in Dublin, romantic and realistic at the same time. Stephen's career as a writer demonstrates his great interest in narrative experimentation; different planes of reality, a fusion of styles and techniques where fairy tale is juxtaposed with comedy, satire, burlesque, and allegory were his characteristic trademarks.

Stephens's fusion of different styles and modes is a good example of the multiple directions that prose fiction took during the Irish cultural revival. While the Irish fictionists did not form a coherent movement, the revival period saw a remarkable growth in fictional output in addition to a great realist tradition, attested to by the appearance of such world-famous masterpieces as *Dubliners, A Portrait*, and *Ulysses*.

## Notes

1. I am greatly indebted to Ina Ferris's illuminating study, *The Romantic National Tale and the Question of Ireland* (Cambridge: Cambridge University Press, 2002).

2. In writing this section, I was assisted by the following sources: Vera Kreilkamp, *The Anglo-Irish Novel and the Big House* (Syracuse: Syracuse

University Press, 1998); Andrew Parkin, "Shadows of Destruction: The Big House in Contemporary Irish Fiction," in *Cultural Contexts and Literary Idioms in Contemporary Irish Literature*, Michael Kenneally, ed. (Toronto: Barnes & Noble, 1988) pp. 306–327; Otto Rauchbauer, ed., *Ancestral Voices: The Big House in Anglo-Irish Literature* (Hildesheim: Olms, 1992).

3. My discussion is indebted to a collection of articles, edited by Maurice Harmon, *The Irish Writer and the City* (Gerrards Cross: C. Smythe, 1983); Gerry Smyth's article "The Right to the City: Re-presentations of Dublin in Contemporary Irish Fiction," in *Contemporary Irish Fiction: Themes, Tropes, Theories*, Liam Harte and Michael Parker, eds. (Basingstoke: Macmillan, 2000) pp. 13–34; Gerry Smyth, *The Novel and the Nation: Studies in the New Irish Fiction* (London: Pluto Press, 1997).

4. My discussion in this section is based on the following studies: Richard Haslam, "'The Pose Arranged and Lingered Over': Visualizing the 'Troubles,'" in *Contemporary Irish Fiction: Themes, Tropes, Theories*, Liam Harte and Michael Parker, eds. (Basingstoke: Macmillan, 2000) pp. 192–212; Liam Harte and Michael Parker, "Reconfiguring Identities: Recent Northern Irish Fiction," in *Contemporary Irish Fiction: Themes, Tropes, Theories*, Liam Harte and Michael Parker, eds. (Basingstoke: Macmillan, 2000) pp. 232–254; Richard Kirkland, "Bourgeois Redemptions: The Fictions of Glenn Paterson and Robert McLiam Wilson," in *Contemporary Irish Fiction: Themes, Tropes, Theories*, Liam Harte and Michael Parker, eds. (Basingstoke: Macmillan, 2000) pp. 213–231; Eve Patten, "Fiction in Conflict: Northern Ireland's Prodigal Novelists," in *Peripheral Visions: Images of Nationhood in Contemporary British Fiction* (Cardiff: University of Wales Press, 1995) pp. 128–148; Gerry Smyth, *The Novel and the Nation: Studies in the New Irish Fiction* (London: Pluto Press, 1997).

5. My discussion of Gothic fiction is indebted to the following sources: David Punter, ed., *A Companion to the Gothic* (Oxford: Blackwell Publishers, 2000); William McCormack's study, *Dissolute Characters: Irish Literary History Through Balzac, Sheridan Le Fanu, Yeats and Bowen* (Manchester and New York: Manchester University Press, 1993); and his article, "Irish Gothic and After, 1820–1945," in *Field Day Anthology of Irish Writing, Vol. 2.* (Derry: Field Day Publications, 1991) pp. 831–854; Hermione Lee, *Elizabeth Bowen* (London: Vintage, 1999); Ina Ferris, *The Romantic National Tale and the Question of Ireland* (Cambridge: Cambridge University Press, 2002); David Sidorsky, "The Historical Novel as the Denial of History: From 'Nestor' via the 'Vico Road' to the Commodius Vicus of Recirculation," *New Literary History* 32.2 (2001) pp. 301–326.

6. I am indebted to James M. Cahalan's informative study, *Great Hatred, Little Room: The Irish Historical Novel* (Syracuse, NY: Syracuse University Press, 1983) and Seamus Deane's illuminating article, "History as Fiction/Fiction as History," in *Joyce in Rome: The Genesis of Ulysses*, Giorgio Melchiori, ed. (Rome: Bulzoni, 1984) pp. 130–141.

7. My discussion of the novels dealing with the 1798 rebellion is indebted to Eileen Reilly's article "Who Fears to Speak of '98? The Rebellion in Historical Novels, 1880–1914," *Eighteenth-Century Life* 22.3 (1998) pp. 118–127.

8. As critics have pointed out, this is best exemplified by Chapter 4, "Harmonice Mundi," which consists of numerous letters written by Kepler and to Kepler. Following the dates of the letters, the elliptical pattern of their ordering becomes apparent. The first one dates from 1605 and the next nine respectively 1607, 1608, 1609, 1609, 1610, 1610, 1611, 1611. The tenth, which bears the date 1612, contains Kepler's statement that he has come to a point in his life where he has to start all over again. After that statement, the letters start moving backward in time, so that the twentieth brings us back to the year 1605, whereby the imitation of the geometrical figure of an ellipse is complete.

9. For studies that analyze Joyce's representation of women (and mothers or motherhood) refer to Bibliography and Further Reading. My discussion of motherhood in contemporary Irish fiction is indebted to the following: Ann Owens Weekes, "Figuring the Mother in Contemporary Irish Fiction," in *Contemporary Irish Fiction: Themes, Tropes, Theories,* Liam Harte and Michael Parker, eds. (Basingstoke: Macmillan, 2000) pp. 100–124; Lorna Rooks-Hughes, "The Family and The Female Body in the Novels of Edna O'Brien and Julia O'Faolain," *The Canadian Journal of Irish Studies* 22.2 (December 1996) pp. 83–97.

10. For a discussion of Irish constitution as a patriarchal cultural narrative see Patrick Hanafin's "Defying the female: the Irish constitutional text as phallo-centric manifesto," *Textual Practice* 11:2 (Summer 1997) pp. 249–273.

11. For a recent discussion of the Irish cultural revival see Clare Hutton, "Joyce and the Institutions of Revivalism," *Irish University Review* 33:1 (Spring/Summer 2003) pp. 117–132. In writing this section I was assisted by the following studies: Augustine Martin, "Prose Fiction in the Irish Literary Renaissance," in *Irish Writers and Society at Large,* Masaru Sekire, ed. (Gerrards Cross: C. Smythe, 1985) pp. 139–162; Declan Kiberd, "The Perils of Nostalgia: A Critique of the Revival," in *Literature and the Changing Ireland,* Peter Connolly, ed. (Gerrards Cross: C. Smythe, 1982) pp. 1–24.

# Chapter Six

# Key Questions

> Oh yeah, the Great Irish Novel, Jesus, man, a computer
> could write that. A bit of motherlove, a touch of suppressed
> lust, a soupçon of masochistic Catholic guilt, a bit of token
> Britbashing, whole shitloads of limpid eyes and flared nos-
> trils and sweaty Celtic thighs, all wrapped up in a sauce of
> snotgreen Joycean wank (O'Connor 137).

In this passage from his first novel, *Cowboys and Indians* (1991),
Joseph O'Connor encapsulates the predicament of contemporary
Irish writers who have had to negotiate their place either in or outside the shadow of the Great Irish Novel. O'Connor's cynical yet
irresistibly convincing recipe reflects the differences and similarities
between the present situation and that of nineteenth-century Irish
literature. For masochistic Catholic guilt and Britbashing—not to
mention flared nostrils and sweaty Celtic thighs—were definitely
not Joycean creations. However, both the existence of a tradition
and one's place within it were relevant issues both in 1991 and two
hundred years ago. Maria Edgeworth, the Banim brothers, Gerald
Griffin, William Carleton, Lady Morgan, and many others endeavored to place their texts outside the English tradition. The tales their
novels were trying to tell were stories of "manners and characters"
which were "unknown in England," as Maria Edgeworth declared in
the "Afterword" to *Castle Rackrent* (1800). In this decided difference resided their desire for an independent tradition and their
claim to a fictional territory, a claim that verged on the political. As
the Banim brothers wrote in the "Introduction" to *The Boyne Water*
(1826): "We, here in Ireland, ought to be anxious to ascertain our
position accurately, if for no other reason than that we may give

ourselves a common country. At present, the Irish, as a people, have no country, while the children of every other soil boast a proud identity with their native land" (Banim xiii). This passage indicates the authors' awareness of having to create a national identity and represent a nation as a political entity within the novel. It also emphasizes that the "common country" was a self-generated concept and that the Irish did not need to emulate a foreign (English) model. The question that still fascinates critics and students alike is whether the realist novel, prevalent at the time, was the suitable mode to accommodate the "unknown" tales of peculiar Irish manners and how Irish authors adapted and adopted that format in order to fit within its framework their aesthetic and political ambitions. Perhaps herein lies the answer to the question of why the Irish tradition seems particularly rich in attempts to experiment with the novel form. As Seamus Deane argued in his essay "Heroic Styles: the Tradition of an Idea" (1983), there are two dominant ways of reading (Irish) history and literature (Deane, "Heroic Styles" 45–58). One is "romantic" and, according to Deane, this is the mode of reading that takes pleasure in the notion that "Ireland is a culture enriched by the ambiguity of its relationship to an anachronistic and a modernized present." The other, denying this ambiguity and seeking to escape from it, locates itself in a "pluralism of the present." Deane saw W. B. Yeats and James Joyce respectively as representatives of these two modes of reading. He distinguished between "hot" and "cold" rhetorics, the first being that of the spiritual heroics of Yeats and the second that of the exile, alienation, and dislocation of Joyce. Writing in the early 1980s, Deane took this division in rhetorics to be an equivalent of the crisis in the North, arguing that the modern Irish condition was a crisis of language.

As the previous chapters of this book indicate, the crisis of language is a long-term condition in Irish culture. Lady Morgan encapsulated the situation in her novel *The Wild Irish Girl* (1806), in which the protagonist, Mortimer, describing the peculiar way in which the Prince of Inismore communicates, notes that the Prince "seems not so much to speak the English language, as literally to translate the Irish" (Owenson 60). Mortimer regards the Prince as an exotic and romantic character and the translated quality of his speech sets him apart from Mortimer, a native English-speaker—the Prince is deceptively close (his grasp of English is excellent), yet he subtly positions himself at a remove from his interlocutor. Mortimer's forefathers may have conquered the Prince's lands and castles but in his linguistic domain the Prince will remain a host and Mortimer an outsider. The Prince's "vernacular idiom" underlines the fundamental gap between the two characters and questions the veracity and accuracy of Mortimer's account. For how could an English person not fluent in Irish understand the subtleties of life at Inismore Castle and penetrate the emotional and intellectual depths of its inhabitants? Lady Morgan, like many of her contemporaries attempted to bridge the gap between the exotic and everyday by incorporating numerous footnotes in order to interpret the "strange," "foreign," and "different" to her English readers in what she saw as understandable terms. Footnotes formed a separate discourse in her novel, as they essentially contained references to other historical or fictional sources. While the footnotes referred to other texts about Ireland, Ireland itself remained stubbornly exotic and resistant to description. This linguistic and textual dilemma indicates that the cultural encounter depicted in the novel took place in a geographical domain that continued to defy description. In addition to the untranslatable residue lost in the communication between the Prince and Mortimer, the country remained stubbornly silent, as Ireland was mainly represented through secondary sources. Thus, authors such as Edgeworth and Morgan subtly point to the untranslatable residue that cannot be described and—if to evoke James Joyce—is left fretting in the shadow of one's soul.

The question remains whether this untranslatable residue is to be mourned as a loss or whether it can be seen as a testimonial of survival. The long greatcoat that Edgeworth's poor Thady wore "winter and summer" is also a subversive accessory. Edgeworth's footnote traced the cloak's ancestry back to Edmund Spenser's *A View of The Present State of Ireland* (1597), in which it is described as a "fit house for an outlaw, a meet bed for a rebel and an apt cloak for a thief." Thady's flattering and cajoling discourse, his seeming subservience to his masters' family, is frequently interpreted by critics as the language of survival, for under his linguistic "cloak" hides a potential rebel and outlaw. Furthermore, by adopting this double discourse in the novel, Edgeworth incorporates feelings of difference and uncertainty on the level of the narrative. Thady's son Jason endangers the (material) well-being of their masters. Edgeworth hints that the Rackrents were native Irish who had changed their name and religion in order to become the owners of their estate. As the estate reverts to Jason, the son of an Irish servant will take over the house of a ruined Irish aristocrat. Edgeworth does not make it clear how this will impact Thady's or Jason's lives or self-identities.

Gerry Smyth's summary of relevant issues to consider in a society grappling with the colonial legacy help to illuminate the potential predicament with which Thady is faced: "Who am I in relation to the groups and the beliefs and the political affiliations I perceive around me? Who am I in relation to the past from which I believe myself to have emerged and the future towards which I believe myself to be moving?" (Smyth 4). Depicting the rise of the M'Quirks and the fall of the Rackrents, Edgeworth's narrative avoids a closer analysis of the future toward which Thady and Jason are moving. Their success as the owners of the Rackrent estate is rendered questionable, hidden under the shadow of the cloak, which had for the entire duration of the story been Thady's until the last of the Rackrents, Sir Condy, is clothed in it. It is not clear whether this signals the disappearance of the Rackrents and the appearance of the M'Quirks. However, the questions formulated by Smyth are relevant both in Thady's case and in present day Ireland.

In Robert McLiam Wilson's *Eureka Street* (1996), one of the characters, Chuckie Lurgan, from a Belfast Protestant background, discovers the usefulness of a linguistic cloak similar to that of Edgeworth's Thady. Having to stand up for himself on the "mean streets" of New York when attacked by three delinquents with a baseball bat, Chuckie, "gripped by lunatic panic," launches into an impression of the Reverend Ian Paisley, a Protestant Unionist MP, the leader of the Democratic Unionist Party, and a leading opponent of the Good Friday Agreement of 1998. The attackers, "stopped dead, frozen in their tracks," glance at each other: "I seen this guy on TV. He's a crazy fucker." And they run off. Chuckie's impersonation skills save him and his wallet; while his Northern Irish accent was considered insufficiently Irish ("he sounds like a fat fuck from North Carolina"), his mimicked Irishness is authentic enough for the young delinquents (Wilson, *Eureka Street* 261–263).

Chuckie's comic survival is not only a theatrical feat of impersonation, but also, on another level, shows the ironic deployment of a national stereotype. The stage Irish or the Paddy from eighteenth-century comedies has become in Wilson's text a well-known political figure whose often televised persona actively participates in the process of self-definition. Stereotypes, which in the nineteenth century were regarded as a deadening imposition, have become a means of survival. Furthermore, Chuckie's imitation skills function as his main claim to a national identity. He is identified as Irish because he can imitate what is considered to be Irish. Chuckie resorts to caricature in the midst of New York's unreality where everyone "behaved like the movies they'd seen, like the movies in which they'd want to star," and where the simulacra of Irishness conform with the stereotype disseminated through television and other mass media. In Maria Edgeworth's and Lady Morgan's novels, the Irish difference was played out against England as a stable entity, from the center of which the Irish otherness was defined. In Wilson's novels "outside" does not offer such a firm anchor for defining Irish reality, for Chuckie's America confirms the inexistence of such a stable and firm center in the contemporary world. As Eve Patten noted about Wilson's first novel, *Ripley Bogle* (1989), comparing the unreality and constructedness of Englishness, Wilson's protagonists are reassured by their equally problematic and constructed Irishness (Patten 128–148).

Anne Enright's *What Are You Like?* takes the example of a postmodern or postnational dilemma further. The novel centers around the depiction of twin sisters, Rose and Maria, who, separated at birth, grow up in England and Ireland respectively. Rose is adopted by an English couple and, although aware of her adoption, lives in ignorance about her (genetic) nationality. She is brought up as a true "English Rose," while Maria bears a name heavy with her country's Catholic heritage. Having discovered her birth parents' nationality, Rose starts wondering about her split inheritance:

> She was Irish.
> Her favourite colour was blue.
> Her favourite colour was actually a deep yellow, but she couldn't live with it.
> She was English.
> She was tidy. She was polite. She hated Margaret Thatcher.
> She was a mess.

> She was someone who gave things up.
> She was someone who tried to give things up and
> failed all the time.
> It was all lies. Rose had a hole in her head and anything
> at all could come out of it (Enright 140).

Rose does not perceive her situation as liberating, for her "native" Irishness and acquired Englishness condemn her to the limbo of an identity crisis. Enright's novel pictures the very contemporary dilemma of non-belonging and non-identity, thus questioning the part that nationality plays in the formation of self-identity. *What Are You Like?* exemplifies the evolution that the question of national and personal identity have gone through since the early nineteenth century. To his delight, Mortimer found Glorvina in *The Wild Irish Girl* to be both "natural and national." Her virginity and the purity of her mind were paralleled and accentuated by the uncontaminated exoticism of her Irishness. With her harp and her singing, the "Sweet Voice" personified Ireland. Enright, on the other hand, indicates that in the contemporary world such a confident location of national and personal identity is at best a contrived, if not altogether impossible, notion.

Recent Irish fiction demonstrates that prevalent among the counter-strategies to combat this postmodern condition of uncertainty is close attention to topographical detail, a Joycean exactness of realist description. Characters in John McGahern, Glenn Patterson, and Robert McLiam Wilson's recent novels map their territories with careful attention to detail. From these texts emerges the present day cityscape (Belfast, London, Dublin, or New York) where an intense attention to territorial markers facilitates the formation of self-identity. National belonging can be problematic, as for instance exemplified in Wilson's hybrid invention of "Ripley Irish British Bogle," however, national longing is located on a concrete and distinct level of streets and districts. While the protagonist of Wilson's *Eureka Street*, Jake, lives on Poetry Street ("the posh end of town," the "bourgeois Belfast, leafier and more prosperous than you might imagine") where his downstairs window opens onto a Belfast deceptively similar to Oxford or Cheltenham, his upstairs window offers a view of West Belfast, where he was born and where he sends his English visitors on a horror tour, "the bold, the true, the extremely rough." Jake acknowledges being torn between his allegiances to different streets and different districts. His split national feelings are reflected in the contrast between his bourgeois pretensions (security, stability, no bombs, no poverty, even his cat is used to a fancy cat food) and the gritty reality of his childhood (Jake "works" on streets similar to the one he grew up in, so he encounters the impoverished part of the city on a daily basis). Jake's story (and its "happy ending") confirms that it is possible to inhabit these two different dimensions and move between these different social groups. Moreover, in addition to the disappearance of the class divide, *Eureka Street* demonstrates that the religious divide between Protestants and Catholics, the main characteristic of the Belfast of news reports and television shows, does not apply to people like Jake and his friends.

Similarly to Joycean Dublin, in contemporary fiction Belfast has become at once real and mythical. Wilson writes in *Eureka Street*:

"Belfast shared the status of the battlefield. The place names of the city and country had taken on the resonance and hard beauty of all history's slaughter venues. The Bogside, Crossmaglen, The Falls, The Shankill and Anderstonstown. In the mental maps of those who had never been in Ireland, these places had tiny crossed swords after their names" (Wilson, *Eureka Street* 14).

The violence that has brought Belfast to the attention of the rest of the world has mapped the districts and streets of the city conferring upon them mythical status of a battlefield. Yet, the group of friends whose collective stories Wilson's novel tells does not show any evidence of arranging their existence according to these "mythological" division lines. Chuckie is the only Protestant in the group, but ecumenical demarcation lines do not have any currency for him or his friends. The mix 'n' match quality of this group identikit is reflected on the level of the street names on which the characters live— Democracy Street, Poetry Street, and Damascus Street. These invented street names contribute to the overall irony of Wilson's representation of Belfast. There seems to be very little that is poetic about the Belfast of 1994, yet, as the authorial voice declares:

Cities are simple things. They are conglomerations of people. Cities are complex things. They are the geographical and emotional distillations of whole nations. But most of all, cities are the meeting places of stories. The men and women there are narratives, endlessly complex and intriguing (Wilson, *Eureka Street* 215).

This lyrical passage demonstrates an authorial yearning for a "meeting place." Wilson's novel exemplifies a contemporaneous desire for the unity of a meeting place of stories and an ironic awareness of how different this yearning is from a stereotypical image of Belfast. Similarly to Maria Edgeworth, Wilson's novel is trying to relate an "unknown tale." The mass media-generated "stories" have no validity in Belfast, which in Wilson's novel has become a meeting place of almost utopian dimensions: Protestant Chuckie meets and falls in love with American Max; liberal, apolitical Jake makes out with republican Aoirghe; and Chuckie's working-class Protestant mother comes out as a lesbian and starts a fulfilling relationship with her school friend Caroline. The improbable-sounding Democracy Street and Poetry Street become "love streets," and, as from a Joycean fusion of the mythical and the realistic, merges and emerges an ironic yet poetic image of late 1990s Belfast.

Painstakingly accurate documentation of reality encompasses both urban and rural locations. John McGahern's most recent novel, *That They May Face the Rising Sun* (2002), maps the daily minutiae of life in a small Irish village. The carefully measured and undisturbed rhythm of McGahern's prose reflects the pace of daily existence on a farm. The narrative unfolds slowly, almost reluctantly, as if the reader is made to wait patiently in order to become trustworthy enough to be given access to the stories of the characters' past. McGahern's narratorial voice relates: "What was unspoken was often far more important than the words that were said. Confrontation was avoided whenever possible. . . . It was a language that hadn't any simple way of saying no" (McGahern 186). The novel reflects the slow progress of the protagonists—Joe, an Irishman, a returning émigré, and his English wife Kate—toward fluency in that non-confrontational meditative language. In their subtle and understated success story is reflected a hope for a success on a larger, national scheme, for Kate and Joe accomplish what eluded Mortimer in *The Wild Irish Girl*. They not only learn to translate the untranslatable residue, but are inhabiting it.

O'Connor's definition of the Great Irish Novel is heavy with weariness and irritation about the constraints such a concept imposes upon an author. For both a tradition and its absence are conditions which generate a (healthy) resistance. While Edgeworth, Morgan, Griffin, and others attempted to fill the lacunae they perceived, writing in the late twentieth century, O'Connor regards tradition as an imposition, constraint, or limitation. The early nineteenth-century authors were resistant to their tales being categorized as part of the English tradition; O'Connor's contemporaries, however, rebel against the limitations of the Irish tradition. It is difficult to locate the exact moment when a lack of tradition was replaced by an existing tradition, which in its turn became an overwhelming imposition. Recalling Virginia Woolf, one could venture to say that the date when human nature (and literary history) changed in Ireland might be located during the time of cultural revival which witnessed both Yeats's passionate attempts to inaugurate an Irish tradition and the birth of a Joycean discourse of alienation and dislocation. These two sides of the Irish coin (Joyce and Yeats) bequeathed to twentieth-century authors an inheritance the weight of which occasionally seems overpowering. In their very different ways Joyce and Yeats reinvented the Irish tradition (in Joyce's case it is not an overstatement to say that he reinvented the entire novel tradition). In the largely Gaelic-speaking West of Ireland, Yeats located what he saw as the "real" Ireland. This idea of an existing Irish community gave a sense of direction to an individual artist like Yeats. He was hoping to locate the hope for a cultural unity, a truly and uniquely Irish tradition in a rural community. Yeats and other revivalists regarded such an act of invention necessary in order for the idea of Ireland to become a cultural and political reality. Joyce moved in the opposite direction; mythic and romantic unity, the idea of a national hero who would save/re-create Ireland, was called into radical doubt. Challenging the concept of self-identity, Joyce questions the validity of the idea of origins from which the cultural and personal sense of unity and identity stem. The radical doubt under which the concepts of national and personal identities are put is reflected on the level of language and form. As Samuel Beckett perceptively noted, in Joyce's texts form is content, content is form, and writing is not about something, it is that something itself. Over the years, Joycean fiction of uncertainty and doubt has found numerous followers.

Richard Kearney noted that a number of modern Irish writers "speak of being in transit between two worlds, divided between opposing allegiances. They often write as émigrés of the imagination, conveying the feeling of being both part and not part of their culture, of being estranged from the very traditions to which they belong, of being in exile even while at home" (Kearney, *Transitions* 14). The old oppositions such as England versus Ireland, city versus countryside, are in Joyce and Beckett's fiction replaced by the simultaneous feeling of being both part and not part, and this inner polarization becomes the imaginative and philosophical center of their writing. Not only national but also personal identity is difficult to locate in that no-man's land of the émigrés of imagination. Writing about Joyce's influence, John Banville confessed that "when I think of Joyce I am split in two. To one side there falls the reader, kneeling speechless in filial admiration, and love; to the other side, however, the writer stands, gnawing his knuckles, not a son, but a survivor" (Banville, "Survivors" 74). Banville touches upon the polarized nature of the predicament where on the one hand lies the desire for unity, definition, tradition, unproblematic allegiance, whether familial or political, and on the other hand stands the defiant declaration of "non serviam," echoing the statement made by Stephen Dedalus in Joyce's *A Portrait of the Artist as a Young Man* and detectable in O'Connor's scathing definition of the Great Irish Novel. [1] As the previous chapters of this book have indicated, concepts such as Irishness and national identity cannot be located in unproblematic polarities or unities of a single definition. Wilson's "Ripley Irish British Bogle" demonstrates how problematic the simple condition of the same people living in the same place, as suggested by Leopold Bloom, can be in the twenty-first-century world of globalism and postnationalism. As the Irish fiction of the last two centuries demonstrates, similarly to many other European countries, Ireland is making a difficult, occasionally painful, transition to modernity.

While trying to locate appropriate critical tools for unraveling the "Irish problem," first and foremost the question remains of whether Ireland is a postcolonial country. There is no question that the English presence on Irish soil has had a profound influence on the Irish psyche and Irish culture. The actual dimensions of this influence are still the subject of an active and vigorous debate. Following this, questions emerge of whether identity has become a polarized formation, structured by the tensions between difference and similarity and locked in an oppositional form of Englishness versus Irishness or Irishness versus Anglo-Irishness. Irish nationalist discourse has tended to disregard any alternatives to its story, which always emphasizes origin and destiny—that Gaelic was Ireland's first language and Catholicism its religion. Critics are still actively debating whether Irish nationalism(s) have now turned into disabling discourses, after performing their historical duty. Gerry Smyth, for instance, argued that with the election of Mary Robinson the Irish demonstrated that a "confident new Ireland" does not need to identify itself in relation to others. However, Northern Ireland with its still fragile peace tends to complicate this argument.

Intertwined with the question of nationalism is the language question, characterized by a paradoxical sense of loss and survival. Early nineteenth-century novels not only reflected social, political, and cultural conditions, but were also written with the aim of actively participating in these discourses and changing society. However, the question remains why these novels, so actively participating in nation building, were written in English. Critics have argued that the (English) language implicates these authors in the demise of Irish culture. The rise of Hiberno-English, the hybrid born out of the encounter between Irish and English, may have hampered the evolution of a stable novel tradition, but at the same time it has provided a fertile ground for its flourishing.

Another problematic factor of these Hiberno-English hybrids is their reader-oriented nature. The introductions to the novels by Edgeworth, Morgan, the Banims, and William Carleton show how acutely aware these authors were of having to compose their tales while bearing in mind their (English) readers and catering to their expectations and tastes. This trend was very much alive during the first half of the twentieth century and even later, as the majority of Irish fiction writers were until very recently still published by British publishing houses. That this was a problematic situation even in the early 1980s is evident in the statement by David Marcus, an editor of *Irish Writing* and the founder of the Poolbeg Press, who said: "Until recently creative writers had to turn to British publishers. But then it became almost impossible for an unpublished Irish writer to find a British publisher unless he or she fit a certain type: a stereotype of what an Irish writer should be. What I call the 'green writers'—

shamrocky" (Davis 68). During the last 30 years the Irish publishing industry has been successful in publishing Irish poetry and drama. In the 1970s and 1980s, Co-op Books, Raven Arts Press, and Tansy Books/The Egotist Press inaugurated a similar mission in the field of prose fiction. Their efforts are carried on today by Blackstaff, Poolpeg, Brandon, Wolfhound, Gallery Press, and New Island. However, in order to reach a wider readership, Irish authors continue to rely on the British publishing industry. The publishing industry and its conditions, and also the role of small magazines in generating a forum for a new generation of Irish writers are important areas of research that are still awaiting deeper critical engagement.

While heralding the arrival of a "Robinsonian" novel, Gerry Smyth claimed that the new Irish novelists of the 1980s and 1990s combined a willingness to confront the formal and conceptual legacies of a received literary (and wider social) tradition alongside a "self-awareness of the role played by cultural narratives in mediating modern (or perhaps it would be better now to say *postmodern*) Ireland's changing circumstances" (Smyth 7). That this is not a straightforward or simple process is evident from Seamus Deane's relatively recent (1983) call for a rewritten and reread politics and literature in order for a new writing and new politics to emerge. The age-old oppositions are still very much alive and the key questions continue to be the same, as is evident from Claire Connolly's recent summary of the questions occupying the critical center of Irish Studies. Connolly defined them very similarly to Gerry Smyth, saying that these questions were: Is Ireland postcolonial? How should the past be remembered? To whom does the term Irish apply? What is the subject matter of Irish Studies? (Connolly, "Introduction" 2). It seems that one is justified in claiming that the conceptual catchphrases in Irish Studies continue to be forgetting and remembering, national and personal identity, language, and representation.

## Notes

1. Stephen declares to his friend Cranly that he will not serve, meaning that he will not perform his Easter duty, requested by his mother. See James Joyce, *A Portrait of the Artist as a Young Man*, Jeri Johnson, ed. (Oxford: Oxford University Press, 2000) p. 201.

# Chapter Seven

# Irish Criticism

"What difference has theory made to the study of Irish culture?" This rhetorical question begins Claire Connolly's informative and insightful article on the current state of Irish cultural criticism, "Theorising Ireland" (Connolly 301).[1] Having enlisted the "anti-theory" emotions and remarks—William J. McCormack's suspicions concerning the "Weetabix Theory, incredibly dense and regular in structure, but lighter than its box"—Connolly proceeds to ponder whether Irish culture is impervious to critical argument (McCormack, *Dissolute Characters* x). Indeed, resistance to "theory" has been strong in some quarters of Irish academe, ranging from the biscuit-based Weetabix criticism to a more scathing attitude evidenced for instance by Edna Longley's oft-quoted abhorrence of "intellectual holiday romances in a postcolonial never-never land" (Longley, *Living Stream* 28). McCormack's critical attitude cannot be taken to signify his anti-theoretical stance; what McCormack, aligning himself with Frederic Jameson and Jerome McGann, is against is the too easy and superfluous application of theory. Speculating on the question of some Irish scholars' peculiar resistance to literary theory, Eamonn Hughes suggested that the original cause of this resentment lies in the fact that Irish Studies as a subject in academic curriculum was a late starter in Ireland (established only in the late 1960s), and once Irish critics finally could move to "their" territory, they discovered it already occupied from "outside," especially America. American literary scholars were, for instance, pioneering Joyce studies (long before Joyce was rescued from the hands of censorship in Ireland) (Hughes 1–15). Thus for instance an American scholar Richard Ellmann has worked extensively on the canonical Irish authors such as Joyce (Ellman's biography appeared in 1959), Yeats (his study on Yeats was published in 1961), and Wilde (biography appeared in 1987), which made Ellmann a central figure in Irish Studies, especially in Joyce studies. That such a "territorial occupation" provoked some resentment in Ireland is evident in Edna Longley's statements such as: "I don't think that Irish literary history has been properly written yet: partly because too many Americans and too few Irish critics have been on the job" (Longley, "Grass-seed" 20).

According to Hughes, the post-war Anglophone academic community, and especially the representatives of the emerging New Criticism (a school of theory which was developed during the 1940s and which is formalist in character, stating that the text should be examined alone, without historical or biographical consideration), were first to discover the Irish "modernists" such as Yeats and Joyce and include them in an "English" literary canon. This canon started with Matthew Arnold and encompassed the works of George Eliot, Charles Dickens, Conrad, James, T. S. Eliot, and D. H. Lawrence. Consequently, the newly established Irish Studies in Ireland were at first largely concerned with attempts to claim the distinctiveness of Irish writers and Ireland itself, opposing the Irish concerns to those of the modernists. For instance, Yeats studies (New Criticism's interest in Yeats) led to studies of the Irish cultural revival as a movement, a shift in critical agenda that consequently led to a greater focus on drama and poetry. Revival became one of the most popular research topics in the departments for Irish Studies that started to appear in the Irish universities around late 1960s.

The Irish Studies scene was challenged and revitalized by the arrival of the Field Day Theatre Company. The Company had been founded in Derry, Northern Ireland, in 1980 by playwright Brian Friel and actor Stephen Rea. The production of Friel's *Translations* in 1980 inaugurated the tradition of an annual theatrical production, which was first staged in Derry, and then toured the entire island. Soon four other directors were invited to join the founding team, poet Seamus Heaney, critic and poet Tom Paulin, folk singer David Hammond, and Seamus Deane. Field Day, founded during the period when sectarian violence continued to affect the North, sought to reexamine Ireland's political and cultural situation. Although there was no manifesto, a statement from the preface to a collection of pamphlets, published in 1985, indicated that Field Day saw its agenda as residing in challenging received opinions, myths, and stereotypes which, as the Company believed, had become "the symptom and a cause of the situation in the North" (*Ireland's Field Day* vii). In 1983, Field Day inaugurated a series of pamphlets in which the nature of Irish situation was explored and reexamined. These pamphlets, composed by the directors of Field Day and their invited guest contributors, established a line of continuity between the late twentieth-century Northern crisis and the contest between Britain and Ireland—a contest deeply embedded in Irish history, politics, and culture. Recognizing that "Ireland has been colonized through conquest and invasion several times and in several ways," Field Day directors acknowledged the influence of postcolonial thought. The pamphlets and a series of monographs on Irish history and culture, "Critical Conditions," constituted an impressive critical contribution that the Company made to the field of Irish Studies. The Company had set the terms for Irish criticism, and others had to align themselves either as reactions against or applications of Field Day's agenda. The most ambitious and monumental of Field Day's projects was the production of a comprehensive anthology of Irish literature. The first three volumes of the *Field Day Anthology of Irish Writing* appeared in 1991. In his "General Introduction," Seamus Deane, the General Editor of the anthology, wrote:

> The island was conquered by pre-Christian invaders, Christian missionaries, the Normans, the pre-Reformation English, the Elizabethans, Cromwellians and by the Williamites. It was dominated by imperial England and it remains, to the present day, in thrall to many of the forces, economic and political, that affect the United Kingdom in its troubled post-imperial decline. But other, internal conquests took place as well, deriving from and modifying the supervening realities of colonial rule. Versions of Ireland and its history and culture were created by many groups within the island—colonists and colonized—in attempts to ratify an existing political and economic system or to justify its alteration or its extinction (Deane, Carpenter, Williams xx).

Stephen Howe has criticized Deane's ambitions, arguing that
the proclaimed pluralist approach, the openness and variousness of
Field Day's practice, were in fact undermined by Deane's own pres-
entation of Ireland's cultural history as bifurcated between colonialism and nationalism. In short, while Field Day's aim was to
expose the worn-out myths, it seems to have replaced them with
new, simplified counter-myths of colonialism and nationalism.
Furthermore, Francis Mulhern detected a fairly traditional concept
of nationalism behind Deane's apparent embrace of plurality. That
this was an ongoing problem in Field Day's ethos is evident from
W. J. McCormack's criticism. McCormack argued long before the
publication of the *Anthology* that Field Day's literary preoccupations indicated the project's unconscious conservatism; while Field
Day emphasized the immediate pre-independence period, it also
stressed the importance of the central period of the directors' and
contributors' own active lives, that is, the 1980s Northern Ireland.
Therefore, McCormack claimed, "officially de-constructing nation-
alism, they effectively by-pass the classic phase of the Irish State as
a stable political entity" (McCormack, *Battle of the Books* 59).
Indeed, Field Day's scale of emphasis left out the founding of the
Irish Free State and the period from 1919 to the 1960s.
McCormack's criticism points toward a persistent gap in Field
Day's project, oddly definable in precise geographical terms.
Namely, the reception of the *Anthology* indicated what some crit-
ics called the "Derry-centrism" of Field Day. In other words, Field
Day regarded Ireland from Northern Ireland and from Derry, and
this viewpoint rendered the Republic marginal. In her stinging criticism of Field Day, Belfast-based critic Edna Longley accused the
Company of having centered its group goals on Derry as "the locus
of Jacobite restoration, the visionary city destined to redeem the
shames of Belfast and Dublin" (Longley, *Living Stream* 39).
Defending the Protestant side, Longley could not forgive what she
read as the Derry-based Catholic nationalist propaganda, speaking
not only for the entire (Northern) community but, even worse
according to Longley, also of Irish nationalism. Longley's resistance
to Field Day's enterprise was increased by her resistance to any
"outsiders" or travelers on "intellectual holiday romances" on the
field of Irish Studies:

It must be admitted that all critics involved in the Irish faction-fight tend to call upon the theoretical support which suits their book—whether feminism, deconstruction, or a more traditional Marxism. Field Day understandably favours theorists who might help to insert Northern Ireland/Ireland into the colonial/post-colonial frame (especially its simpler models). At the same time, the theorists in question [Terry Eagleton, Edward Said, and Frederic Jameson] could have been productively exposed to data about Ireland since the era of Yeats and Joyce. Strange collusions are taking place: intellectual holiday romances in a post-colonial never-never land (Longley, *Living Stream* 28).

Field Day's wholehearted embrace of the concept of an Ireland that suffered from colonialism was also criticized by Shaun Richards, who blamed Field Day for reading Northern Ireland as "unambiguously colonial" and censoring work that did not fit their nationalist preconceptions. According to Richards, Field Day rejected Frank McGuinness's play *Observe the Sons of Ulster Marching Towards the Somme*, which examined the psyche of the Ulster Protestants and did not fit within Field Day ethos (Richards, "To Bind the Northern" 56). This incident clashed with Field Day's declared concern with the "fifth province." The concept of the fifth province originates from Mark Patrick Hederman, a co-editor of the journal *The Crane Bag*, who in an editorial suggested that the problems of the four provinces of Ireland could be solved in "a no-man's land, a neutral ground, where all things can detach themselves from all partisan and prejudiced connection" (Richards, "Fifth Province" 140). This fifth province was the "secret center" and the place where "all oppositions were resolved." The concept was taken up by Richard Kearney and Seamus Deane, both associated with Field Day, who suggested that Hederman's "secret center" and the place where "all oppositions were resolved" could be defined as "an equivalent center from which the four broken and fragmented pieces of contemporary Ireland might be seen in fact as coherent" (Richards, "Fifth Province" 140). In short, while advocating multiplicity, plurality, and variety, Field Day's ethos was carried by the idea of unity. The problems that originated from this problematic ambiguity are best summed up by Shaun Richards who said that "it is not that

Field Day is a 'nationalist' movement in the sense of being hard-line republican, but there is a real political-cultural consequence of reading Ulster's situation as colonial, in that while there is the desire for a non-sectarian republic . . . there is also the necessity of dealing with those whose sense of political/cultural—and religious—being is predicated upon the maintenance of the fact of Union" (Richards, "Fifth Province" 142). According to Longley and Richards, even though there was no programmatic unity within the Company, and despite its oft-declared plurality of views, the statements made by the Field Day circle appeared intellectually and politically limiting. As Longley claimed, Field Day was trying no more or less than to exclude Northern Protestants from history.

Limitation, definition, and the creation of boundaries became the polemical and critical cornerstones on which critics founded their attacks on the *Field Day Anthology of Irish Writing*. In accordance with Field Day's aim to do away with the established opinions, myths, and stereotypes, the *Anthology* sought to re-present a series of representations of Ireland, the earliest of which dated to the year 550. In this three-volume monumental work were unearthed and republished a number of little known or inaccessible texts. The *Anthology* was chronologically arranged in subsections, which were introduced and edited by different contributors, all well-known and established Irish scholars. Seamus Deane claimed in "General Introduction" that "there is no attempt here to establish a canon," however, an anthology by definition establishes a tradition, and the Field Day tradition was seen by critics to be a male-centered one; the underrepresentation of women writers in the *Anthology* caused uproar and controversy, which led to the commissioning of an additional volume that concentrated on women's writing. The two additional volumes finally appeared in 2002, edited by a team of eight women scholars and critics. It can be argued that by assigning (belatedly) two volumes exclusively for women, Field Day did not exonerate its name, for women's writing was represented as separate, an "addition" to the tradition, which still excluded them from the "main tradition." Indeed, as Edna Longley scathingly remarked, the "afterthought"—the additional volume(s)—could be called, echoing Gilbert and Gubar, "The Mad Woman in the Annex" (Longley, *Living Stream* 35).

By covering a remarkable temporal territory—Irish writing of the last 1,500 years—the first three volumes of the *Anthology* tried to accomplish something that, according to Deane, had never been done before. The earlier attempts to achieve a representation of Irish writing on such a scale dated to 1879, when the four-volume *The Cabinet of Irish Literature* was published, and to 1911, when the ten-volume *Irish Literature* appeared, edited by Justin McCarthy. Volumes Four and Five of the *Field Day Anthology of Irish Writing* had a precedent in Brigid J. McCarthy's two-volume *The Female Pen* (1944, 1947) which covered women's writing from the period between 1621 and 1818. Underrepresentation of women writers in the first three volumes of the *Anthology* and the 11-year-long publishing process of the additional volumes caused a gap in Irish Studies of which women authors were painfully aware. This is for instance evident in another anthology, *The Wildish Things: An Anthology of New Irish Women's Writing*, edited by Ailbhe Smyth and published in 1989. In the "Introduction," Smyth claimed that the anthology "virtually imposed itself" on her as a "necessary statement of the fact of Irish women's writing now." According to Smyth, *The Wildish Things* had to save the work of women authors who otherwise would continue to be "altogether denied, ignored or only grudgingly admitted to the jealously male-guarded territory of 'Irish literature'" (Smyth 15). She finished by stating that it is "good for us and for others to know that we speak proudly, independently in an anthology published by an Irish women's press," a statement in which rings the dissatisfaction with the male-dominated Field Day.[2]

As the example of Field Day's *Anthology* indicated, making Irish women's voices heard was a complicated and long-winded process. This is also the case of feminist or gender criticism in Irish Studies, fields which have only recently witnessed an upsurge of interest. Toni O'Brien Johnson and David Cairns, in the "Introduction" to a collection of essays, *Gender in Irish Writing* (1991), conceded that although interest in gender in Irish society, culture, and politics had grown, studies of Irish literature in which gender is foregrounded were few and far between (Johnson and Cairns 1). This complaint is echoed by Catherine Lynette Innes, who in her study *Woman and Nation in Irish Literature and Society, 1880–1935*, published in 1993, pointed to the fact that Irish critical writing tended to focus obsessively on authors like Yeats, Joyce, Synge, O'Casey, and Beckett while ignoring the role of Irish women in the struggle for Irish national independence and identity.

Trying to find an explanation for the lack of popularity of feminist criticism, O'Brien Johnson and Cairns suggested that the pivotal positions within Irish institutions were held by people who were not interested in gender issues. It has to be noted, however, that by late 1980s and early 1990s, many Irish universities had already established centers for women's studies: Centre for Gender and Women's Studies at Trinity College in Dublin was established in 1988, the same year that saw the foundation of Women's Studies Centre at National University of Ireland in Galway; in 1990 Women's Education Research and Resource Centre at University College Dublin was formally set up; in 1999 the Queen's University in Belfast incorporated its already existing Centre for Women's Studies into the School of Humanities. It appears thus that by 1991 women's studies as a discipline had been institutionalized, while the publishing industry was still waiting to take off. Success seems evident, as eight years later David Alderson and Fiona Becket noted in the "Introduction" to the chapter on gender in *Ireland in Proximity: History, Gender, Space* that contemporary Irish Studies have become "increasingly preoccupied with questions of gender" (Alderson and Becket 61).

The difficulties encountered by feminist and gender studies are mainly due to the overwhelming importance accorded to nationalism, which has tended to overshadow feminism while also complicating the feminist argument. Carol Coulter pointed to the dangerous faultiness in the assumption that nationalism and feminism are opposites, the first being a patriarchal ideology founded in traditional Catholicism and the second a modern and international outlook, which surfaced in Ireland in the 1970s with the foundation of the modern Irish women's movement (Coulter 3). Recent scholarship has shown that in the nineteenth century, Irish women were actively involved in the nationalist struggle and played a significant part in the nationalist movements of the early twentieth century. The newly founded Irish Free State tried to exclude women from active political life, institutionalizing the most traditional and conservative elements of cultural and religious traditions. During these years, women's organizations had to find new ways to negotiate within the established framework of the conservative regime of the Irish Free State. Studies such as Carol Coulter's *The Hidden Tradition: Feminism, Women and Nationalism* (1993) and C. L. Innes's *Woman and Nation in Irish Literature and Society*, and also collections of essays such as *Gender and Sexuality in Modern Ireland* (1997) and *Representing Ireland: Gender, Class, Nationality* (1997) are good examples of the analysis of the relationship between feminism and nationalism in Ireland.[3] Writing about the mythicization of Ireland as female, C. L. Innes examined how the gendered representation of Ireland has influenced male writers, their perception and their portrayal of Irish women, male-female relations and women's response to male-generated rhetoric. She concludes that in the writings of Yeats, Joyce, and Synge, women became identified with Ireland both as images of an ideal order they sought to restore, and as images of an Ireland that had been betrayed, or had collaborated in its own betrayal. Innes claimed that if women, constructed as representations of Ireland, spoke their own version of the Irish conscience, they were ridiculed, reviled, or ignored (Innes 178–179).[4] Demystification of sexual politics has been the main object of Patricia Coughlan and Emer Nolan, who seek to revise the debilitating national myths of Irishness and point to the conceptual difference between woman as nation and woman as nationalist.[5]

A new departure for gender criticism can be detected in Colin Graham's essay, "Subalternity and Gender: Problems of Postcolonial Irishness," which focuses on the ideas of subalternity and the way this can be applied to gender issues in the Irish context (Graham, "Subalternity and Gender" 150–159). The "subaltern" in postcolonial studies usually designates oppressed groups within society. Drawing upon Gayatri Chakravorty Spivak's criticism of the Subaltern Studies historians, Graham argued that in the Irish context, gender should be allowed to exist within, outside of, and in opposition to the State and the nation. Graham endeavored to find a way in which gender can exist "inside" nation but is not dominated or stratified by it. According to Graham, gender and nation have to become subversive and affiliative concepts, resisting homogeneity.

James Joyce's work has frequently been subjected to feminist and gender criticism. Joyce's paradoxical statements about women, ranging from his declaration of his hatred to the celebration of women's intellect, have not deterred feminist critics, for Joyce's representation of female characters such as Molly Bloom and Anna Livia Plurabelle invites interpretations of his texts in which he challenged Western conceptions of the hero and the heroine. As Vicky Mahaffey argued in her essay "*Ulysses* and the End of Gender," Joyce attacks the unreality and counterproductiveness of such traditional ideals. *Ulysses* has been the favorite subject of feminist and gender critics, the principal examples of which are Vicki Mahaffey's *Reauthorizing Joyce* (1988), Bonnie Kime Scott's *Joyce and Feminism* (1984), Suzette Henke's *James Joyce and the Politics of Desire* (1990), and Joseph Valente's *James Joyce and the Problem of Justice: Negotiating Sexual and Colonial Difference* (1995).[6] Indeed, Derek Attridge and Marjorie Howes identified a shift in Joyce criticism that occurred in the 1990s, which they called an "Irish turn," but which essentially constituted a reconsideration of the Irish dimension in Joyce scholarship in the light of postcolonial theory (Attridge and Howes 15).

The last two decades have witnessed the growing popularity of the postcolonialist approach in Irish Studies. Acknowledging the colonial dimension of Irish experience has allowed Irish critics to compare their work with other scholars working with analogous materials in other cultures and literatures and to analyze Irish literature and culture in conjunction with the literatures from the West Indies and Africa.[7] However, postcolonial criticism has seen a rigorous resistance from some quarters of Irish academe. Glenn Hooper has distinguished three categories of reasons offered by critics hostile to a postcolonial reading of Ireland: 1) that Ireland was never really a colony, 2) that Ireland may once have been a colony, but since it was treated differently from, say, other British-governed territories in East Africa or Asia, the postcolonial models available to us are inappropriate; or 3) that Irish literary studies—whether these models are applicable or not—should simply be divorced from the "true," sometimes simply the aesthetic, intentions of their authors (Hooper 3). Edna Longley, a fierce critic of postcolonialism, claimed that while "the term 'colonial' may fit some aspects of Irish experience, most historians would qualify or specify its uses, and dispute the one-size-fits-all zeal of most theorists" (Longley, *Living Stream*

30). Stephen Howe's *Ireland and Empire: Colonial Legacies in Irish History and Culture* (2000) challenged the work of the majority of Irish postcolonialists and offered a well-argued and thoroughly-researched refutation of the concept of Ireland as a postcolony.[8] These counter-arguments and the growing importance of postcolonial approach have made postcolonialism the most vibrant field of criticism in Irish Studies today.

One of the most prominent and controversial proponents of postcolonialist Ireland is Declan Kiberd. Central to Kiberd's critical agenda is the notion of Irishness as a colonial creation: "If Ireland had never existed, the English would have invented it; and since it never existed in English eyes as anything more than a patchwork-quilt of warring fiefdoms, their leaders occupied the neighboring island and called it Ireland. . . . Ireland was soon patented as not-England, a place whose peoples were, in many important ways, the very antitheses of their new rulers from overseas" (Kiberd, *Inventing Ireland* 9). Thus it follows from Kiberd's argument that the notion of Englishness is defined and conceived through its "non-Irishness" and vice versa. As Stephen Howe pointed out, this is a "surely over-played" notion that most historians would refute by claiming that the French had more influence on the formation of the English national identity than the Irish (Howe 121). In his best-known study to date, *Inventing Ireland* (1995), Kiberd deployed Edward Said's Orientalist paradigm, as well as Albert Memmi and Franz Fanon's ideas. *Inventing Ireland* is the most comprehensive example of the application of colonial and postcolonial ideas to Irish litera-ture. Concerned both with "high art and popular expression," Kiberd charts the postcolonial Irish experience from Oscar Wilde and Somerville and Ross to 1990s Ireland. In the process he treats most of the well-known Irish authors such as Yeats, Synge, Brendan Behan, and Beckett as colonial or postcolonial. Kiberd's declared aim in *Inventing Ireland* was not to write a literary history of Ireland —although critics have viewed the book as an attempt to set out a canon—this ambition was accomplished in his next book, *The Irish Classics* (2000). His analysis in *Inventing Ireland* is thought provok-ing and challenging, his reading of Yeats illuminating—*Inventing Ireland* remains one of the most useful studies for students of Irish literature.[9]

Luke Gibbons's critical writings utilize features of postcolonialism, while subscribing to poststructuralist and cultural nationalist
ideas. His essays in the *Field Day Anthology of Irish Writing* (1991),
"Constructing the Canon: Versions of National Identity" and
"Challenging the Canon," constituted a fresh and interesting move
in Irish Studies toward analyzing criticism as a form of cultural production. In his study *Transformations in Irish Culture* (1996),
Gibbons distinguished between "European conceptions of nationalism" (characterized by coherence, abstraction, clarity) and the
peripheral variants of the European model (excluded from the public sphere, these fugitive experiences constructed by marginalized
subjects from the fragments of popular culture make up the dissident, insurrectionary tradition). Gibbons saw these two modes of
nationalism competing in nineteenth-century Ireland, where the
official, constitutional nationalism of Daniel O'Connell, Home
Rule, and Young Ireland was engaged in a struggle with the dissident
insurrectionary mode espoused by agrarian secret societies and
expressed in popular ballads. The latter mode pictured its cultural
self-image in allegorical terms. It is an "unverbalized" or "figural
practice" that originates from and thrives in an "instability of reference and contestation of meaning to the point where it may not be
all clear where the figural ends, and where the literal begins"
(Gibbons, *Transformations* 20). This insurrectionary allegory infil-
trates numerous cultural and political fields, introducing contradic-
tory inflections into official nationalism and other "official"
discourses, preventing their narratives from achieving unity, identity,
and closure.

The Irish literary historian David Lloyd has been influenced by
the ideas of Frantz Fanon and Jacques Derrida while deploying concepts developed in the writing of Gilles Deleuze and Félix Guattari,
Paul Ricoeur, Claude Levi-Strauss, and Immanuel Kant. He has
written extensively on Irish cultural nationalism, and his study on
James Clarence Mangan, *Nationalism and Minor Literature: James
Clarence Mangan and the Emergence of Irish Cultural Nationalism*
(1987), remains an outstanding example of a rigorous application
of the Deleuze-Guattari concept of minor literature to Irish literature. Lloyd's main argument is that the universalizing and homog-
enizing narrative of imperialism seeks to integrate Irishness and Irish

cultural nationalism within that narrative, rendering it as an inauthentic and conservative construct that locks Ireland in a self-justifying imperialist tale of a primitive community trying to make a necessary transition to a modern nation-state. Lloyd concentrates on the relationship between the official nationalism (promoted by state-building elites) and modes of resistance to this official narrativization. Recognizing nationalism as a progressive force at one stage of its history, Lloyd argues in the essays that constituted *Anomalous States: Irish Writing and the Post-Colonial Moment* (1993) that nationalism at its later stage of development tends to grow into a reactionary concept, because of its obsession with racial identity and its formal identity with imperial ideology. Consequently, Lloyd dismissed the work of Seamus Heaney as "profoundly symptomatic of the continuing meshing of Irish cultural nationalism with the imperial ideology which frames it," and celebrated the modernist writing of Beckett, Yeats, and Joyce. The latter's work, according to Lloyd, provided a form of non-collusive colonial resistance. Lloyd's prime example was Joyce's *Ulysses*; he claimed that while giving the Irish nation the desired national epic, Joyce utilized the anti-epic features of contingency and ambivalence.

Lloyd's more recent work shows a growing tendency to locate Ireland and Irish cultural concerns in a more global context, as he has frequently compared Ireland with other European countries, the United States, and India. This is evident, for example, in *Anomalous States*, but also in his latest publication, a collection of essays entitled *Ireland after History* (1999). The latter constitutes a new departure for Lloyd, as there he examines the cultural phenomena that resist the dictates of modernity. His ahistorical or post-historical vision was inspired by his endeavors to find new ways to speak about Irish culture, which he calls neither modern nor traditional, but which he sees occupying a space that is uncapturable by any such conceptual models. Somewhat paradoxically, this non-modern set of spaces emerges "out of kilter with modernity" but is still in a dynamic relationship to it; it is not traditional, not even subaltern, but "a space where alternative survives."

Cultural imperialism and the resistance to it in Ireland form the critical center of the arguments put forward by Shaun Richards and David Cairns. The theoretical agenda purported by Cairns and

Richards is formed on three premises: Edward Said's concept of Orientalism, Antonio Gramsci's notion of hegemony, and Michel Foucault's ideas on discourse analysis. This theoretical framework is supported by extensive and in-depth empirical reference drawing upon examples from Irish literature. Cairns and Richards's theories are informed by their readings of such authors as Samuel Ferguson, Thomas Davis, Standish O'Grady, Patrick Pearse, W. B. Yeats, James Joyce, Sean O'Casey, and Seamus Heaney. Their best known work to date, *Writing Ireland: Colonialism, Nationalism and Culture* (1988), examines the historic relationship of Ireland with England as a relationship of the colonized and the colonizer, focusing on the ways in which the making and remaking of the identities of both parties have been inflected by this relationship. Cairns and Richards saw it as a process that takes place through discourse. Their conclusions aligned them with Seamus Deane, for Cairns and Richards argued that the English-Irish relationship has to be "re-thought" and "re-read" in order to bring about a cultural renewal and a new politics.

Colin Graham's work shows evidence of a wide theoretical perspective; a representative of the younger generation of postcolonial critics, Graham extends the theoretical framework of Fanon and Said usually applied by Irish critics and utilizes critical concepts of such thinkers as Homi K. Bhabha, Ranajit Guha, and Gayatri Chakravorty Spivak.[10] His essay on Maria Edgeworth's *Castle Rackrent* is a good example of how the concept of "sly civility" developed by Homi Bhabha can be applied to an Irish text (Graham, "History, Gender and the Colonial Moment").

Gerry Smyth's *Decolonisation and Criticism* (1998) draws upon the ideas of Deane, Kiberd, Gibbons, and Lloyd, and he is also influenced by his reading of Bhabha and Spivak. Smyth constructs a binary model of cultural decolonization, viewing nationalism as organized around a fundamental split between discourses of "sameness" and "difference" which in their turn give rise to two main modes of colonial resistance, "liberal" and "radical." The liberal mode is mainly identified with the settler Anglo-Irish community and is a form of resistance in which subordinate colonial subjects (such as settlers or natives) seek equality with the dominant colonialist identity. The radical mode emerges from nationalism's impulse toward difference, aggression, and anti-universalism. Radical decolonization involves the rejection of imperial discourse, a celebration of difference and otherness, and the attempted reversal of the economy of power that constructs the colonial subject as inferior.

The internationally renowned Marxist literary critic Terry Eagleton first became associated with Irish Studies as an invited contributor to the Field Day pamphlet series. His essay, "Nationalism: Irony and Commitment" (1988), proclaimed that since, "from the standpoint of the advanced societies, [Ireland] is already a kind of nonplace and nonidentity, it can lend itself peculiarly well to a cosmopolitan modernism for which all places and identities are becoming progressively interchangeable" (Eagleton 35). That such a nonplace and nonidentity lends itself easily as a testing site or a laboratory for competing ideological concepts or cultural theories (and theorists) is evident in Eagleton's article, in which he declared that "the ideological category of Irishness signifies on the one hand roots, belonging, tradition, *Gemeinschaft*, and on the other hand, again with marvellous convenience, exile, diffusion, globality, diaspora. . . . With wonderful economy, it signifies a communitarianism nostalgically seductive in a disorientatingly cosmopolitan world, while offering itself at the same time as a very icon of that world in its resonance of political defeat, hybridity, marginality, fragmentation."[11] Irish Studies and Ireland became a testing site for Eagleton's artistic ambitions; his play, *Saint Oscar* (published in 1989), was staged by Field Day, and he published a book-length study called *Heathcliff and the Great Hunger: Studies in Irish Culture* (1995), in which he sought to "bear on Ireland the language of contemporary cultural theory." He further claimed that his eight essays constituted one of the first sustained projects to examine the "neglected categories of class, state, revolution, ideology, material production" in Irish Studies. In this book Eagleton attempts to "insert Irish history into cultural theory" and challenge what he sees as the current repressions and evasions of theory. The cultural theory he deploys is influenced by Antonio Gramsci and his concept of hegemony, in which the dominated party is under the illusion that its coercion is voluntary. This gives Gramscian critics an opportunity to analyze texts counter-intentionally, and examine the unwitting challenging of or submission to existing power relations. Eagleton's critical agenda made him well equipped to detect unresolved tensions and previously undiscovered gaps in the last two hundred years of Irish culture.[12] His two most interesting chapters, "Ascendancy and Hegemony" and "Form and Ideology in the Anglo-Irish Novel" deal respectively with class and ideology and the (im)possibility of a great realist novel tradition in Ireland.

Richard Kearney's views on modern Irish culture differ sharply from the postcolonialist critical stand. Kearney's *Transitions: Narratives in Modern Irish Culture* (1988) analyzes modern Irish culture by counterposing the concepts of traditional and modernist, national and revivalist, discontinuous and foreign. Influenced by his reading of hermeneutical philosophy, especially Paul Ricoeur, Kearney proposed a transitional (postmodern) mode of cultural creation that mediates between these oppositions. In a collection of essays entitled *The Irish Mind* (1985), Kearney put forward a theory of "the Irish mind," characterized by its ability to hold the traditional oppositions of Western philosophy (the dualist logic of either/or principle) together in a creative confluence. Organizing the Irish mind according to the "both/and" principle, Kearney suggested that categories such as Irishness and Englishness cannot be disposed of or replaced, as the Irish mind is simultaneously constructive and deconstructive, both engaged in decolonizing activity and displaced, aware of its own arbitrariness. Thus Irish culture operates through a rhythm of affirmation and skepticism. Kearney's thinking is characterized by his embracing of postmodernist ideas, a move evident in his editorial for *Across the Frontiers: Ireland in the 1990s* (1990) and the study *Postnationalist Ireland: Politics, Culture, Philosophy* (1997). Subscribing to the postmodern ideas of fragmentation of identities and narratives, *bricollage*, and pastiche allowed Kearney to form a critical paradigm where nationalist solidarities and borders are broken down in a postnationalist vision of a future that lies beyond the nation-state. In *Postnationalist Ireland*, he proposed the idea of a "Council of the Islands of Britain and Ireland," which would eventually evolve toward a "federal British-Irish archipelago in the larger context of a Europe of Regions" (Kearney, *Postnationalist Ireland* 11). Kearney urged the citizens of Britain and Ireland to think of themselves as "mongrel islanders," and argued that every nation is a hybrid construct, an imagined community that can be re-imagined in alternative versions. The fifth province espoused by Field Day has become in Kearney's later thinking a need to acknowledge the process of ongoing hybridization.

## Notes

1. I am greatly indebted to the following studies: Claire Connolly, ed., *Theorizing Ireland* (Basingstoke: Palgrave, 2003); Claire Connolly, "Theorizing Ireland," *Irish Studies Review* 9:3 (2001) pp. 301–315; Stephen Howe, *Ireland and Empire: Colonial Legacies in Irish History and Culture* (Oxford: Oxford University Press, 2000).

2. See also Ann Owens Weekes, *Unveiling Treasures: The Attic Guide to the Published Works of Irish Women Literary Writers* (Dublin: Attic Press, 1993) as an example of an attempt to produce a comprehensive guide to the published works by Irish women writers.

3. See Maryann Gialanella Valiulis and Anthony Bradley, eds., *Gender and Sexuality in Modern Ireland* (Amherst: University of Massachusetts, 1997); Susan Shaw Sailer, ed., *Representing Ireland: Gender, Class, Nationality* (Gainesville: University Press of Florida, 1997).

4. Note also Patricia Coughlan's pioneering essay, "'Bog Queens': The Representation of Women in the Poetry of John Montague and Seamus Heaney," in *Gender in Irish Writing*, Toni O'Brien Johnson and David Cairns, eds. (Milton Keynes/Philadelphia: Open University Press, 1991) pp. 88–111.

5. This distinction is made by Emer Nolan in her study *James Joyce and Nationalism* (London: Routledge, 1995).

6. There have been numerous studies and articles published on this topic. Students might want to consult for example Karen Lawrence's article "Joyce and Feminism," in *The Cambridge Companion to James Joyce*, Derek Attridge, ed. (New York: Cambridge University Press, 1990) pp. 237–258; Sheldon Brivic, *Joyce's Waking Women* (Madison: University of Wisconsin Press, 1995); Suzette Henke and Elaine Unkelness, eds., *Women in Joyce* (Urbana: University of Illinois Press, 1982); and Margot Norris, *Joyce's Web: The Social Unraveling of Modernism* (Austin: University of Texas, 1992). See also the Suggestions for Further Reading in Chapter Nine.

7. See, for instance, essays by Tim McLoughlin, Steven Matthews, and Joshua Esty in *Irish and Postcolonial Writing: History, Theory, Practice*, Colin Graham and Glenn Hooper, eds. (Basingstoke/New York: Palgrave, 2002); the pioneering work in this field was Catherine Lynette Innes's *The Devil's Own Mirror: The Irishman and the African in Modern Literature* (Washington, D.C.: Three Continents Press, 1990).

8. According to Glenn Hooper, "at least some of [Howe's work's] impact derives from an implicit association between support for postcolonial criticism in Ireland and sympathy for the IRA." See Hooper's "Introduction," p. 16.

9. For criticism of *Inventing Ireland* see Colin Graham, "Post-colonial Theory and Kiberd's 'Ireland'," *The Irish Review* 19 (Spring/Summer 1996) pp. 62–67; Colm Tóibín, "Playboys of the GPO," *London Review of Books* (18 April 1996) pp. 14–16; Stephen Howe, *Ireland and Empire: Colonial Legacies in Irish History and Culture*, pp. 121–125.

10. In a footnote, David Lloyd links his notion of "adulteration" with Bhabha's concept of "hybridity," see David Lloyd, *Anomalous States: Irish Writing and the Post-Colonial Moment* (Durham, NC: Duke University Press, 1993) p. 124.

11. Howe, *Ireland and Empire: Colonial Legacies in Irish History and Culture* (Oxford: Oxford University Press, 2000) p. 2.

12. Eagleton's book caused a controversy in Irish Studies, for insightful criticism of *Heathcliff and the Great Hunger* see for example Joep Leerssen, "Theory, History and Ireland," in *The Irish Review* 17–18 (Winter 1995) pp. 167–175.

# Chapter Eight

# Glossary

**Absenteeism** Many Protestant landlords resided permanently in England, dependent on the income that came from their Irish estates but never interested enough to invest in Ireland. Their affairs were taken care of by "middlemen." The absenteeism essentially came to symbolize the corruptness of the landlord system.

**Catholic Emancipation** The long political struggle to get civil rights for Roman Catholics. In 1829, finally, "An Act for the relief of His Majesty's Roman Catholic subjects" was passed, and Catholics were granted the right to vote and become members of Parliament. Catholics were not allowed to become regent, chancellor, or lord lieutenant, but apart from these restrictions they were allowed to hold all civil and military offices.

**Daniel O'Connell's Catholic Association** Daniel O'Connell (1775–1847), a lawyer and politician, became involved in the Catholic Committee, which was attempting to win Catholic emancipation. He founded the Catholic Association in 1823, which attracted thousands of followers and became a mass organization. In 1826, O'Connell was elected as an MP for County Clare, which made him the first Catholic MP since the seventeenth century. In 1829, Catholic emancipation was finally won, a feat that earned him a popular title "the Liberator" among the Catholics.

**Easter Rising** An insurrection on Easter Monday of 1916 organized by Ulster Volunteers, Irish Republican Brotherhood, and the working-class citizens army led by James Connolly. Patrick Pearse, a Gaelic-speaking poet, read the Proclamation of a Republic outside the General Post Office on April 24, 1916. The insurrection lasted less than a week; the rebels surrendered on April 29, and between May 3 and 12, fourteen of the leaders were executed.

**Grattan's Parliament**   Irish legislature between 1782 and 1800. Henry Grattan (1746–1820) has been commonly credited with achieving the legislative independence. The "independence" of 1782 was largely a symbolic gesture, essentially what was changed was a Poynings' Law procedure that meant that after 1782 the Irish privy council could not alter or suppress an Irish parliamentary measure. This remained essentially an experiment in power sharing between Ireland and England.

**Great Famine, The (1845–1849)**   The potato blight hit Ireland in 1845, affecting mainly the east of Ireland; the following year the catastrophe was complete as the crop failed everywhere, and continued to do so for the next four years. Potato was the staple diet of the poorest class of the overpopulated Ireland, and affected most seriously the rural countryside. It is estimated that over a million people died of malnutrition. Some historians argue that the effects of the Famine lasted as long as 1852.

The Great Famine caused a mass emigration, as almost two million people left the country during the Famine years.

**Home Rule**   A term denoting the restoration of an Irish parliament in Dublin (while still being subordinate to Britain). Isaac Butt founded the Home Government Association in 1870, which in 1873 became the Home Rule League. In the general elections of 1874, fifty Home Rulers were elected to the parliament, and they formed the Irish Parliamentary Party, or Home Rule Party. While Butt hoped that Home Rule would appeal to both Catholics and Protestants, Charles Stewart Parnell, who became the leader of the Home Rulers in 1880, saw Home Rule as a step toward Ireland's complete independence from Britain. This was, however, a private view, as publicly Parnell supported Home Rule. The first Home Rule Bill was defeated in 1886; in 1893 the second one passed the Commons but not the House of Lords. The third Home Rule Bill was introduced in 1912, was again vetoed by Lords and, finally, in 1914, got the royal assent.

**Penal Laws**  Known as "Property Acts" in the eighteen century. A body of legislation restricting civil rights of Catholic population that was first introduced in 1695.

**Repeal**  A general and widespread demand to repeal the Act of Union of 1800 in order to reestablish an independent Irish Parliament.

**United Irishmen**  A movement founded in 1791 in Belfast by a radical organization called the Presbyterian Volunteers. The United Irishmen wanted to achieve parliamentary reform and Catholic emancipation. In order to achieve these aims, they believed that Catholic and Protestant Irishmen should join forces. Having managed to get France into their alliance, the United Irishmen tried to organize an insurrection, which failed fatally. In 1798, several local insurrections were soon thwarted by the government's control. The movement deepened the sectarian strife, and the failed insurrection of 1798 was among the main reasons propelling the Protestant Ascendancy to agree to the Act of Union.

# Chapter Nine

# Bibliography and Further Reading

Alderson, David, and Fiona Becket, "Introduction," in *Ireland in Proximity: History, Gender, Space*, Scott Brewster, Virginia Crossman, Fiona Becket, and David Alderson, eds. (London and New York: Routledge, 1999) pp. 1–6.

Arnold, Matthew, *On the Study of Celtic Literature* (London: Smith, Elder and Co, 1867).

Attridge, Derek, and Marjorie Howes, *Semicolonial Joyce* (Cambridge, MA: Columbia University Press, 2000).

Banim, John, and Michael Banim, *The Boyne Water by The O'Hara Family. A New Edition, with Introduction and Notes by Michael Banim, Esq., the survivor of "the O'Hara family"* (Dublin: James Duffy, 1865).

Banville, John, "Survivors of Joyce," in *James Joyce the Artist and the Labyrinth*, Augustine Martin, ed. (London: Ryan Publishing, 1990) pp. 73–81.

———, "A Talk," *Irish University Review* 11 (1981) pp. 13–17.

Beckett, Samuel, *The Complete Dramatic Works* (London: Faber, 1986).

———, *Worstward Ho* (London: John Calder, 1983).

Briggs, Julia, "The Ghost Story," *A Companion to the Gothic*, David Punter, ed. (Oxford: Blackwell Publishers, 2000) pp. 122–131.

Brown, Stephen J., *A Readers' Guide to Irish Fiction* (London: Longmans, 1910).

Cahalan, James, M., *Great Hatred, Little Room: The Irish Historical Novel* (Syracuse, NY: Syracuse University Press, 1983).

———, *The Irish Novel: A Critical History* (Dublin: Gill and Macmillan, 1988).

Cairns, David, and Shaun Richards, "Discourses of Opposition and Resistance in Late Nineteenth and Early Twentieth Century Ireland," *Text and Context* 2:1 (Spring 1988) pp. 76–84.

Carty, Ciaran, "Out of Chaos Comes Order," *The Sunday Tribune* (14 September 1986) pp. 18.

Connolly, Claire, "'I accuse Miss Owenson': *The Wild Irish Girl* as Media Event," *Colby Quarterly* 36:2 (June 2000) pp. 98–115.

———, "Introduction: Ireland in Theory," in *Theorizing Ireland*, Claire Connolly, ed. (Basingstoke: Palgrave, 2003) pp. 1–13.

———, "Theorizing Ireland," *Irish Studies Review* 9:3 (2001) pp. 301–315.

Coulter, Carol, *The Hidden Tradition: Feminism, Women and Nationalism in Ireland* (Cork: Cork University Press, 1993).

Cronin, John, "The Creative Dilemma of Gerald Griffin," *Canadian Journal of Irish Studies* 12:2 (June 1968) pp. 105–118.

Cuddon, J. A., *Dictionary of Literary Terms and Literary Theory* (London: Penguin, 1992).

Cullen, Louis M., *The Hidden Ireland: Reassessment of a Concept* (Dublin: The Lilliput Press, 1988).

Davis, Kenneth, C., "Ireland: A New Flowering," *Publisher's Weekly* (23 January 1981) pp. 63–66, 68, 72–73, 76–80.

Deane, Seamus, "Heroic Styles: the Tradition of an Idea," in *Ireland's Field Day* (London: Hutchinson, 1985) pp. 45–58.

———, "History as Fiction/Fiction as History," in *Joyce in Rome: The Genesis of Ulysses*, Giorgio Melchiori, ed. (Rome: Bulzoni, 1984) pp. 130–141.

———, *A Short History of Irish Literature* (London: Hutchinson, 1986).

———, *Strange Country: Modernity and Nationhood in Irish Writing since 1790* (Oxford: Clarendon Press, 1997).

Deane, Seamus, Andrew Carpenter, and Jonathan Williams, eds., *Field Day Anthology of Irish Writing*, 3 Vols. (Derry: Field Day Publications, 1991).

Donoghue, Emma, "Coming Out a Bit Strong," *Index on Censorship* 24:1 (Jan/Feb 1995) pp. 87–88.

Duffy, Séan, et al., *Atlas of Irish History* (Dublin: Gill & Macmillan, 1997).

Eagleton, Terry, *Heathcliff and the Great Hunger: Studies in Irish Culture* (London: Verso, 1995).

———, "Nationalism: Irony and Commitment" in *Nationalism, Colonialism, and Literature*, Fredric Jameson and Edward W. Said, eds. (Minneapolis: University of Minnesota Press, 1990) pp. 23–39.

Enright, Anne, *What Are You Like?* (London: Jonathan Cape, 2000).

Ferris, Ina, *The Romantic National Tale and the Question of Ireland* (Cambridge: Cambridge University Press, 2002).

Foster, Roy, *Modern Ireland, 1600–1972* (London: Penguin, 1989).

Gibbons, Luke, "Challenging the Canon: Revisionism and Cultural Criticism," in *Field Day Anthology of Irish Writing*, Vol. 3 (Derry: Field Day Publications, 1991) pp. 561–568.

———, "Constructing the Canon: Versions of National Identity," in *Field Day Anthology of Irish Writing*, Vol. 2 (Derry: Field Day Publications, 1991) pp. 950–1020.

———, *Transformations in Irish Culture* (Cork: Cork University Press & Field Day, 1996).

Graham, Colin, "History, Gender and the Colonial Moment: *Castle Rackrent*," *Irish Studies Review* 14 (1996) pp. 21–24.

———, "Subalternity and Gender: Problems of Postcolonial Irishness," in *Theorizing Ireland*, Claire Connolly, ed. (Basingstoke and New York: Palgrave, 2003) pp. 150–159.

Harmon, Maurice, *The Irish Writer and the City* (Gerrards Cross: C. Smythe, 1983).

Harte, Liam, and Michael Parker, "Reconfiguring Identities: Recent Northern Irish Fiction," in *Contemporary Irish Fiction: Themes, Tropes, Theories,* Liam Harte and Michael Parker, eds. (Houndmills and New York: Macmillan, 2000) pp. 232–254.

Haslam, Richard, "'The Pose Arranged and Lingered Over': Visualizing the 'Troubles,'" in *Contemporary Irish Fiction: Themes, Tropes, Theories,* Liam Harte and Michael Parker, eds. (Houndmills and New York: Macmillan, 2000) pp. 192–212.

Hooper, Glenn, "Introduction," in *Irish and Postcolonial Writing: History, Theory, Practice,* Glenn Hooper and Colin Graham, eds. (Basingstoke and New York: Palgrave, 2002) pp. 3–31.

Hough, Graham, "George Moore and the Novel," in *George Moore's Mind and Art,* Graham Owens, ed. (Edinburgh: Oliver and Boyd, 1968) pp. 166–175.

Howe, Stephen, *Ireland and Empire: Colonial Legacies in Irish History and Culture* (Oxford: Oxford University Press, 2000).

Hughes, Eamonn, "Forgetting the Future: An Outline History of Irish Literary Studies," *The Irish Review* 25 (Winter/Spring 1999–2000) pp. 1–15.

Innes, Catherine Lynette, *Woman and Nation in Irish Literature and Society, 1880–1935* (New York: Harvester Wheatsheaf, 1993).

*Ireland's Field Day* (London: Hutchinson, 1985).

Johnson, Toni O'Brien, and David Cairns, eds. *Gender in Irish Writing* (Milton Keynes and Philadelphia: Open University Press, 1991).

Joyce, James, *Letters of James Joyce,* Stuart Gilbert, ed., 3 Vols., (New York: The Viking Press, 1966).

———, *A Portrait of the Artist as a Young Man,* Jeri Johnson, ed. (Oxford: Oxford University Press, 2000).

———, *Ulysses,* Jeri Johnson, ed. (Oxford: Oxford World Classics, 1993).

Kearney, Richard, *Postnationalist Ireland: Politics, Culture, Philosophy* (London and New York: Routledge, 1997).

————, *Transitions: Narratives in Modern Irish Culture* (Manchester: Manchester University Press, 1988).

Kiberd, Declan, *Inventing Ireland* (London: Jonathan Cape, 1995).

————, "The Perils of Nostalgia: A Critique of the Revival," in *Literature and the Changing Ireland*, Peter Connolly, ed. (Gerrards Cross: C. Smythe, 1982) pp. 1–24.

————, "Story-telling: The Gaelic Tradition," in *The Irish Short Story*, Patrick Rafroidi and Terence Brown, eds. (Lille, France: Pubs. de l'Université Lille, 1979) pp. 13–25.

Kiely, Benedict, "Introduction," in *The Penguin Book of Irish Short Stories* (London: Penguin Books, 1981) pp. 8–12.

Kinsella, Thomas, "The Irish Writer," in *Davis, Mangan, Ferguson? Tradition & The Irish Writer*, Thomas Kinsella and W. B. Yeats, eds. (Dublin: Dolmen Press, 1970) pp. 57–66.

Kirkland, Richard, "Bourgeois Redemptions: The Fictions of Glenn Paterson and Robert McLiam Wilson," in *Contemporary Irish Fiction: Themes, Tropes, Theories*, Liam Harte and Michael Parker, eds. (Houndmills and New York: Macmillan, 2000) pp. 213–231.

Kreilkamp, Vera, *The Anglo-Irish Novel and the Big House* (Syracuse, NY: Syracuse University Press, 1998).

Larkin, Emmet, "A Reconsideration: Daniel Corkery and His Ideas on Cultural Nationalism," *Éire-Ireland* 8:1 (Spring 1973) pp. 42–51.

Le Fanu, Joseph Sheridan, *The House by the Churchyard* (London: Anthony Blond, 1968).

Lee, Hermione, *Elizabeth Bowen* (London: Vintage, 1999).

Lloyd, David, *Anomalous States: Irish Writing and the Post-Colonial Moment* (Durham, NC: Duke University Press, 1993).

Longley, Edna, *The Living Stream: Literature and Revisionism in Ireland* (Newcastle upon Tyne: Bloodaxe Books, 1994).

————, "Writing, Revisionism and Grass-seed: Literary Mythologies in Ireland," in *Styles of Belonging: The Cultural Identities of Ulster*, Jean Lundy and Aodáin MacPóilin, eds. (Belfast: Lagan Press, 1992) pp. 11–21.

Mahaffey, Vicki, "*Ulysses* and the End of Gender," in *A Companion to James Joyce's Ulysses*, Margot Norris, ed. (Boston: Bedford Books, 1998) pp. 151–168.

Martin, Augustine, *James Stephens: A Critical Study* (Dublin: Gill and Macmillan, 1977).

———, "Prose Fiction in the Irish Literary Renaissance," in *Irish Writers and Society at Large*, Masaru Sekire, ed. (Gerrards Cross: C. Smythe, 1985) pp.139–162.

McCormack, William J., *The Battle of the Books: Two Decades of Irish Cultural Debate* (Mullingar: Lilliput Press, 1986).

———, *Dissolute Characters: Irish Literary History through Balzac, Sheridan Le Fanu, Yeats and Bowen* (Manchester and New York: Manchester University Press, 1993).

———, "Irish Gothic and After, 1820–1945," in *Field Day Anthology of Irish Writing*, Vol. 2 (Derry: Field Day Publications, 1991) pp. 831–854.

McGahern, John, *That They May Face the Rising Sun* (London: Faber and Faber, 2002).

Moore, George, *The Lake* (London: Heinemann, 1921).

Moynahan, Julian, *Anglo-Irish: The Literary Imagination in a Hyphenated Culture.* (Princeton, NJ: Princeton University Press, 1995).

O'Brien, Edna, *Mother Ireland* (London: Penguin Books, 1984).

O'Connor, Joseph, *Cowboys and Indians* (London: Sinclair-Stevenson, 1991).

Owenson, Sydney, *The Wild Irish Girl: A National Tale*, Claire Connolly and Stephen Copley, eds. (London: Pickering & Chatto, 2000).

Parkin, Andrew, "Shadows of Destruction: The Big House in Contemporary Irish Fiction," in *Cultural Contexts and Literary Idioms in Contemporary Irish Literature*, Michael Kenneally, ed. (Toronto: Barnes & Noble, 1988) pp. 306–327.

Patten, Eve, "Fiction in Conflict: Northern Ireland's Prodigal Novelists," in *Peripheral Visions: Images of Nationhood in Contemporary British Fiction* (Cardiff: University of Wales Press, 1995) pp. 128–148.

Power, Arthur, *From The Old Waterford House* (Waterford: Carthage Press, 1940).

Punter, David, ed., *A Companion to the Gothic* (Oxford: Blackwell Publishers, 2000).

Rauchbauer, Otto, ed., *Ancestral Voices: The Big House in Anglo-Irish Literature* (Hildesheim: Olms, 1992).

Richards, Shaun, "Field Day's Fifth Province: Avenue or Impasse?" *Culture and Politics in Northern Ireland 1960–1990* (Milton Keynes: Open University Press, 1991) pp. 139–150.

———, "To Bind the Northern to the Southern Stars: Field Day in Derry and Dublin," *The Irish Review* 4 (Spring 1988) pp. 52–58.

Robinson, Hilary, *Somerville & Ross: A Critical Appreciation* (New York: Gill and Macmillan, 1980).

Said, Edward S., "Reflections on Exile," in *Reflections on Exile and Other Literary and Cultural Essays* (London: Granta Books, 2001) pp. 173–186.

Scott, Walter, *Waverley*, Claire Lamont, ed. (Oxford: Clarendon Press, 1981).

Sheehan, Ronan, "Novelists on the Novel: Ronan Sheehan talks to John Banville and Francis Stuart," *Crane Bag* 3:1 (1979) pp. 76–84.

Smyth, Ailbhe, ed., *Wildish Things: The Anthology of New Irish Women's Writing* (Dublin: Attic Press, 1989).

Smyth, Gerry, *The Novel and the Nation: Studies in the New Irish Fiction* (London: Pluto Press, 1997).

———, "The Right to the City: Re-presentations of Dublin in Contemporary Irish Fiction," in *Contemporary Irish Fiction: Themes, Tropes, Theories*, Liam Harte and Michael Parker, eds. (Houndmills and New York: Macmillan, 2000) pp.13–34.

Weekes, Ann Owens, "Figuring the Mother in Contemporary Irish Fiction," in *Contemporary Irish Fiction: Themes, Tropes, Theories,* Liam Harte and Michael Parker, eds. (Houndmills and New York: Macmillan, 2000) pp. 100–124.

————, *Unveiling Treasures: The Attic Guide to the Published Works of Irish Women Literary Writers* (Dublin: Attic Press, 1993).

Welch, Robert, ed., *The Oxford Companion to Irish Literature* (Oxford: Clarendon Press, 1996).

Wilson, Robert McLiam, *Eureka Street* (London: Vintage, 1998).

————, *Ripley Bogle* (Dundonald: Blackstaff, 1989).

Yeats, W. B., *Representative Irish Tales* (Gerrards Cross: C. Smythe, 1979).

————, *Uncollected Prose by W. B. Yeats,* John P. Frayne, ed., 2 Vols. (London: Macmillan, 1970).

Zimmern, Helen, *Maria Edgeworth* (London: Walter Allen & Co, 1883).

# Suggested Further Reading

### 1. General (these books give you a good background, and are essential for a beginner):

Bourke, Angela, et al., eds., *The Field Day Anthology of Irish Writing,* 2 Vols. (Cork: Cork University Press and Field Day, 2002).

Cahalan, James M., *The Irish Novel: A Critical History* (Dublin: Gill and Macmillan, 1988).

Deane, Seamus, *A Short History of Irish Literature* (London: Hutchinson, 1986).

Deane, Seamus, Andrew Carpenter, and Jonathan Williams, eds., *Field Day Anthology of Irish Writing,* 3 Vols. (Derry: Field Day Publications, 1991).

Jeffares, A. Norman, *Anglo-Irish Literature* (London: Macmillan, 1982).

Kiberd, Declan, *Inventing Ireland: The Literature of the Modern Nation* (London: Jonathan Cape, 1995).

Mahony, Christian Hunt, *Contemporary Irish Literature: Transforming Tradition* (New York: St. Martin's Press, 1998).

McCormack, William J., *Ascendancy and Tradition in Anglo-Irish Literary History from 1789 to 1939* (Oxford, Clarendon Press, 1985).

Mercier, Vivian, *Modern Irish Literature: Sources and Founders* (Oxford: Clarendon Press, 1994).

Vance, Norman, *Irish Literature: A Social History* (Dublin: Four Courts Press, 1999).

Welch, Robert, ed., *The Oxford Companion to Irish Literature* (Oxford: Clarendon Press, 1996).

## 2. Fiction in Irish:

Cahalan, James M., *The Irish Novel: A Critical History* (Dublin: Gill and Macmillan, 1988).

Kiberd, Declan, *The Irish Classics* (London: Granta, 2000).

Leerssen, Joep, *Mere Irish and Fior-Ghael: Studies in the Idea of Irish Nationality, its Development and Literary Expression Prior to the Nineteenth Century* (Amsterdam: John Benjamins Pub. Co., 1997).

## 3. Irish History:

Beckett, J. C., *The Making of Modern Ireland, 1603–1923* (London: Faber, 1966).

———, *A Short History of Ireland from Earliest Times to the Present Day* (London: Hutchinson, 1952).

Brown, Terence, *Ireland: A Social and Cultural History, 1922–1979* (London: Fontana, 1981).

Foster, R. F., *Modern Ireland 1600–1972* (London: Allen Lane, 1988).

Lyons, F. S. L., *Ireland Since the Famine* (London: Weidenfeld and Nicolson, 1975).

McCaffrey, Lawrence J., *Ireland: From Colony to Nation State* (Englewood Cliffs, NJ: Prentice-Hall, 1979).

Moody, T. W., and F. X. Martin, *The Course of Irish History* (Cork: The Mercier Press, 1967).

### 4. Theoretical and Historical Perspectives on Irish Literature:

Brewster, Scott, Virginia Crossman, Fiona Becket, and David Alderson, eds., *Ireland in Proximity: History, Gender, Space* (London and NY: Routledge, 1999).

A collection of essays that surveys the fields of history, gender, and space in Irish Studies. It draws upon a variety of theoretical approaches.

Cairns, David, and Shaun Richards, *Writing Ireland: Colonialism, Nationalism and Culture* (Manchester: Manchester University Press, 1988).

Analyzes Irish culture, literature, and identity in Ireland in the nineteenth and twentieth centuries. Utilizing Gramscian's theory of discourse and postcolonial theories, the authors offer incisive readings of key texts in Irish literature. Indispensable for anyone interested in postcolonial criticism.

Connolly, Claire, "Theorizing Ireland," *Irish Studies Review* 9:3 (2001) pp. 301–315.

A "must" for students interested in theoretical perspectives on Irish literature and culture. An excellent overview of recent scholarship.

Corcoran, Neil, *After Yeats and Joyce: Reading Modern Irish Literature* (Oxford: Oxford University Press, 1997).

Good discussions of contemporary Irish writing, chapters on Big House fiction, representations of Dublin, and Northern Irish writers.

Coulter, Carol, *The Hidden Tradition: Feminism, Women and Nationalism in Ireland* (Cork: Cork University Press, 1993).

A pioneering study on feminism and nationalism. A good starting point if you are investigating the subject, but don't forget to consult more recent studies.

Deane, Seamus, *Strange Country: Modernity and Nationhood in Irish Writing since 1790* (Oxford: Clarendon Press, 1997).

Intellectually challenging but stimulating discussions on national character and national tradition in Irish writing from the French Revolution onward.

Eagleton, Terry, *Crazy John and the Bishop and Other Essays on Irish Culture* (Cork: Cork University Press and Field Day, 1998).

An interesting collection of provocative readings of Irish texts from the eighteenth century to the present day. Among the authors discussed are Thomas Moore, Maria Edgeworth, Samuel Beckett, and Francis Stuart. A stimulating, if occasionally challenging, read.

Fegan, Melissa, *Literature and the Irish Famine 1845–1919* (Oxford: Clarendon Press, 2002).

Examines the impact of the Great Famine on Irish fiction and nonfiction. The chapter on William Carleton is especially interesting.

Fogarty, Anne, "Uncanny Families: Neo-Gothic Motifs and the Theme of Social Change in Contemporary Irish Women's Fiction," *Irish University Review* 30:1 (Spring/Summer 2000) pp. 59–81.

In this well-argued article, Anne Fogarty examines Mary Morrissy's *Mother of Pearl*, Anne Haverty's *One Day as a Tiger*, Jennifer Johnston's *Two Moons*, and Mary O'Donnell's *The Elysium Testament* in the light of recent changes in women's situation in contemporary Ireland.

Foster, John Wilson, *Fictions of the Irish Literary Revival: A Changeling Art* (Syracuse, NY: Syracuse University Press, 1987).

An indispensable study of the prose fiction of the Irish literary revival, also analyzes such genres as autobiography and folklore.

Gibbons, Luke, *Transformations in Irish Culture* (Cork: Cork University Press and Field Day, 1996).

A thought-provoking collection of essays, examines the questions of culture and politics, nation and state, and high and popular culture.

Graham, Colin, "Subalternity and Gender: Problems of Postcolonial Irishness," in *Theorizing Ireland*, Claire Connolly, ed. (Houndmills & New York: Palgrave, 2003) pp. 150–159.

Homi Bhaba's ideas are deployed in an Irish context. A challenging read, but worth a try.

Harmon, Maurice, ed., *The Irish Writer and the City* (Gerrards Cross: C. Smythe, 1984).

Excellent collection of thought-provoking essays from great scholars. Perhaps the best essays are Edna Longley's analysis of Belfast and Julian Moynahan's discussion of the city in nineteenth century fiction.

Harte, Liam, and Michael Parker, eds., *Contemporary Irish Fiction: Themes, Tropes, Theories* (Houndmills and New York: Macmillan, 2000).

A very useful collection of essays for students working on contemporary fiction. Irish fiction is here analyzed from a variety of theoretical perspectives. Joseph McMinn's essay on Banville, Gerry Smyth's essay on representation of Dublin, and Harte and Parker's essay on recent Northern fiction are perhaps the finest in this impressive collection.

Hooper, Glenn, and Colin Graham, *Irish and Postcolonial Writing: History, Theory, Practice* (Basingstoke: Palgrave, 2002).

An indispensable collection of essays for anyone interested in postcolonial perspective on Irish writing. Part Two draws comparisons between Irish texts and other postcolonial writing (Zimbabwe, West Indies, African, and Cape Colony).

Howe, Stephen, *Ireland and Empire: Colonial Legacies in Irish History and Culture* (Oxford: Oxford University Press, 2000).

This is a definite must-read for students working on postcolonialism and Irish literature. Howe's critique of postcolonialist Irish scholars is incisive, well argued, and researched.

Innes, Catherine Lynette, *Woman and Nation in Irish Literature and Society, 1880–1935* (New York: Harvester Wheatsheaf, 1993).

A very useful study on women writers and nationalism, well-researched and well written.

Johnson, Toni O'Brien, and David Cairns, eds., *Gender in Irish Writing* (Milton Keynes and Philadelphia: Open University Press, 1991).

A useful collection of essays; a good starting point for anyone interested in gender studies and Irish literature. Do consult more recent studies on the subject to get more updated information.

Kennedy-Andrews, Elmer, *Fiction and the Northern Ireland Troubles Since 1969: De-constructing the North* (Dublin: Four Courts Press, 2003).

A very good survey of the Troubles novels; contains chapters on individual novels and novelists.

Kirkpatrick, Kathryn, ed., *Border Crossings: Irish Women Writers and National Identities* (Tuscaloosa and London: The University of Alabama Press, 2000).

An excellent collection of essays on Irish women writers. Perhaps the most interesting among these essays is Julia Anne Miller's fascinating analysis of Edgeworth and Owenson.

Lloyd, David, *Anomalous States: Irish Writing and the Post-Colonial Moment* (Durham, NC: Duke University Press, 1993).

A collection of essays on modern Irish writing in which Lloyd explores the formation of Irish identity, starting from the nineteenth century. A challenging read at times, Lloyd offers a good analysis of postcolonialism and cultural politics in Ireland.

Longley, Edna, *The Living Stream: Literature & Revisionism in Ireland* (Newcastle upon Tyne: Bloodaxe Books, 1994).

Continuing her critique on postcolonial approaches to Irish literature and culture, Longley's incisive essays offer an illuminating perspective on Northern Irish writers.

————, "The Writer and Belfast," in *The Irish Writer and the City*, Maurice Harmon, ed. (Gerrards Cross: C. Smythe, 1984) pp. 65–89.

A seminal article on the image of Belfast in Northern Irish literature.

McCarthy, Conor, *Modernisation, Crisis and Culture in Ireland, 1969–1992* (Dublin: Four Courts Press, 2000).

Well-argued and engagingly written, McCarthy's study analyzes the writing of Brian Friel, John Banville, and Dermot Bolger. In the last chapter of this book McCarthy offers a thought-provoking and controversial discussion of Edna Longley and Seamus Deane's intellectual politics.

McMinn, Joseph, "Contemporary Novels on the 'Troubles,'" *Études Irlandaises* 5 (December 1980) pp. 113–121.

Examines the ways in which contemporary novels represent the Troubles, tries to detect general patterns rather than give a detailed analysis of a single work. McMinan concludes that the novels under discussion prefer psychological characterization to a historical explanation of the origins of the Troubles.

Morash, Christopher, *Writing the Irish Famine* (Oxford: Clarendon Press, 1995).

An excellent study on the subject; analyzes the concept of famine as a moment of absence and examines works by William Carleton, Anthony Trollope, James Clarence Mangan, John Mitchel, and Samuel Ferguson.

Moynahan, Julian, *Anglo-Irish: The Literary Imagination in a Hyphenated Culture* (Princeton, NJ: Princeton University Press, 1994).

An excellent collection of essays on Anglo-Irish writers such as Maria Edgeworth, William Carleton, Charles Lever, Charles Robert Maturin, Joseph Sheridan Le Fanu, George Moore, and Somerville and Ross.

———, "The Image of the City in Nineteenth Century Irish Fiction," in *The Irish Writer and the City*, Maurice Harmon, ed. (Gerrards Cross: C. Smythe, 1984) pp. 1–17.

A thought provoking article that charts the evolution of the image of the city in nineteenth-century Irish fiction, covering authors from Edgeworth to Joyce.

Ní Anluan, Clíodhna, ed., *Reading the Future: Irish Writers in Conversation with Mike Murphy* (Dublin: The Lilliput Press, 2000).

Interviews with such contemporary Irish authors as John Banville, John McGahern, Edna O'Brien, and William Trevor. Useful and interesting read.

Smyth, Gerry, *The Novel and the Nation: Studies in the New Irish Fiction* (London: Pluto Press, 1997).

Part One of Smyth's study considers a number of theoretical perspectives such as postcolonial and postmodernist, whereas Part Two offers readings of individual texts. While Smyth's study is commendable for the discussions of lesser-known novelists, such as Robert McLiam

Wilson, Colin Bateman, Desmond Hogan, Joseph O'Connor, and Kate O'Riordan, there are several gaps in his overview of recent Irish fiction. The most striking is the absence of John Banville. However, it is a very useful overview of recent Irish fiction.

Smyth, Gerry, *Decolonisation and Criticism: The Construction of Irish Literature* (Sterling: Pluto Press, 1998).

Smyth charts the history of Irish criticism from the foundation of the Republic. Recommended for students interested in theoretical approaches to Irish literature and culture.

St. Peter, Christine, *Changing Ireland: Strategies in Contemporary Women's Fiction* (Basingstoke: Macmillan, 2000).

This study examines recent fiction by women writers who are working both in exile and in Ireland. Chapters on feminist fiction, historical fiction, war literature, exilic writing, and fictionalized memoirs.

Walshe, Éibhear, ed., *Sex, Nation and Dissent in Irish Writing* (Cork: Cork University Press,1997).

A good collection of excellent essays on sexuality and nationalism. Definitely consult the essays by Patricia Coughlan and Declan Kiberd.

## 5. Some criticism on individual authors (note that these entries do not supply you with exhaustive bibliographies but a few examples which get you started on the subject):

### 5.1. Maria Edgeworth

Bilger, Audrey, *Laughing Feminism: Subversive Comedy in Frances Burney, Maria Edgeworth, and Jane Austen* (Detroit: Wayne State University Press, 1998).

Studies the intersection of feminism and comedy in the eighteenth century, arguing that writing comic novels allowed authors like Austen, Burney, and Edgeworth to contribute to the ongoing debate about women's proper place in society.

Butler, Marilyn, *Maria Edgeworth: A Literary Biography* (Oxford: Clarendon Press, 1972).

An excellent book that gives an overview of Edgeworth's life and contextualizes her culturally, intellectually, and politically. Highly recommended for students interested in Edgeworth.

Caraher, Brian, "Edgeworth, Wilde and Joyce: Reading Irish Regionalism through 'the cracked lookingglass' of a Servant's Art," in *Ireland in the Nineteenth Century: Regional Identity*, Leon Litvack and Glenn Hooper, eds. (Dublin: Four Courts Press, 2000) pp. 123–139.

Offers an excellent overview of Maria Edgeworth and literary regionalism. Proposes a triadic matrix of regionalism. Occasionally a challenging read, but worth the effort.

Dunne, Tom, *Maria Edgeworth and the Colonial Mind*, the 26th O'Donnell lecture, delivered at University College Cork on 27 June 1984 (National University of Ireland, 1984).

An extremely well-written and thought-provoking piece on Edgeworth's language in *Castle Rackrent*. Definitely worth consulting.

Graham, Colin, "History, Gender and the Colonial Moment: *Castle Rackrent*," *Irish Studies Review* 14 (1996) pp. 21–24.

A postcolonial take on *Castle Rackrent*.

Murray, Patrick, *Companion to Castle Rackrent* (Dublin: Educational Company, 1991).

Gives a brief outline of the novel, its historical background, discusses characterization, comedy, and irony in the novel. Unfortunately it has no bibliography, footnotes, or bibliographic references of any sort.

## 5.2. Lady Morgan (Sydney Owenson)

Dunne, Tom, "Fiction as 'the Best History of Nations': Lady Morgan's Irish Novels," in *The Writer as Witness: Literature as Historical Evidence*, Tom Dunne, ed. (Cork: Cork University Press, 1987) pp. 133–159.

An illuminating discussion of Lady Morgan's use of history in her Irish novels. A "must" for students interested in Lady Morgan or in nineteenth century Irish fiction.

Leerssen, Joep, "How *The Wild Irish Girl* Made Ireland Romantic," *Dutch Quarterly Review of Anglo-American Letters* 18:3 (1988) pp. 209–227.

An interesting article that theorizes the use and significance of footnoted discourse in *The Wild Irish Girl*.

————, "On the Treatment of Irishness in Romantic Anglo-Irish Fiction," *Irish University Review* 20:2 (Autumn 1990) pp. 252–263.

Leerssen introduces the concept of "auto-exoticism" for analyzing *The Wild Irish Girl*. His argument centers around the way in which nineteenth century novels articulated an Irish cultural identity.

### 5.3. John and Michael Banim

Cahalan, James M., *Great Hatred, Little Room: The Irish Historical Novel* (Syracuse, NY: Syracuse University Press, 1983).

See Chapter 3 for a good discussion of *The Boyne Water*. Cahalan analyzes the novel by comparing it to Scott's model of historical fiction. A good analysis, which also gives you a detailed close reading of the text.

Flanagan, Thomas, *The Irish Novelists, 1800–1850* (New York: Columbia University Press, 1958).

The chapter on the Banim brothers is dated by now. Flanagan gives a good overview of their work, but you should definitely consult more recent studies or reference works.

### 5.4. Gerald Griffin

Cronin, John, "The Creative Dilemma of Gerald Griffin," *Canadian Journal of Irish Studies* 12:2 (June 1968) pp. 105–118.

————, *Gerald Griffin (1803–1840): A Critical Biography* (Cambridge: Cambridge University Press, 1978).

John Cronin's articles and his excellent biography of Griffin remain the best introduction to Griffin's life and writings. Highly recommended.

Davis, Robert, *Gerald Griffin* (Boston: Twayne, 1980).

A very good overview of Griffin's works; detailed close readings of his texts.

### 5.5. William Carleton

Haslam, Richard, "The Prose Arranged and Lingered Over: Visualizing the Troubles," in *Contemporary Irish Fiction: Themes, Tropes, Theories,* Liam Harte and Michael Parker, eds. (Houndmills and New York: Macmillan, 2000) pp. 192–212.

Haslam draws interesting parallels by comparing Carleton's short story, "The Wildgoose Lodge," to Eoin McNamee's *Resurrection Man* and Bernard McLaverty's *Cal*. His argument centers around the treatment of violence in these texts.

Orel, Harold, "William Carleton: Attitudes toward the English and the Irish," in *Literary Interrelations: Ireland, England and the World*. Volume 3. *National Images and Stereotypes*, Wolfgang Zach and Heinz Kosok, eds. (Tübingen: Narr, 1987) pp. 85–93.

An interesting study of Carleton's attitude toward the Irish and the English.

Sullivan, Eileen A., *William Carleton*, Twayne's English Authors Series, 376 (Boston: Twayne, 1983).

An excellent starting point for students interested in Carleton: gives a very good overview and close readings of Carleton's texts.

## 5.6. Charles Lever

Bareham, Tony, ed., *Charles Lever: New Evaluations*, Ulster Editions and Monographs 3 (Gerrards Cross: C. Smythe, 1991).

An excellent collection of essays on Lever. Chris Morash's essay on post-Famine landscapes is perhaps the most interesting of these stimulating new perspectives on Lever's work.

Haddelsey, Stephen, *Charles Lever: The Lost Victorian* (Gerrards Cross: C. Smythe, 2000).

A good overview of Lever's life and career. A good point of reference, but perhaps not the most illuminating or exciting of discussions.

## 5.7. Sheridan Le Fanu

McCormack, William J., *Sheridan Le Fanu and Victorian Ireland* (Oxford: Clarendon Press, 1980).

A definite "must"—a superb biography that offers an excellent analysis of Le Fanu's fiction and an illuminating overview of Ireland during the Victorian era. Occasionally a bit challenging read, but highly recommended.

Melada, Ivan, *Sheridan Le Fanu* (Boston: Twayne Publishers, 1987).

An accessible overview of Le Fanu's life and work; offers close readings of Le Fanu's texts.

Sullivan, Kevin, "*The House by the Churchyard*: James Joyce and Sheridan Le Fanu," in *Modern Irish Literature: Essays in Honor of William York Tindall*, Raymond Porter and James D. Brophy, eds. (New York: Iona College Press and Twayne Publishers, 1972) pp. 315–334.
Examines *The House by the Churchyard* as an intertext for Joyce's *Finnegans Wake*.

## 5.8. Somerville and Ross

Chen, Bi-Ling, "De-Mystifying the Family Romance: A Feminist Reading of Somerville and Ross's *The Big House of Inver*," in *Notes on Modern Irish Literature* 10 (1998) pp. 17–25.
Chen examines *The Big House of Inver* as a family romance. Although a bit of a challenging read, this is an interesting example of a feminist take on Somerville and Ross.

Greene, Nicole Pepinster, "Dialect and Social Identity in *The Real Charlotte*," *New Hibernia Review* 4:1 (2000 Spring) pp. 122–137.
An analysis of Somerville and Ross's novel in relation to dialect and social identity.

Stevens, Julie Anne, "The Staging of Protestant Ireland in Somerville and Ross: The Real Charlotte," in *Critical Ireland: New Essays in Literature and Culture*, Alan A. Gillis and Aron Kelly, eds. (Dublin: Four Courts Press, 2001) pp. 188–195.
An interesting reading of *The Real Charlotte*. Stevens analyzes the imagery of polarity and circular motion in relation to theater and performance.

## 5.9. George Moore

Davison, Neil R., "Representations of 'Irishness' in *The Untilled Field*: Deconstructing Ideological Ethnicity," *Textual Practice* 12:2 (Summer 1998) pp. 291–321.
Occasionally a challenging read, but offers a fascinating analysis of Moore's short stories examining his treatment of Irish identity in relation to gender, social class, and ideology.

Devine, Paul, "Leitmotif and Epiphany: George Moore's *Evelyn Innes* and *The Lake*," in *Moments of Moment: Aspects of the Literary Epiphany*, Wim Tigges, ed., *Studies in Literature* 25 (Amsterdam: Rodopi, 1999) pp. 155–175.

This is an excellent article on a fascinating topic—Moore's use of epiphany. This is a must read for students interested in Moore's influence on James Joyce.

Frazier, Adrian, *George Moore, 1852–1933* (New Haven, CT: Yale University Press, 2000).

An excellent biography of Moore—highly recommended.

## 5.10. James Joyce

Attridge, Derek, ed., *The Cambridge Companion to James Joyce* (Cambridge: Cambridge University Press, 1990).

A very useful collection of essays for a beginner, which covers all of Joyce's works. Karen Lawrence's chapter on Joyce and feminism, Jennifer Levine on *Ulysses*, and John Paul Riquelme's study of *Stephen Hero*, *Dubliners*, and *A Portrait* are highly recommended.

Attridge, Derek, and Marjorie Howes, *Semicolonial Joyce* (Cambridge: Cambridge University Press, 2000).

An extremely useful collection of essays that examine Joyce's writing from postcolonial perspective.

Bowen, Jack, and James F. Carens, eds., *A Companion to Joyce Studies* (Westport, CT: Greenwood Press, 1984).

An indispensable reference tool for anyone interested in Joyce. Covers every work ever written by Joyce, has chapters on textual and publishing history, biographical information, poems, letters, Joyce's aesthetic theory and critical writings, and charts the history of Joyce criticism and scholarship. Excellent scholarship, accessible, intelligent, and well written.

Deane, Seamus, "Fiction as History—History as Fiction," in *Joyce in Rome: The Genesis of Ulysses*, Giorgio Melchiori, ed. (Rome: Bulzoni Editore, 1984) pp. 130–141.

A very useful essay on Joyce's ideas on history, nationalism, and the Irish cultural revival.

Kenner, Hugh, *Ulysses* (London: George Allen & Unwin, 1980).
A classic study of Joyce's masterpiece. Accessible and insightful, well written and argued. Highly recommended.

Mahaffey, Vicki, "*Ulysses* and the End of Gender," in *A Companion to James Joyce's Ulysses*, Margot Norris, ed. (Boston: Bedford Books, 1998) pp. 151–168.
An excellent analysis of *Ulysses* in the context of gender studies; a challenging read but should definitely be consulted.

Potts, Willard, *Joyce and the Two Irelands* (Austin: University of Texas Press, 2000).
A fresh reading of Joyce's response to the Irish cultural revival.

### 5.11. Samuel Beckett

Acheson, James, *Samuel Beckett's Artistic Theory and Practice. Criticism, Drama and Early Fiction* (Basingstoke: Macmillan, 1997).
An interesting analysis of Beckett's artistic theory, based on Achenson's reading of Beckett's essays and reviews.

Alvarez, A., *Beckett* (London: Fontana Press, 1973).
A classic study of Beckett. This is a very good introduction to Beckett, which covers his major works.

Connor, Steven, *Samuel Beckett: Repetition, Theory and Text* (Oxford: Basil Blackwell, 1988).
A reading of Beckett's works from a poststructuralist perspective. Connor utilizes ideas drawn from Jacques Derrida and Gilles Deleuze's writings. A challenging read.

Pilling, John, ed., *The Cambridge Companion to Beckett* (Cambridge: Cambridge University Press, 1994).
An excellent collection of essays, indispensable for a beginner.

### 5.12. James Stephens

Putzel, Steven, "James Stephens's Paradoxical Dublin," in *The Irish Writer and the City*, Maurice Harmon, ed. (Gerrards Cross: C. Smythe, 1984) pp. 103–114.

A very useful article for students interested in Stephens or representations of Dublin. Putzel examines Stephens's novels *The Crock of Gold* and *The Charwoman's Daughter* as well as his short stories.

————, "Portraits of Paralysis: Stories by Joyce and Stephens," *Colby Library Quarterly* 20:4 (December 1984) pp. 199–205.
An interesting comparison of Stephens and Joyce and their uses of paralysis.

## 5.13. Flann O'Brien

Booker, M. Keith, "The Bicycle and Descartes: Epistemology in the Fiction of Beckett and O'Brien," *Éire-Ireland* 26:1 (Spring 1991) pp. 76–94.
An excellent analysis of O'Brien and Beckett's skeptical world-view. An interesting and well-written article.

Clissmann, Anne, *Flann O'Brien: A Critical Introduction to His Writing* (New York: Barnes and Noble, 1968).
This is the best book to consult if you are interested in O'Brien; a thorough and well-written study of his works. Highly recommended.

Clune, Anne, and Tess Hurson, eds., *Conjuring Complexities: Essays on Flann O'Brien* (Belfast: The Institute of Irish Studies at Queen's, 1997).
A good collection of essays examining Flann O'Brien's works. Hugh Kenner's essay "The Fourth Policeman" is a must.

## 5.14. Sean O'Faolain

Harmon, Maurice, *Sean O'Faolain: A Critical Introduction* (Dublin: Wolfhound Press, 1967).
Harmon's study charts the evolution of O'Faolain's aesthetic and critical thinking. An excellent biographical overview.

————, *Sean O'Faolain: A Life* (London: Constable, 1994).
The first full biography of O'Faolain. Well written and researched.

## 5.15. Frank O'Connor

Tomory, William M., *Frank O'Connor* (Boston: Twayne Publishers, 1980).

This study centers around an examination of O'Connor's short fiction, his theory and practice of short story writing. Tomory also gives a biographical overview and the book contains a chapter on O'Connor's translations of Gaelic poetry.

## 5.16. Liam O'Flaherty

Cahalan, James M., *Liam O'Flaherty: A Study of the Short Fiction*, Twayne's Studies in Short Fiction 23 (Boston: Twayne, 1991).
An accessible and useful overview of O'Flaherty's short stories. Good analysis. Well written and researched.

Sheeran, Patrick F., *The Novels of Liam O'Flaherty: A Study in Romantic Realism* (Atlantic Highlands: Humanities, 1976).
Although might seem a bit dated, this is still a good study for students interested in O'Flaherty's novels.

## 5.17. Kate O'Brien

Fogarty, Anne, "The Ear of the Other: Dissident Voices in Kate O'Brien's *As Music and Splendour* and Mary Dorcey's *A Noise from the Woodshed*," in *Sex, Nation, and Dissent in Irish Writing*, Éibhear Walshe, ed. (New York: St. Martin's, 1997) pp. 170–201.
A fascinating examination of the role of dissent and lesbianism in O'Brien's *As Music and Splendour*.

Reynolds, Lorna, *Kate O'Brien: A Literary Portrait* (Gerrards Cross: C. Smythe, 1987).
A pioneering study of O'Brien's novels. Sensitive and intelligent readings of O'Brien's works.

Walshe, Eibhear, ed., *Ordinary People Dancing* (Cork: Cork University Press, 1993).
A very useful collection of essays on Kate O'Brien. Covers her novels, travel writing, and journalism. Includes essays from feminist perspective but also offers readings on lesbianism in Kate O'Brien's fiction.

## 5.18. Elizabeth Bowen

Glendinning, Victoria, *Elizabeth Bowen: Portrait of a Writer* (London: Weidenfeld & Nicolson, 1977).

An excellent biography, which offers sensitive and well-informed readings of Bowen's novels. A good point of departure for students interested in Bowen.

Lee, Hermione, *Elizabeth Bowen: An Estimation* (London: Vintage, 1981).

A superb biographical study of Bowen's fiction. Thematically arranged, well written, accessible, and well researched, Lee's study is highly recommended for anyone interested in Bowen.

### 5.19. Francis Stuart

Caterson, S. J., "Joyce, the Künstlerroman and Minor Literature: Francis Stuart's *Black List, Section H*," *Irish University Review* 27:1 (Spring/Summer 1997) pp. 87–97.

Caterson draws interesting parallels between Stuart's novel and Joyce's *A Portrait*, analyzing these texts as belonging to the genre of Künstlerroman.

Caterson, Simon, "Francis Stuart, Hitler, and Lure of Fascism," *Irish Studies Review* 16 (Autumn 1996) pp. 18–22.

A very interesting article which examines the most controversial aspect of Stuart's life and fiction—his stay in Nazi Germany.

McCartney, Anne, *Francis Stuart: Face to Face: A Critical Study* (Belfast: The Institute of Irish Studies, 2000).

A thorough examination of Stuart's life; accessible and well written. McCartney gives a good analysis of Stuart's philosophy and tries to place him in the Irish literary tradition.

### 5.20. Brian Moore

O'Donoghue, Jo, *Brian Moore: A Critical Study* (Montreal: McGill-Queen's University Press, 1991).

An excellent study covering most of Moore's published works. Highly recommended for students interested in Moore's fiction.

Sullivan, Robert, *A Matter of Faith: The Fiction of Brian Moore* (Westport, CT: Greenwood, 1996).

Although Sullivan analyzes Moore's fiction primarily in relation to the writer's treatment of faith, this is a good point of departure for anyone interested in Moore's novels.

## 5.21. William Trevor

Morrison, Kristin, *William Trevor,* Twayne's English Authors Series 501 (New York: Twayne, 1993).
The best introduction to Trevor's fiction. Accessible and well researched, this guide covers all of Trevor's fiction.

Tracy, Robert, "Telling Tales: The Fictions of William Trevor," *Colby Quarterly* 38:3 (September 2002) pp. 295–307.
A good analysis of Trevor's fiction, which concentrates on his treatment of Ireland.

St. Peter, Christine, "Consuming Pleasures: Felicia's Journey in Fiction and Film," *Colby Quarterly* 38:3 (September 2002) pp. 329–339.
An excellent analysis of Trevor's novel, *Felicia's Journey,* and its adaptation for cinema. St. Peter utilizes postcolonial theory in order to examine both the film and the novel.

## 5.22. Edna O'Brien

Ingman, Heather, "Edna O'Brien: Stretching the Nation's Boundaries," *Irish Studies Review* 10:3 (December 2002) pp. 253–265.
Ingman's article is very useful for anyone interested in politics in O'Brien's fiction. An interesting analysis of Irish nationalism in O'Brien's work.

St. Peter, Christine, "Petrifying Time: Incest Narratives from Contemporary Ireland," in *Contemporary Irish Fiction: Themes, Tropes, Theories*, Liam Harte and Michael Parker (Houndmills and New York: Macmillan, 2000) pp. 125–144.
St. Peter's study examines O'Brien's recent fiction, concentrating on father-daughter relationships and the treatment of incest in O'Brien's novels. Intriguing and well argued, this article offers an interesting reading of *Down By the River*.

## 5.23. Jennifer Johnston

Lynch, Rachael Sealy, "Public Spaces, Private Lives: Irish Identity and Female Selfhood in the Novels of Jennifer Johnston," in *Border Crossings: Irish Women Writers and National Identities,*

Kathryn Kirkpatrick, ed. (Tuscaloosa: University of Alabama
Press, 2000) pp. 250–268.
Lynch offers an excellent study of female self in relation to the prob-
lematics of Irish identity in Johnston's novels.

Rooks-Hughes, Lorna, "The Family and the Female Body in the
Novels of Edna O'Brien and Julia O'Faolain," *Canadian Journal
of Irish Studies* 22:2 (December 1996) pp. 83–97.
An excellent study of such topics as motherhood, sexuality,
Catholicism, and the female body as depicted in O'Brien and Johnston.

Rosslyn, Felicity, "The Importance of Being Irish: Jennifer
Johnston," *Cambridge Quarterly* 32:3 (2003) pp. 239–249.
Rosslyn's article is a good example of a psychological analysis of repre-
sentation of Irish identity in Jennifer Johnston's fiction.

## 5.24. Roddy Doyle

Donnelly, Brian, "Roddy Doyle: from Barrytown to the GPO," *Irish
University Review* 30:1 (Spring/Summer 2000) pp. 17–31.
An excellent article that examines Doyle's treatment of Irish culture.

White, Caramine, *Reading Roddy Doyle* (Syracuse, NY: Syracuse
University Press, 2001).
A good introduction to Doyle's fiction. Analyzes humor, familial rela-
tionships, and treatment of Irish identity.

## 5.25. John McGahern

Holland, Siobhán, "Re-citing the Rosary: Women, Catholicism and
Agency in Brian Moore's *Cold Heaven* and John McGahern's
*Amongst Women*," in *Contemporary Irish Fiction: Themes, Tropes,
Theories,* Liam Harte and Michael Parker, eds. (Houndmills and
New York: Macmillan, 2000), pp. 56–78.
An illuminating analysis of McGahern's treatment of women in his
Booker-nominated novel *Amongst Women*. A "must" read for students
interested in McGahern.

Sampson, Denis, *Outstaring Nature's Eye: the Fiction of John
McGahern* (Dublin: The Lilliput Press, 1993).
A useful (and so far the only) comprehensive study of McGahern's
prose. Sampson provides excellent close readings of McGahern's texts.

## 5.26. John Banville

Hand, Derek, *John Banville: Exploring Fictions* (Dublin: The Liffey Press, 2002).
An excellent study on Banville, a rare example of postcolonial approach to his fiction.

Imhof, Rüdiger, *John Banville: A Critical Introduction*, 2nd revised edition (Dublin: Wolfhound Press, 1997).
A good study that analyzes Banville from a formalist point of view. Imhof tries to place Banville in the context of contemporary metafiction. Very useful discussions of intertextuality in Banville's novels.

McMinn, Joseph, *The Supreme Fictions of John Banville* (Manchester: Manchester University Press, 1999).
An excellent study, the best existing book-length introduction to Banville's works. In contrast to Imhof, McMinn analyzes Banville in the context of Irish literature. Highly recommended.

## 5.27. Eoin McNamee

Haslam, Richard, "The Pose Arranged and Lingered Over: Visualizing the 'Troubles'," in *Contemporary Irish Fiction: Themes, Tropes, Theories*, Liam Harte and Michael Parker, eds. (Haundmills and New York: Macmillan, 2000) pp. 192–212.
A fascinating, if occasionally challenging, study which investigates the treatment of violence in McNamee's, Carleton's, and McLaverty's novels.

McCarthy, Dermot, "Belfast Babel: Postmodern Lingo in Eoin McNamee's *Resurrection Man*," *Irish University Review* 30:1 (Spring/Summer 2000) pp. 132–148.
An excellent analysis of McNamee's novel, McCarthy examines violence and narrative technique in *Resurrection Man*.

## 5.28. Colm Tóibín

Harte, Liam, "History, Text, and Society in Colm Tóibín's *The Heather Blazing*," *New Hibernia Review* 6:4 (Winter 2002) pp. 55–67.
A historical and socio-political reading of *The Heather Blazing*. A well-argued and interesting study.

Herron, Tom, "ContamiNation: Patrick McCabe and Colm Tóibín's Pathographies of the Republic," in *Contemporary Irish Fiction: Themes, Tropes, Theories*, Liam Harte and Michael Parker, eds. (Houndmills and New York: Macmillan, 2000) pp. 168–191.

Herron analyzes the treatment of Irish nationalism and politics in McCabe and Tóibín. Incisive and well-argued analysis.

## 5.29. Anne Enright

Felter, Maryanne, "Anne Enright," in *Dictionary of Irish Literature*, Robert Hogan, ed., Vol. 1 (Westport, CT and London: Greenwood Press, 1996) pp. 410–411.

Moloney, Caitriona, "Anne Enright," in *Dictionary of Literary Biography: Twenty-first-Century British and Irish Novelists*, Vol. 267 (Detroit: Bruccoli Clark Layman, 2003) pp. 88–93.

These dictionary entries give a good overview of Enright's fiction to date. Caitriona Moloney's article is especially insightful and useful, as she discusses Enright's use of intertextuality.

Weekes, Ann Owens, "Anne Enright," in Unveiling Treasures: The Attic Guide to the Published Works of Irish Women Writers: Drama, Fiction, Poetry (Dublin: Attic Press, 1993) pp. 120–121.

## 5.30. Emma Donoghue

Quinn, Antoinette, "New Noises from the Woodshed: the Novels of Emma Donoghue," in *Contemporary Irish Fiction: Themes, Tropes, Theories*, Liam Harte and Michael Parker, eds. (Houndmills and New York: Macmillan, 2000) pp. 145–167.

An excellent overview of Donoghue's novels to date. Highly recommended.

# Index

green
press
INITIATIVE